Peet van Biljon and Alexandra Reed Lajoux
**Making Money**

Peet van Biljon and Alexandra Reed Lajoux

# Making Money

---

The History and Future of Society's Most
Important Technology

**DE GRUYTER**

ISBN 978-1-5474-1723-0
E-ISBN (PDF) 978-1-5474-0111-6
E-ISBN (EPUB) 978-1-5474-0113-0

**Library of Congress Control Number: 2019948693**

**Bibliographic information published by the Deutsche Nationalbibliothek**
The Deutsche Nationalbibliothek lists this publication in the Deutsche Nationalbibliografie;
detailed bibliographic data are available on the Internet at http://dnb.dnb.de.

© 2020 Peet van Biljon and Alexandra Reed Lajoux
Published by Walter de Gruyter Inc., Boston/Berlin
Typesetting: Integra Software Services Pvt. Ltd.
Printing and binding: CPI books GmbH, Leck

www.degruyter.com

To my wife, Liesel, and my sons, Stefan and Benjamin, who are a constant reminder that there are things in life more precious than gold.
    Peet van Biljon


To Bernard, my better half, who teaches me every day by example that a penny saved is a penny earned.
    Alexandra Reed Lajoux


S.D.G.

# Preface

Money—which we experience as the paper bills or coins in our wallets, the checks we write, the balances we see in our online accounts or mobile devices, and the like—is so integral to our lives that we don't ponder its properties that often. We are practical people: We know money exists, that there are things we'd like to spend it on, and that we need to make enough of it to live. And we also know that most of us are somewhere in the middle between those who have a lot of it (the "rich") and those who do not have nearly enough (the "poor"). But we rarely consider the true nature of money, how it enables our society to function every day, and how it may change in the future. This book does exactly that. We feel that it is time to demystify "money" and how it is "made," in every sense of these words.

Most books about money focus on one aspect, such as the history of money, the workings of the economy, income distribution in society, the role of central banks and other financial institutions, or the latest developments in fintech, cryptocurrencies, and blockchain. As such, most of us have a fragmented view of money, never really understanding it as a broad social phenomenon. To provide you with the whole picture, we have resolved to be more ambitious and cover all of these topics in one book.

This book is about "making money" in every sense of the term—how society had to invent money for it to function, how banks create money every day to put into circulation for use in a growing economy, how we as individuals make money for ourselves and our families, and how the global financial system helps us to move money around, from those who have a surplus of money (the savers) to those who have a deficit (the borrowers).

Readers of this book will journey through this entire terrain. We begin with a fundamental definition of money as a constantly evolving innovation that serves the needs of the society of the day. We explain why money is one of society's biggest inventions, and trace the monetary innovations that have occurred since then, up to present-day fintech and cryptocoins like bitcoin.

Our book is organized into four parts:

- **Part I, Money and Society,** explores the origins of money and faces the question of distribution: Why do some have so much and some so little?
- **Part II, Central Banks and Global Finance,** reveals the roles of central banks and treasuries, and the dynamics of global financial markets.
- **Part III, Money and Technology,** explains what is happening with fintech and cryptocurrencies, the frontiers of money innovation today.
- **Part IV, Beyond Money,** looks at other applications of blockchain, and the coming era of a cashless society.

https://doi.org/10.1515/9781547401116-202

Throughout this book we maintain our unyielding commitment to both economic freedom and economic fairness. We believe that the best way to preserve both is a continuing inquiry into the truth of how money is made. Without such an understanding, we are all prey to myths, "fake news," popular misconceptions, panics, and a myriad of other social ills. But armed with such an understanding, we can take better care of our own financial lives as well as the financial lives of those in our economic sphere. Furthermore, if all of us in the general population have a good understanding of money, our chances of overall prosperity will increase. How we think about money influences not only our economics, but also our politics. There may be no right or wrong answers in absolute terms, but ill-informed opinions and misconceptions about the role of money in society are certainly not helpful to our political debates.

While we are not utopians, we believe that an informed citizenry can be much more effective than a misinformed one, or one biased by only piecemeal information. Furthermore, we believe that our *perception* of money plays a large role in its generation and distribution—how much of it there can be for how many, and what would happen if we change the rules. The best perception is always based in truth, and we vow to tell it fully and exclusively in the following pages.

# Acknowledgments

It would be impossible for us to thank all the many colleagues, mentors, and scholars who have had a role in the inspiration and creation of this book. We would be remiss, however, if we did not acknowledge the valuable contributions of De Gruyter, including our publisher, Jeffrey M. Pepper, as well as Jaya Dalal, editorial assistant, Natalie Jones, copy editor, and André Horn, production editor.

https://doi.org/10.1515/9781547401116-203

# Contents

## Part II: **Central Banks and Global Finance**

## Chapter 6
**What's New about Cryptocurrencies and What's Not —— 153**

## Part IV: **Beyond Money**

# About the Authors

**Peet van Biljon** is the founder of BMNP Strategies LLC, an advisory company. He serves clients on strategy, innovation, and business transformation. His focus is on challenges related to Industry 4.0, and the impact of disruptive technologies such as AI, digitization, fintech, and IoT. Mr. Van Biljon was a management consultant at McKinsey & Company, where he also managed its global innovation practice, and he has held executive positions in several companies internationally. He is an adjunct professor at Georgetown University's McCourt School of Public Policy, where he teaches a graduate course on innovation. Mr. Van Biljon coauthored a book on business ethics, *Profit with a Higher Purpose*. Articles on innovation and R&D management that he coauthored have been published in *MIT Sloan Management Review*, *Research-Technology Management*, and on mckinsey.com. He holds an electrical engineering degree from the University of Stellenbosch, and accounting and economics degrees from the University of South Africa. He is licensed as a professional engineer in Ontario, Canada, and is a member of IEEE. Mr. Van Biljon is involved in initiatives to set ethical guidelines for technology, and currently co-chairs the General Principles Committee of the IEEE Global Initiative on Ethics of Autonomous and Intelligent Systems (A/IS).

**Alexandra Reed Lajoux** is Series Editor for Walter De Gruyter, Inc. The series has an emphasis on governance, corporate leadership, and sustainability. Dr. Lajoux is Chief Knowledge Officer emeritus (CKO) at the National Association of Corporate Directors (NACD) and founding principal of Capital Expert Services, LLC (CapEx), a global consultancy providing expert witnesses for legal cases. She has served as editor of *Directors & Boards*, *Mergers & Acquisitions*, *Export Today*, and *Director's Monthly*, and has coauthored a series of books on M&A for McGraw-Hill, including *The Art of M&A* and eight spin-off titles on strategy, valuation, financing, structuring, due diligence, integration, bank M&A, and distressed M&A. For Bloomberg/Wiley, she coauthored *Corporate Valuation for Portfolio Investment* with Robert A. G. Monks. Dr. Lajoux serves on the advisory board of Campaigns and Elections, and is a Fellow of the Caux Round Table for Moral Capitalism. She holds a BA from Bennington College, a PhD from Princeton University, and an MBA from Loyola University in Maryland. She is an associate member of the American Bar Association and is certified as a Competent Communicator by Toastmasters International.

https://doi.org/10.1515/9781547401116-205

Part I: **Money and Society**

# Chapter 1
# A Great Human Invention: The Role of Money in Society

*All the Perplexities, Confusions and Distresses in America arise not from defects in their Constitutions or Confederation, not from a want of Honour or Virtue, So much as from downright Ignorance of the Nature of Coin, Credit and Circulation.*

—John Adams, Letter to Thomas Jefferson, August 25, 1787[1]

## Why We Invented Money and What It Does for Us

Let's start our journey by exploding a myth: Money did not begin in barter—we know that from the work of many anthropologists. This is an old fallacy propagated into modern economic discourse by Adam Smith. Even though other concepts introduced by this great philosopher—such as the *labor theory of value* (see the next chapter)—have long been discarded, many economic textbooks still like to start by explaining that money solves the major inconvenience associated with barter, the need for a so-called *confluence of needs*. However, that particular inconvenience was not the primary problem that money was invented to solve, and we will therefore not start our story there.

Money was invented to solve a much more profound problem: how to keep track of—literally to count—the obligations people have to one another in a society where any form of value needs to be exchanged.

Money is an *invention* that serves, and always must serve, a beneficial social purpose. It is therefore a technology that will always keep evolving through *innovation* along with the society it serves, while retaining its defining characteristics. That is why we concur with Felix Martin[2] that money is first and foremost a "*social technology.*" This is also why money and the management of money have always been controversial. You cannot take a position on the role of money in the economy and in society at large without attracting some controversy or disagreement with people who have a different economic and political philosophy.

What does this all mean? We can best explain by telling a simple story of how we would have to invent money all over again if we did not have it.

https://doi.org/10.1515/9781547401116-001

## A Money Parable

Imagine a dozen of us getting shipwrecked on an island on the way to a global conference. We have lost all contact with the modern world and have to revert to living off the land as hunter-gatherers of old. In order to make sure that everyone contributes to our little community, we agree on a system whereby we award points for chores. More points are rewarded for more difficult and more valuable contributions. For example, gathering a load of firewood is one point, carrying a pale of freshwater from the distant spring is three points, catching a sizable fish for all to eat is worth ten points, and so on. We keep score on a large rock close to our base, where we have written down everyone's names and make notches to tally up each individual's contribution.

This tally system is a proto-monetary system. It fulfills one of the main roles economists usually associate with money—that of acting as a *unit of account*. But it is not yet money.

After some experience with what it takes to survive and thrive on the island, our island council mandates that every person contributes chores totaling at least three points, or three tally marks per day, on average taken across a week. We decide to give each person one day off per week to rest from the grueling work. Therefore, each of us owes the community 18 points per week. At the end of each day, we gather around the big stone and make notches to tally up everyone's individual contributions, and at the end of each week, we check the totals.

Spearfishing is quite tricky—it requires a sharp spear, keen eyes, and quick reflexes, and most of us aren't any good at it. However, let's say that "Joe" has developed into an excellent spear fisherman. He is so good at it now that he finds that he can spear two fish on Monday, get 20 points of credit for them, and take the rest of the week off.

This introduces another role of money—that of being a *store of value*. Is our proto-monetary system now money? Close, but not quite yet. There is one very important element still missing.

Our island council meets again. There is some discontent with the way things are going. The community seems to be surviving, but not thriving. It seems that everyone is just doing the bare minimum. In particular, the people who haul wood and water every day resent that Joe, the spear fisherman, takes extra days off. The problem, we realize, is that there is no incentive for enterprise, for going above and beyond the minimum we are obligated to do. We decide that in the future, people can trade with one another, using the same tally system that we had earlier devised to keep track of their transactions. If a transaction is worth five points, the seller will be credited with five fresh tally marks on the stone, while five tally marks will be scratched out on the buyer's account.

Now Joe can catch fish every day, so he gets extra points that he can trade with individuals who would like to eat more fish. In return, Joe gets more of the things he wants, like maybe fruits and berries to improve his diet. People start specializing in what they like doing more and are better at. Sarah weaves clothes from plant leaves, Pedro collects coconuts, Mapula grows root vegetables, Aarav constructs a wheeled cart to make hauling wood and water easier, and so on. In other words, people are investing and specializing. When they trade their goods with one another, they record the transactions by adding tally marks on the rock for the seller and scratching out the equal amount of tally marks for the buyer.

We have created *a medium of exchange*, the third and most important role of money. Our tally marks on stone are now money, in every sense of the word. Note how modern this all seems; the stone with tally marks acts as a primitive ledger. There is conceptually no difference between this scratched database on a rock and a spreadsheet on a PC, or a database on a bank's computer. We have created a cashless monetary society without the computers.

However, you may say, where are the seashells or other physicals tokens that we thought primitive societies used as money? While it is true that some societies used such tokens, they are not essential to money. Our little island community certainly does not need tokens, at least not yet. The stone with the marks is there for everyone to see. Why would we need to exchange some object to confirm the transaction we have already recorded?

Our island example is not so unrealistic. There are indeed many examples of primitive societies with monetary systems similar to our fictitious island example here. To varying degrees, these societies have all developed some form of economic accounting, storage, and/or exchange.

## Stone Money

In 1903 a young American adventurer and anthropologist named William Henry Furness visited the island of Yap in Micronesia in the Pacific Ocean. What he discovered on his two-month visit and described in a book[3] published some years later has been a source of fascination for economists ever since. Yap was a tiny island with only a few thousand inhabitants and untouched by outside influences. However, Furness found a complex society with a caste system and rich native cultural and religious traditions. But the most fascinating aspect of this society was its monetary system.

With only a few products on the island, Furness expected to find a barter economy. Instead, he found a quite sophisticated monetary system. What made it even more intriguing was that it was essentially operating as a cashless economy. A long time ago, large, heavy stone wheels (Figure 1.1, licensed under Creative Commons attribution) called *fei* had been quarried on an island some 300 miles away and transported with great difficulty by boat to Yap. These stone discs were like coins, representing different denominations. They were so unwieldy that they were impractical to physically move from one owner to the other. (For the same reason, theft was rather uncommon.) Physical possession was in fact not required to claim ownership. After transactions, debts were simply offset against each other, with outstanding balances carried forward to be used in future exchanges. There was even a very wealthy family who were supposedly the owners of an enormous fei that no one has seen for generations because it was lost in a shipwreck in transit. Yet this family was still wealthy because the Yap society kept crediting them with the worth of that stone which was lying somewhere on the sea floor.

Furness's book would have languished in obscurity had it not come to the attention of a young and later famous economist, John Maynard Keynes, who

**Figure 1.1:** Yap island stone money (Fig. Note 1.1).

thought that it held important lessons about the nature of money.[4] Later on, another great twentieth century economist, Milton Friedman, was just as fascinated. He kicked off his book on monetary history with a chapter titled, "The Island of Stone Money," copying the title of Furness's book. Friedman compared the stone money to the gold standard:

> For a century and more, the civilized world regarded as a concrete manifestation of its wealth a metal dug from deep in the ground, refined at great labor, transported great distances, and buried again in elaborate vaults deep in the ground. Is the one practice really more rational than the other?[5]

Indeed, just as other societies took something that they valued, like gold, and made it the basis of their money, the Yap islanders used the stones which they acquired at great cost and treasured. But once they started using it as a medium of exchange, they did not need the precious object anymore. Contrast this with our fictional island of modern castaways. The exchange mechanisms are remarkably similar, but on our fictional island, there is no underlying object of value underpinning the money. On our island we have *fiat money*, like today's dollar notes, which are not backed by anything other than the word of the U.S. government that these paper bills are money.

A contemporary archaeologist, Scott Fitzpatrick, recently called the Yap stone money the precursor of bitcoin and blockchain-based transactions (to be discussed in Chapters 6 and 7). The great effort involved in quarrying the big stone disks on a distant island and then transporting them by boat is analogous to the mining effort in the creation of cryptocoin. Similarly, the tallying system can be seen as the forerunner of the blockchain-based ledger system.[6]

### Counting Our Obligations

Tally sticks go back very far in early human history. Several prehistoric examples of tally sticks have been unearthed. Some of the very oldest tally sticks are bones with some series of notches on them. The Ishango bone (Figure 1.2, licensed under Creative Commons attribution) found in the Congo is dated at 20,000 years and has 168 notches, arranged into sixteen groups and three rows. The oldest tally stick found to date, a 43,000 year-old baboon fibula recovered in the Lebombo Mountains on the border between South Africa and Eswatini, has 29 markings on one side.[7]

Humans have been counting things for a long time indeed. But what have they been counting?

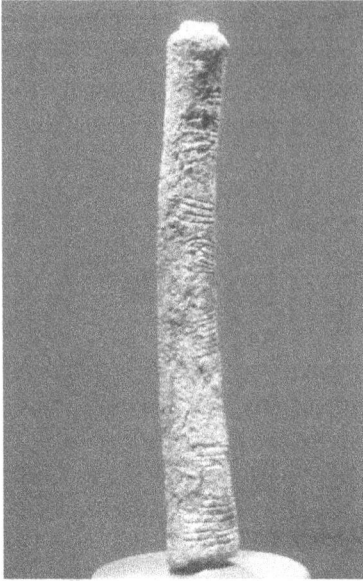

**Figure 1.2:** The Ishango bone (Fig. Note 1.2).

The problem with monetary history, as with all history, is that we only have artifacts that survived to look at. This means typically stone, ceramic, or metal objects, and the occasional dried bone. What we call the Stone Age, was probably more like the "Wood Age," except it is the stone objects from that age that survived, not the objects made from wood.

For 600 years, until the early nineteenth century, debts in Britain were recorded on pieces of willow about 8 inches (20 cm) long. They were called tally sticks (Figure 1.3, licensed under Creative Commons attribution) and each stick had the amount and debtor recorded on it, then split in half from one end to the other. The distinctive grain of the willow meant that two unique halves would only match each other. The one half called the *foil* would go to the debtor, and the other half called the *stock* would go to the creditor. Creditors found that they could use stocks with the name of creditworthy debtors as a convenient means of payment at close to the nominal value of the amount on the stick. These stocks thus became convenient forms of money. Sadly, only a few tally sticks survived, because when the system was abolished in 1834 in the move to a paper ledger system, the sticks were burned in a coal-fired stove in the House of Lords. But the fire got out of control and it burned down the House of Lords and the House of Commons, and most of the Palace of Westminster.[8]

**Figure 1.3:** Medieval tally sticks (Fig. Note 1.3).

What this story teaches us—aside from not burning historical artifacts in an unsafe way or, better yet, at all—is that debt can become money. An IOU that I write you with the words, "I promise to pay my debt of $100 to the bearer of this note" becomes transferable and can be used as a means of payment.

But how is the value of something in money determined? Why $100 rather than $50 for something? We alluded to that distinction in the island parable above, where spearing fish was worth more than hauling wood. But what if some of our castaways succeeded in weaving plant fibers together into rope, and used that rope to construct an effective fishing net? Such a technological innovation would result in more fish being caught for the island society to eat, but it would decrease the relative value of spearfishing skills, to the disadvantage of the specialist spearfisher. In the next chapter, we shall review economic theories of value. For now, another simple illustration will suffice: Think about the typical family household as a miniature service economy. If there is any desire to distribute chores equitably among members of the household, the fundamental issues of pricing and valuation immediately come up.

Maybe a simple exchange agreement is that one person cooks and the other does the dishes. It could be argued that cleaning up is the more unpleasant chore and should be worth more, but on the other hand, cooking requires more skill than washing dishes, which elevates the value of cooking as an activity. (In restaurants, chefs get paid more than dishwashers, which is the verdict of the free market on these two competing arguments.) For activities that require equal amounts of skill, like cleaning different rooms, the "exchange rate" that is typically bargained by family members is based on some combination of the amount of time it takes to clean a room and the level of unpleasantness of the task. In this system of exchange, cleaning the bathroom is worth more than cleaning the living room.

Even though no money changes hands, an exchange system has been established that reflects a societal agreement. Even without any token money, it is possible to keep a full account of who has done which chores as long as there is a central ledger open for all to see. Imagine a household where this arrangement is institutionalized by allocating a fixed number of credits per chore, and everyone is required to do chores equal to a particular number of credits per week. A chore sheet is posted on the fridge with check marks to show completion against names.

The next logical evolution of this system is where people exchange chores using the relative values determined by the assigned credits. For example, washing the dishes two times is exchanged for cleaning the bathroom once.

It is merely one step further to say that an individual can promise to do one of these things instead of doing it. In that case, the one who receives the promise becomes a creditor holding promissory notes (a fancy name for an IOU), which, in turn, might have some value. The invention of such promissory notes was the beginning of money as a store of value. They can be passed on and used by whomever the owner is at the time.

The power of promissory notes is illustrated in one of the most famous (and some say disturbing) episodes of the long-running Fox animated series *The Simpsons*, when the ten-year old Bart Simpson sells his soul for $5 to his best friend Milhouse, by writing "Bart Simpson's soul" on a piece of paper. Bart uses the proceeds to buy toys, but soon regrets selling his soul. He begs Milhouse to sell it back to him. Milhouse tells Bart that he traded the paper at the comic book store. Bart races to the comic book store where the owner tells him that he already sold the paper representing Bart's soul to someone else, but refuses to tell Bart who the mysterious buyer is. Dejected and desperate, Bart walks home in the pouring rain, praying to God for his soul. Suddenly the paper floats down from above. Bart grabs it and eats it, which immediately puts his troubled mind at ease. He later learns that his sister, Lisa, had bought it back for him.[9]

Of course, most promissory notes have a more economic purpose—as the British tally sticks showed. A more recent historical example of how easily debt can become money is what happened during the Irish bank strike of 1970. Every major bank in Ireland was closed for a period that dragged on for six months due to a countrywide labor dispute between the banks and their employees. This was before internet or even telephone banking and credit cards. People had stockpiled cash in anticipation of the strike, but the major reason the Irish economy kept going was that people kept writing each other checks. A check is an instruction to your bank to pay the person's name on the check, or the bearer, whatever the case may be. So, how could checks be useful when all the banks were closed and the payments could not get cleared? If your local pub owner knows you well, he would be happy to accept a check as payment of your bar tab. He may then pass that check on to one of his suppliers, along with other checks he collected to pay for the next keg of beer. Remarkably, the system kept working because shop owners and bar keepers knew their customers well enough to know whose checks to trust.[10] The checks were money as long as people were willing to accept them as money.

Those who believe that money and debt are virtually indistinguishable are adherents of what is known as the *credit theory of money*—explored and confirmed in Chapter 3 on central banks and treasuries, along with competing theories. According to the credit theory, money is not a commodity but an accounting device. This stands in contrast with *metallism*, the belief that money should be a precious metal like gold or silver or be fully convertible into one. In his book, *Debt: The First 5,000 Years*,[11] the anthropologist David Graeber takes the credit theory even further by arguing that all original money systems were effectively debt-based, and most subsequent systems were too.

As a social technology, credit has social as well as economic implications. There is a psychological transition when the credits we accumulate start to be seen as something "owed" to us. That is why people with lots of money often come across as entitled.

The evolution of language reveals the close connection between money and our sense of obligations to and from others. Consider the word *finance* in English (and similar words in other modern languages, including *la finance* (French), *die Finanz* (German), and *las finanzas* (Spanish).[12] They all trace their roots via Old French to the Latin verb *finire*, meaning "to finish," because financial soundness is associated with final repayment of debt.[13]

## Trust

This leads us to another vitally important element of money: *trust*. The reason I may not accept a scruffy piece of paper with an IOU from you, may well be that I don't know you or I don't trust you, or both. For me to accept an IOU from you as payment, I have to trust you in terms of both your ability and your willingness to pay your debts. But for your IOU to become money, not only do I have to trust you, but I also have to believe that other people will too, otherwise I will not be able to pass your IOU on to the next person. When you give me a piece of token money, a bill signed by the Secretary of Treasury of the United States, I trust that. Why? Because I trust the U.S. government to tell me what is money that I can accept for payment and, even more important, I know everyone else will trust the U.S. government too.

But what of an unfortunate country which is in a state civil war with the government contested, and the national reserves depleted? Even though I may be offered a bank note from such a country with similar print and design quality to the U.S. dollar, I would prefer not to accept it.

The reason laws governing the issue of money (bills and coins) always state that the government will accept said money as "legal tender" in return for debts payable to it, particularly taxes, is to demonstrate this trust for all to see (and also to start the circulation of that money). The declaration also means that the government's creditors (for example, anyone who buys a government bond) must accept its currency in payment. But what if I don't trust the government? Well, then I need something else that I can trust in, like the currency of another country, or something that is universally valued, such as gold. That is why gold coins are often favored by people who mistrust governments of all stripes, and why the demand for gold—and hence its price tends to increase during times of economic or political trouble.

It is hard for people to trust the abstract. And the more we fear, the less we trust. The less trusting we are, the more we want forms of money that provide "proof" of the value of the currency.

Think of cigarettes being used as money in a prison. The inmates are unlikely to trust one another enough to keep a central ledger as our idyllic community of honest island dwellers did, but exchanging cigarettes solves that problem. Having a tangible token that has value in itself reassures receivers of the currency that they can trust it.

It is so easy to be tricked by the tangible, because it is very human to want to associate money with something that we can touch, something that looks and feels valuable. Even when we go to the ATM to withdraw the money we have in our bank accounts, we feel slightly richer at an emotional level when we stuff $200 dollars of crisp, new notes in our wallets. This is despite the fact that our bank accounts have just been debited by the same amount. We are not richer—we only feel richer.

Have you ever had a somewhat damaged $20 bill in your wallet? Chances are you passed it along as soon as you had the opportunity. Even though damaged U.S. paper currency is still legal tender, we all have the instinct to get rid of any money that looks dodgy. There is a name for this—it is called

*Gresham's law.* Also known as "bad money drives out good," it refers to situations where there are two or more types of money in circulation with the same face value but different quality. Gresham's law has been operative throughout the history of money. When emperors started debasing their coin by minting it with cheaper metal, people hoarded the purer coins, and passed along the impure ones as soon as they could in payment for goods or services. It's always better to have the next person be stuck with the doubtful money.

Gresham's law comes back again and again in many different forms, but the principle is always the same: When two types of money have the same face value, but one is more desirable than the other, the less desirable money will be passed on. It applies even in cases where money is not debased, but a difference in value emerges for some other reason. A modern-day example can be found between the Namibian and South African currencies: The southern African country of Namibia pegs its currency, the Namibian Dollar (NAD, or N$), at par to the Rand (ZAR), the currency of neighboring South Africa. Both N$ and Rand are legal currency in Namibia, but tourists find it useful to have N$ for local cash transactions. However, international travelers are advised to use all their N$ before leaving the country. That is because outside of Namibia, foreign exchange dealers will give you a less favorable rate of exchange for converting your Namibian dollars to U.S. dollars, euros, or British pounds than they would give you for the same amount in South African Rands. Namibia's economy (GDP U.S. $13 billion) is dwarfed by the size of South Africa's economy (GDP U.S. $350 billion).[14] Therefore, the Rand is more welcomed by foreign exchange dealers—they know they will soon be able to sell the South African currency they buy, while Namibian currency will be much harder to offload.

### The Essence of Money

Earlier, in our island parable, we mentioned the three textbook roles of money:
- A unit of account that assigns value to different kinds of goods and services
- A store of value that can be used to defer consumption
- A medium of exchange that can be used to trade goods and services efficiently

Does money have to fulfill all these roles to be true money as we implied? Can money be a medium of exchange without being a store of value?

The difference between the medium-of-exchange function of money and the store-of-value function of money can be illustrated by thinking of a typical town fair with amusement rides. At such events, ride operators typically do not accept cash but only tickets that have to be bought at a central ticket office. This reduces *transaction costs*, as ride operators don't have to worry about safely storing cash or handing out change. For example, you might buy 20 tickets for 15 dollars, and then use them to pay for rides that may cost three, four, or five tickets each. At the fair, the tickets are the only *medium of exchange* acceptable for rides, while the dollars in your pocket are not an acceptable medium of exchange for this purpose. However, the tickets become worthless once the fair ends, so they are not a *store of value*, unlike the dollar notes that stay in your pocket. Are the fair tickets actually money, even if just for a day?

In a thought-provoking paper titled "Cigarettes, Dollars, and Bitcoins," Smit, Beukens and Du Plessis[15] assert that the medium-of-exchange role of money is the *only* essential role, and that money is typically acquired in order to reduce transaction costs. Unlike an asset required as an investment, hoping that its value will increase, money is acquired to lower transaction costs through a form of social coordination. As Smit et al. say in their paper, "Currencies are tools of social coordination for, all else being equal, the transaction costs incurred by an economic agent decreases as a function of the amount of agents that she transacts with that transact in the same currency." This is, of course, just another instance of what is known as the *network effect*. A telephone is only useful to me if many other people have one too. The value to each user belonging to a social media network such as Facebook or LinkedIn increases the more other people join.

Smit et al.[16] take issue with the store-of-value role of money in so far as it refers to the desire to sell currency at a later date. Withdrawing money from, say, an interest-bearing account means that the owner of that money is sacrificing some value for the convenience of being able to have cash to use as a medium of exchange. Hence the medium-of-exchange role is the real role of money. The authors also argue that the unit-of-account role of money (the first one mentioned in our island parable) is not essential either, offering the example of a fiat currency during times of hyperinflation. They point out that even when it is still being used as a medium of exchange, it loses its practical ability to be a unit of account, so stores and restaurants denominate their prices in other units of value.

Using the language of computer technology, it is best to think about money as software, not as a piece of hardware that you can touch or hold in your hand. As software, it represents a protocol in the form of points on a ratio scale, very much like the tally marks we scratched out on the stone in our island parable. For someone to gain five points, credits, or dollars, another has to give up five. This is the true essence of money as software and, more generally, as a social technology.

## Inflation and Equity

Let's return to our county fair example, where tickets to ride are money for the day. Now let's suppose it is a slow day at the fair, so that by early afternoon the ticket office starts discounting the tickets. Instead of paying $15 for 20 tickets, people can now pay only $10 for 20 tickets. This leads people to buy more tickets and take more rides. Are the ride operators happy? Well, they now have more people handing over more tickets to pay for more rides. So at least initially they will be happy. Money creation always boosts the economy, at least for a while.

Whether the ride operators stay happy depends on what their arrangement with the ticket office is. If they get a fixed amount of dollars per ticket collected, they will be very happy because the ticket office carries the full cost of the discount. If, on the other hand, they get a percentage of the total proceeds in line with the proportion of tickets they collected, however the exact formula is constructed, they will not stay happy. That is because they will realize that the tickets used to buy rides from them are now worth less than before. Operators will respond by raising prices—for example, by charging five tickets per ride when they originally only asked for four tickets per ride. This is the process we call *inflation*, which means a general increase in the price level or, conversely, a decline in the purchasing power of money. The opposite of inflation is *deflation*, which means a general decrease in the price level.

Given enough time, the whole system will reach a new equilibrium: the price of rides settling at a higher cost in the soft currency (tickets) while returning to the same cost in the hard currency (dollars) it was before the discount. But if the fair ends before they can make these adjustments, the ride operators will bear the full cost of the discount offered by the central ticket office. This is but a small illustration of the basic arbitrariness of money as a medium of exchange in the hands of various issuers and other parties who have control over it.

Maybe you suspect that inflation is associated with using fiat currency not backed by any commodity. Oh, how we may long for the good old days when money was solid gold coins!

If money were only based on something intrinsically valuable, like gold, would we still have inflation?

Let's take a step back to examine the argument behind this question. Money is indeed a complete abstraction, but sometimes people will need more convincing in order to trust in its value. That is where gold or silver coins come in handy, because people believe that these commodities have intrinsic value. Why do these commodities have intrinsic value? It is mostly because of their desirability—gold always looks pretty, will not tarnish, and can be used in jewelry.[17] More important, gold is scarce.

What happens to money based on supposedly scarce commodities like gold when those commodities become more abundant? We don't have to speculate. When the Spanish started bringing back shiploads full of gold from the Americas, it lowered the value of money denominated in those metals and caused inflation throughout Europe. Having commodity-backed currency does not guarantee the absence of inflation, nor does it prevent deflation.

A monetary policy that allows or causes unexpected inflation to happen—expected inflation typically gets built into expectations over time and is less disruptive, as in our county-fair-ticket example—will inevitably make winners and losers of different parties in the economy, depending on the positions they hold. Debtors generally like inflation because they can settle their debits by sacrificing less purchasing power than they borrowed, and creditors obviously hate getting paid back in less valuable currency than they loaned out.

Deflation is not good either—in fact, it is usually more destructive than inflation, because falling prices impoverish holders of assets (think of the plummeting house prices after the 2007–2008 financial crises) and reduce wages.

This arbitrariness of how money is exchanged and how its value fluctuates immediately raises fundamental questions of fairness and social justice. No monetary system can be created or sustained without society having to deal with the implications of who has more and who has less, who wins and who loses, and what is ultimately desirable from a societal point of view. We will explore this theme in more depth in the next chapter, as we ask why some people have more money than others.

---

**Note 1.1 The Need for Society to Manage Money**

Clearly, money needs to be properly managed by the society it serves. It cannot be put on autopilot. In Chapter 2 on economic disparities, we will see how attributes of money can affect wealth and poverty. In Chapter 3 on central banks and treasuries, and Chapter 4 on the global financial system, we will see how various institutions play the role of manager on behalf of society at large. Chapters 5 through 8—on fintech, cryptocoins, blockchains, and the cashless society—explore new forms of money. To understand how to manage them, we must return to our monetary roots.

## The Early History of Money

The earliest forms of money have a lot in common with the latest forms of money, more so than with the coins and notes that came in between. These are but physical manifestations of what money truly is—namely, a way to keep track of our material obligations to one another. Money is, at its heart, a system of debits and credits. This is a crucial point often missed by histories of money that start by telling you that the first money was minted by the Lydians in the sixth century BC—these may have been the first coins but they were not the first money: coins are just tokens that have appeared, disappeared, and reappeared through the history of money. Even precious metals, called *species money* when used in gold or silver coins, do not convey the essence of what money is.[18]

We have already introduced most of the essential elements of money, and explained how they operate. Now we will take a short look at the history of money's evolution over the ages to see how societies used (and sometimes misused) their money. Often this is a story of two steps forward and one step back, because the progression of this social technology is never without challenges and setbacks. As we will see, money is always changing and is always being reinvented to serve the needs and values of the society of the day. Therefore, we cannot ask what money is without also asking what it is being used for at the time. Every generation goes through a new monetary order. Nothing about money is ever settled—from the way it is produced to the way it is valued, and on what basis.

### Money from Ancient to Medieval Times

In its earliest forms, the use of money was not widespread in society as it is today. It was more typically reserved for particular purposes.

The earliest mention of money in the Bible can be found in the book of Genesis, thought by modern scholars to be written somewhere between the fifth and sixth centuries BC. Sadly this reference is in the context of slavery, as the author literally refers to a particular category of people as those "bought with money."[19]

The ancient Greek historian Herodotus, writing in the fifth century BC, noted disapprovingly how the young women of Lydia sold themselves into marriage. In the same passage, he also noted that the Lydians were the first people to have coined gold and silver and used it for trade:

> All the young women of Lydia prostitute themselves, by which they procure their marriage portion; this, with their persons, they afterwards dispose of as they think proper ... The manners and customs of the Lydians do not essentially vary from those of Greece, except in this prostitution of the young women. They are the first people on record who coined gold and silver into money, and traded in retail.[20]

The reason Lydia needed money was that it was a small trading nation located between the Mediterranean and the Near East. As a crossroads for trade, it needed portable money to transact with travelers of all kinds. Metal was already in use as money, but the great invention of the Lydians was to standardize the metal coins, which they minted from a gold-silver alloy called electrum. Soon, this invention was copied by other trading nations around the Mediterranean. These coins served the merchants in the societies of their day who needed to trade and the rulers who need to establish their authority. It is easy for modern people to assume that everyone at the time was using those coins, but it was only the people who needed them, like we today might need a business credit card. The majority of people were subsistence farmers without the purchasing power or need for money.

The Greek conqueror Alexander the Great was the first head of state who put his likeness on a coin. No doubt he had a huge ego, but stamping the coins with his face on them helped people across his far-flung empire to trust the coins.

The Roman Empire is well-known for its use of metal currency, which facilitated trade across the known world (Figure 1.4, under Pixabay license). Many Roman coins have survived to this day and can be easily purchased by collectors.

After the fall of Rome, and the start of the so-called Dark Ages, the usage of coins in the West declined sharply, since the societies of the day were insular and had less use for them. By the era of the Crusades, however, coins had made a comeback in Europe, being used on both sides of this storied conflict as well as in the Byzantine Empire, where many battles were waged.[21]

But what of paper currency? The first paper banknotes appeared in China as early as the ninth century AD, soon after paper became widely available. Thus, paper became another new technology that was turned into financial technology by human innovation. In the thirteenth century, China was ruled by the Mongol emperor Kublai Khan, the grandson of the fearsome Genghis Khan. Kublai Khan decreed that gold and silver were no longer currency and that traders had to accept his paper notes on pain of death. When Marco Polo visited Kublai's court, he was very impressed with the efficient system of paper money he found and documented it in his famous travel journal.[22]

**Figure 1.4:** Various Roman coins (Fig. Note. 1.4).

## Growing Money

The invention of paper money was only one in a series of monetary inventions that did not require precious metal. As noted by the famed economist John Kenneth Galbraith, tobacco started to be used as money in Virginia soon after the first English colonists settled Jamestown in 1607.[23] In 1642 the colony's General Assembly declared it to be legal tender, outlawing contracts that called for payment in gold or silver (tobacco farmers were well represented in the General Assembly). The beauty of this arrangement was that farmers could literally grow money. A glut of wheat or any other crops would lead to a drop in the crop price, making it hard for farmers to service their inevitable debts. But those who grew tobacco could always pay their creditors.

The exchange rate between England's pound sterling, and the currency of Virginia was therefore the price of tobacco in sterling. This was a floating, not fixed, exchange rate. Using tobacco as money both meant a money supply that expanded with the growth of the tobacco economy, and a floating exchange rate. This flexible arrangement has remarkable similarities to the modern monetary system, and probably explains the endurance of tobacco money in Virginia. This was a type of money that served the needs of a largely tobacco-growing society very well.

To address the problem of inferior grades of tobacco leaf being passed on as payment while the best leaves were kept behind (Gresham's law in action again), tobacco leaves came to be weighed and graded in public warehouses, with certificates being issued for quantity and quality. We can think of these warehouses as tobacco banks. Interestingly, as we will see in Chapter 3 on central banks, this is very similar to one of the world's earliest central banks, located in Holland, which cleared up the uncertainty surrounding too many types of coins in circulation by weighing and grading the coins. In 1727 tobacco certificates or notes became legal tender, and continued to be until the end of the nineteenth century. Galbraith points to the remarkable fact that tobacco money survived in Virginia for nearly two centuries (until the federal government took over the issue of money). This lasted nearly twice as long as the gold standard.[24]

### Fuel for Revolutions

Meanwhile in England, the British Parliament had banned paper money, but when the American colonies rebelled, this ban was yet another oppression they immediately cast off. The Continental Congress did not have taxation power, and the rebellious citizenry of the colonies were in no mood to be taxed, given that taxes were what triggered the revolution. And it would also have been a practical and logistical nightmare to collect taxes from the unwilling colonists when parts of the country were in enemy hands. Yet, making war is an expensive business, so the American Revolution was largely financed by the aggressive issue of paper money:

> Between June 1775 and November 1779, there were forty-two currency issues by the Continental Congress with a total face value of $241,600,000. In the same years the states issued another $209,500,000. Domestic borrowing, much of it rendered in the notes just mentioned, brought in less than $100,000,000.[25]

The bills were called *continentals*. Not surprisingly, with the flood of new money being put in circulation into the economy, prices started climbing and inflation eventually turned into hyperinflation. Creditors hid from debtors lest they be repaid with worthless money, and those who relied on interest income were devastated. The phrase "not worth a continental" was coined. Yet, as we know, the colonies won their freedom, something they could not have achieved without the aggressive issue of their fiat currency. This was exactly the type of money that particular society needed to help them accomplish their most important goal at the time. Victory was more important than low inflation, or having "sound" money.

The French Revolution was also financed by paper money, called *assignats.* To help people trust this new type of money issued by the revolutionaries, the assignats were initially backed by claims on land previously owned by the Church, which the revolutionaries had appropriated. Unlike gold and other precious assets, land could not be smuggled out of the country by the fleeing nobility. Initially the assignats were very sound money and people were happy to accept them. Unfortunately, the demands of war forced the issue of many subsequent rounds of the assignats, no longer convertible to land, eventually rendering them worthless. As Galbraith says:

> It was the fact of scarcity, not the fact of intrinsic worthlessness, that was important. The problem of paper was that, in the absence of convertibility, there was nothing to restrict its supply. Thus it was vulnerable to the unlimited increase that would diminish or destroy its value.[26]

The convertibility of assignats to land was not in itself what gave them value. It was the fact that it made them scarce enough for people to trust.

## Features and Bugs of Money

We explained earlier why money is both an important human invention and an essential social technology on which society relies for its proper functioning. We have also said that money is more akin to software than hardware, since it is not tangible (even though it sometimes makes use of tokens like notes and coins) but rather can be thought of as a set of rules that we as a society implement.

Anyone who knows even a little bit about software knows that it has both *features*, the intended functioning of the system, and *bugs*, the unintended and mostly unwanted ways in which the system functions or malfunctions. To illustrate some of the more glaring bugs, we shall start with that famous monetary system: the gold standard. It had many good features, but also a couple of fatal bugs.

## The Gold Standard

Ever since its demise roughly a century ago, the gold standard has been a source of nostalgia for those who long for the good old days when money was sound and backed by a truly valuable substance. People who want to return to the gold standard typically fear inflation more than anything else and they don't trust the government to contain it. They believe that the discipline of a limited supply of gold will control inflation by putting a cap on the money the government may put in circulation. That is as far as their views on monetary policy go.

But their desire for the gold standard is also motivated by a preference for a very strict fiscal policy. They want the government to be tied down by gold, so it cannot spend money it doesn't have on causes they consider unworthy. Most often, proponents of a gold standard come from the libertarian part of the political spectrum (like former U.S. Congressman Ron Paul), and have a strong ideological aversion to "big government" and hence deficit spending by governments. Therefore, the debate about the gold standard is also a very political debate.

Let us look at the gold standard, its heyday, and consider its features.

At the end of the eighteenth century and the beginning of the nineteenth century, Britain first was at war with its American colonies, and then with Napoleon in Europe. War being expensive and reserves running low, the government pressured the Bank of England to print money (Bank of England notes) to pay for its campaigns. Not surprisingly, inflation resulted. In 1810, the House of Commons impaneled the Select Committee on Gold Bullion to figure out why the value of Bank of England notes had fallen while the price of gold had risen. Galbraith calls the debate that ensued the most famous debate on money in all of history. It surfaced two opposing viewpoints of money that survive until today and keep coming back in slightly different forms:

> Where does economic change originate? Does it begin with those who are responsible for money—in this case with those who made loans and thus caused the supply of notes and deposits to increase? (From this then comes the effect on prices and production, including the stimulating effect of rising prices on production and trade.) Or does change begin with the production? Does it originate in business activity and prices with consequent effect on the demand for loans and thence on the supply of notes and deposits, which is to say the supply of money? *In short, does money influence the economy or does money respond to the economy?*[27] (Emphasis added.)

In crude terms, the two views of money may be thought of as a supply theory and a demand theory. The supply theory, known today as the *quantity theory of money*, is that the more money you put into circulation, all other things being equal, the more goods and services will cost in terms of money. The *demand theory* is that production and business activity will drive the demand for money, which in turn will lead to the creation of more money in a growing economy. We shall return to this important debate later.

During the epic nineteenth-century House of Commons debate, the later-famous economist David Ricardo counseled that money should have an invariable value so that it should not be subject to the whims of the issuers of money. Of all the precious metals, gold was deemed the most suitable for this purpose. As there were still wars to finance, it took a decade, but Ricardo's argument prevailed and was put into action soon after peace returned to the continent. The Bank Charter Act of 1844 perfected the system, which had the following features: First, the note issue of the Bank of England was limited to a specified amount to be secured by government bonds. Second, beyond that specified amount, notes could only be issued if there were enough gold and silver (the junior partner to gold) in the Bank's vault.

Two key instruments of central bank policy were essential features of this system: the bank rate at which the Bank of England loaned funds to other banks, and open-market transactions, whereby the Bank bought and sold financial securities on the market. We will return to these policy instruments later in Chapter 3 on central banks and treasuries.

In 1876, the other leading industrial countries of Europe also signed up to the gold standard, which meant that within each country, bank notes (and deposits) could be freely exchanged for gold at a fixed rate. This also implied that a fixed exchange rate existed between the currencies of these countries.[28] The gold standard locked the participating industrial economies into a system in which their economies were coordinated and tended to be in equilibrium with one another: If one country's economy was experiencing a boom, prices would rise, and goods would flow in from the other countries. Gold was used to pay for these goods. With gold flowing out from the boom countries, the decrease in gold reserves there would cause interest rates to rise, and that would slow the economy down by cutting prices, output, and employment. At the same time, the new gold arriving in the other countries would stimulate their local economies.

The gold standard seemed like a very solid system with great features, but there was a catch—it was always dependent on gold retaining its relative scarcity. And herein lay an enormous irony: the use of scarce commodity like gold gave rise to deflation that hurt the poor, and thus cause a democratic uprising that could vote against gold. Here again, we see the importance of money as a social technology. When different classes in society have different preferences for the nature of their money—the rich abhorring a reduction in value of money, while the working class would benefit from its depreciation—the resolution becomes a profoundly political game.

But the immediate vulnerability of gold was war. The gold standard was a peace-time standard. What would happen if it were to be tested by a war? Well, the answer came swiftly when World War I (known as the Great War during this time) broke out in 1914. The main belligerents, Germany, France, Austria, and Britain suspended specie payments, meaning that notes and bank deposits were no longer redeemable in gold. In short, they went off the gold standard. The United States, which remained neutral until 1917, stayed on the gold standard, though there was much initial concern that Europeans would sell their investments in the United States and repatriate their proceeds in gold. However, with German U-boats prowling the Atlantic, there was not too much appetite for shipping gold back to Europe. Then the unexpected happened— gold started to flow into the United States in large quantities:

> Soon the United States had more gold than any country had ever possessed before—the increase was from $1.5 billion at the end of 1914 to $2.0 billion at the end of 1915 to $2.9 billion at the end of 1917. It was a flood with a double effect. It destroyed the gold standard in the countries whence it came and also in the country where it went.[29]

Why was all this gold coming to the United States? It was in payment for American goods—everything from grain to munitions, which were in high demand by the warring powers in Europe. The gold reserves in the Bank of England and the Bank of France got depleted. Paper money replaced gold coins. Before the war, gold coins and paper bills in circulation had equal status, with people giving no thought to exchanging one for the other. But then gold became scarce and special, so people preferred to hold on to it and pass along paper money—Gresham's Law at work.

After the war and a couple of tough economic cycles that followed it, many people in Britain longed for a return to the gold standard. They had fond memories of the golden days of the British Empire when gold and sterling (British pounds) were interchangeable. In 1925, Winston Churchill made one of his trademark thundering speeches, concluding with these words:

> Thus over the wide area of the British Empire and over a very wide and important area of the world there has been established at once one uniform standard of value to which all international transactions are related and can be referred. That standard may, of course, vary in itself from time to time, but the position of all the countries related to it will vary together, like ships in a harbour whose gangways are joined and who rise and fall together with the tide. ... [S]uch a foundation is important to all countries and to no country is it more important than to this island whose population is larger than its agriculture or its industry can sustain, which is the centre of a wide Empire, and which, in spite of all its burdens, has still retained, if not the primacy, at any rate the central position, in the financial systems of the world.[30]

The speech convinced Parliament to return to the gold standard, despite some ringing cries of "No!" interrupting the speech at the end.

It was a calamity. The biggest mistake was restoring the gold standard at the prewar exchange rate between gold and sterling. In the post-war economy, this ratio was far too high, which implied that prices of goods and services were too high. Anyone who had pounds could do much better to exchange them for foreign currency and buy the much cheaper equivalent goods abroad. The adjustment required by the gold standard was a painful British depression which would lower the prices of goods, services, and wages. By 1931, after an eventful six years which included the 1929 U.S. market crash, the British government went off the gold standard again.

The fatal bug in the gold standard is its rigidity and restrictiveness. It only works under a narrow set of conditions and cannot be adjusted fast enough to changing circumstances. The money supply is essentially fixed and does not automatically expand with the growth of the economy. It also requires all countries who are on the gold standard to manage their economies in synchronization with one another. This is often not practical or even possible. (The astute reader may wonder if the latter problem is not a flaw of the euro too. While the euro is a fiat currency with growth in its supply not constrained by any physical quantity but managed by a central bank, the participating countries all decide independently on their fiscal policies with some constraints applying. Thus, the euro zone has a modern fiat currency with a single monetary policy but diverse fiscal policies. The synchronization problem applies, but only to euro zone fiscal policy.)

### Money and the Real Economy

Another feature and "bug" of money is its link to the real economy, a topic that has divided economists in different camps. Money may be an abstract concept, but in the real economy people have jobs (or not), produce goods (or not), and build and buy houses (or not). In their extreme form, we have, on one hand, the monetarist proposition that money causes income, and on the other hand, the Keynesian proposition that income causes money. In the middle between these two extremes, there are various altogether more reasonable propositions that each causes, and is caused to some extent, by the other. These more complex but pragmatic propositions are the more likely, which shifts the extent to which variable influences the other, according to empirical economic research.

In our introduction, we debunked the often-told story that societies move from barter to money as a superior method of trading value. As appealing as it may be, it is most likely a myth. Anthropologists have been complaining for years about this misstatement beloved by economists, because no one has been able to find any credible evidence supporting it in their research on ancient societies.

There is a dirty little secret as to why economists seem so comfortable with the barter idea. It can be found in any undergraduate microeconomics textbook: Basic microeconomic models implicitly assume a barter economy. While economists who use these models do not claim that we live in a barter economy, they assume that the economy can be analyzed as if it were one. For the purpose of simplification, they are ignoring the mechanism of exchange. This assumption that money has no real effect on the economy is sometimes referred to as the "classical veil." The purpose of monetary economics, on the other hand, is to analyze the role that money plays in the economy.

So, what is the link between the monetary or financial sector of the economy, and the real or goods sector? Most economists use models in which the rate of interest is the crucial link (or transmission mechanism) between the monetary and the real sectors.[31] The reason is that the rate of interest is both a financial measure (the inverse of the price of financial assets), and a real measure (the rate of return on capital invested). The housing market is a well-known example of this linkage: when interest rates go up, mortgages become more expensive, and fewer homes are built or remodeled. A lowering of the interest rate boosts the construction of new homes and the remodeling of existing homes.

### Inflation and Hyperinflation

Whether money is made of an intrinsically valuable substance like gold, issued as paper bills fully convertible into such a valuable substance, or made only of paper (fiat money), the assessment of its value is based on a belief in its scarcity. Since gold is scarce—there is only a limited quantity of it on our planet and there will never be more, as gold can only be made inside a star—we find it quite plausible to believe in the scarcity of this attractive yellow metal. When money is not linked to a scarce substance, as in the case of fiat money, we need to be convinced in other ways that the money is scarce and going to stay scarce.

Most governments don't just print money willy-nilly. If they did, people would lose faith in the value of currency. That is why (as we shall explain in more detail in Chapter 3) central banks conduct their operations to maintain the faith in the value of the currency by carefully managing its supply. Most modern economists believe that this is a better strategy than linking the value of money to gold, which, as mentioned, has a fixed supply that cannot grow with the economy. And it is also why (as we shall see later) bitcoin's founders limited the total amount of this cryptocoin that can be issued, and why the creation of new cryptocurrency is designed to be a difficult and energy-intensive process. It is to artificially create this scarcity.

In the case of ordinary inflation, the monetary authorities have been unable or unwilling to manage increases in the price level to a desirable range. Inflation can therefore be seen as a flaw in the monetary system. Or as Milton Friedman famously said, "Inflation is always and everywhere a monetary phenomenon in the sense that it is and can be produced only by a more rapid increase in the quantity of money than in output."[32]

Hyperinflation, on the other hand, occurs when money becomes almost completely worthless—when it literally takes wheelbarrows full of paper bills to buy bread or when prices cannot be posted anymore because they change too fast.

Inflation and hyperinflation are thus two distinct phenomena. Hyperinflation is not merely the most extreme form of inflation. Rather, hyperinflation is associated with societal breakdown and deep flaws in the political system. Often, there is internal or external strife, and governments that confiscate assets from their citizens. Whether it is Weimar Germany in the 1920s, or Zimbabwe (see Figure 1.5, licensed under Creative Commons attribution) in the first

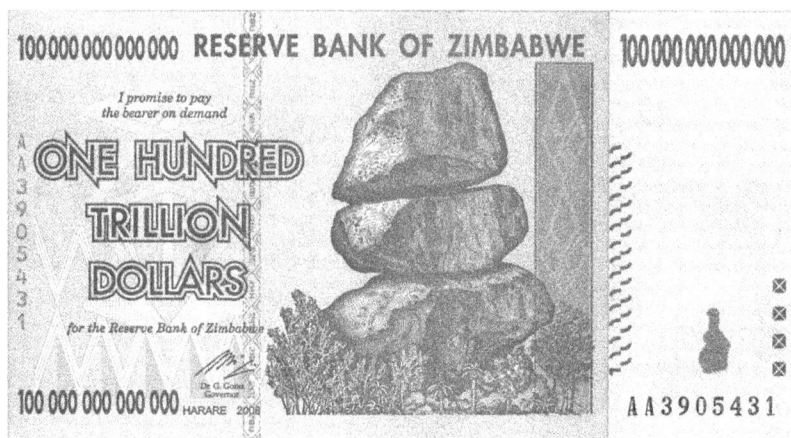

**Figure 1.5:** Zimbabwean one hundred trillion dollar note, 2008 (Fig. Note 1.5).

decade of the twenty-first century or present-day Venezuela, hyperinflated money reflects the deep distress of the society it is supposed to serve.

## Money and Policy

Clearly, given the importance of money to society, it is important to have a policy governing it. As stated earlier, to be considered "money," a thing must function as a unit of account, a store of value, and a medium of exchange. For the purpose of monetary policy, economists focus on a definition that synthesizes all three of these functions: *that money is any asset generally acceptable in payment for debt.* This definition implies that, like beauty, money is in the eye of the beholder, and that the definition may change from time to time. Remember our example of the county fair where ride operators would only accept tickets as payment for rides, not dollar bills.

Another more technical definition is that money is a perfectly liquid asset. *Liquidity* depends on the speed, cost, and certainty in which an asset can be converted into purchasing power. A house is a most illiquid asset because it takes time to sell, incurs significant transaction costs like brokerage fees and taxes, and you are not sure how much you will get for it.[33] Your money market fund is a lot more liquid and may be sold at low transaction costs, with the proceeds credited to your bank account within days or less.

Keynesians believe in a liquidity spectrum, where assets can be ranked by liquidity with relatively small differences between adjacent assets on the spectrum. Monetarists, on the other hand, see a large gap between money (cash and other financial assets that are close substitutes) and all other assets.

It is widely understood that government monetary policy affects the money supply. It is perhaps less widely understood that government fiscal policy (taxes and spending) also affects the money supply. By definition, money can be created (through an increase in the money supply) or destroyed (a decrease in the money supply) only by increases or decreases in any of the four following activities:[34]

1. *Bank lending to the non-bank private sector, as when the bank extends a loan to you and me.* Such loans create money. When the loans are paid off, money is destroyed.
2. *Non-bank private sector lending to the government, like when private individuals buy government savings bonds.* Such purchases destroy money. When the bonds are paid out, money is created.
3. *Public sector borrowing, when the government spends more than it receives in taxes, it creates money.* This is because taxes destroy money, but

government expenditures create money. If the difference between the two is a deficit, net money creation is happening. Conversely, when the government runs a surplus (an altogether rare occurrence), net money destruction is happening.

4. *Transactions with overseas entities.* Travelers buying foreign currency for a vacation abroad destroy their domestic currency, while exporters selling foreign currency (received in payment) to get domestic currency create money. Loans to overseas borrowers create money domestically just as they would for domestic borrowers. Government purchases of domestic currency create money, while government purchases of foreign currency destroy money.

On the fiscal side, we can thus see that government spending will increase the money supply unless these are financed by taxes, by borrowing, or by selling foreign currency.

Money is an important technology on which society depends. As such, it needs to be well understood and carefully managed. Monetary authorities do not have an easy job. Along with their fiscal counterparts, they have to balance multiple, often competing objectives, and must wrestle with important social questions we all have about money.

## Our Money Journey Will Continue

We hope that this book will help improve the understanding of money and how it works for society. The journey we will travel in this book is organized into eight chapters, each an answer to an important question about money. In this first chapter, we have attempted to answer this question: What exactly is money, and what role does it play in society?

In the remaining seven chapters we will address the following questions:

Chapter 2—Why do some people make more money than others?

Chapter 3—How do banks and treasuries create and control the money?

Chapter 4—How does the global finance system help societies to make efficient use of money?

Chapter 5—How is financial innovation changing our relationship with money?

Chapter 6—What is new about cryptocurrencies like bitcoin, and what is not?

Chapter 7—How will blockchains change the way business is done?

Chapter 8—How close are we to a cashless society, and what are the upsides and downsides to living in one?

On this journey we shall see that monetary innovations often start on the fringes of society, but eventually get adopted by the establishment. The establishment loves so-called "sound money," because they have much to lose and can afford to be risk-averse. Those who have less to lose and more to gain tend to be more open to innovation and more willing to experiment. And so money keeps evolving with the needs of the society it serves.

# Chapter 2
# Why Some People Have So Much Money and Others Have So Little

*Men possessed of money, like men earlier favored by noble birth and great title, have infalli-*
*bly imagined that the awe and admiration that money inspires were really owing to their*
*own wisdom or personality.* —John Kenneth Galbraith[1]

## How Money Is Earned

In our preface we explored the phrase "making money." In our opening chapter, we have seen that money can be created seemingly out of nothing by the
monetary system, a topic we shall further explore in the next chapter. But unlike the government or banks, the rest of us cannot create money out of nothing. Running a printing press at home making counterfeit currency will soon
result in a knock on the door by the authorities who take a dim view of others
appropriating their special privileges[2] to create money. Therefore, for most people who work for a living, "making money" simply means earning an income.
More generally, making money means any transactions that will thicken your
wallet or increase the money in your bank accounts.

Of course, in the economy, money circulates all the time, like water circulates all the time through the earth's biosphere. My income is your expense,
and your expense is someone else's income. The government also takes part
when it taxes Sally and spends the money on Joe. (But if the government
spends money on Joe without offsetting that spending with taxes elsewhere, it
is also creating the money that Joe receives, as discussed in the last chapter.)

At some point the question arises: How is money exchanged in the economy
between different parties, and why do some have so much more than others?

Let's take a closer look at the major money issues that have had economists
arguing for ages. The first has to do with who gets rewarded for economic activity, and what they get paid.

### Factor Payments: A Key Concept

If you think about it, there are only a few ways to earn, or make, money.
Economists call them *factor payments*. Each factor has a different way of getting paid, and the payment is called a different term for each factor:

https://doi.org/10.1515/9781547401116-002

- *Rent* is the payment that the landlord of privately owned land or real estate demands for its use.
- *Wages* are what workers demand in return for their *labor*.
- *Interest* is what owners demand in return for the use of their *capital* (which includes money, equipment, and other resources invested in production).
- *Profit* is the reward that businesses (called *entrepreneurs* in economic literature) earn for their enterprise, and is equal to *revenue less cost*.

**Is the Return to Intellectual Capital a Distinct Factor Payment?**
In the twenty-first century economy, the returns to *intellectual capital* are viewed by some commentators[3] as a factor payment on par, or even superior, to the traditional factor payments listed above. But often the return to intellectual capital resembles one or the other of the traditional factors of production. For example, a royalty paid for use of a patent or a copyrighted work seems similar to rent paid for the use of land, while professionals are paid premium fees (i.e. wages) for their unique knowledge. Then others call intellectual capital a new type of capital, which of course would imply that interest is the factor payment. This requires classifying royalties as interest. Given these competing considerations, we are not quite ready to call the return to intellectual capital a separate factor payment yet.

The sizes of the factor payments relative to one another are hugely consequential, not just for the growth of total national income or Gross Domestic Product (GDP),[4] but also for how money is distributed between people, and ultimately for determining who has power and how society is structured.

In order to be complete, we should also mention *taxes* and *government transfer payments* here. These are not factor payments, but ways in which the government can take money from some people and give it to others (redistribution), spend the money on the provision of government functions, or purchase goods and services from suppliers. In the latter case, the suppliers could make profits in the same way they would if they were supplying any other customer.

Last, you may wonder how buying and then selling an asset like a security at a "profit" falls into this schema of factor payments. A transaction like that would indeed put money in your pocket, but it would be more accurate to refer to this type of windfall as a *capital gain* rather than a profit in economic terms. The capital gain may be attributed to a true appreciation driven by a change in underlying factor payments like interest or profit, but it can also come from speculative forces not associated with any factor. As an example of the first case, the price of a bond is inversely related to the prevailing interest rate, as we will explain in Chapter 4 on Global Finance. A drop in interest rates would therefore increase the price of the bond. Someone who bought it at the old price could sell it at a gain at the new price.

Another example of a factor payment change would be an increase (or de-crease) in the value of farmland because of favorable (or unfavorable) climate changes; the factor at work here is rent. The stock of a company may go up due to increased expectations of future profit—a clear example of the factor pay-ment for profit affecting the price of a security. The price of a security may therefore change based on any changes in the various underlying factor pay-ments that influence the value of the security.

It is also true, however, that the prices of securities—or any type of other asset like land—may be driven purely by speculation. *Speculation* is the invest-ment in some asset in the hope that it will be worth more in the future just be-cause you think other people will be willing to pay more for it, without having any proper economic rationale for how factor payments will make that asset *earn* more in the future. Successful speculators love to think of themselves as enterprising, smart investors. But this should not fool us into thinking that money was earned or invested in the true sense of the word. As John Kenneth Galbraith defined it so well:

> Speculation occurs when people buy assets, always with the support of some rationaliz-ing doctrine, because they expect their prices to rise. That expectation and the resulting action then serve to confirm expectation. Presently, the reality is not what the asset in question—the land or commodity or stock or investment company—will earn in the fu-ture. Rather, it is only that enough people are expecting the speculative object to advance in price to make it advance in price and thus attract yet more people to yet further fulfill expectations of yet further increases.[5]

In his classic book on *The Alchemy of Finance*, billionaire George Soros empha-sized the role of perception in financial markets, citing economist John Maynard Keynes:

> The fact that a thesis is flawed does not mean that we should not invest in it as long as other people believe in it and there is a large group of people left to be convinced. The point was made by John Maynard Keynes when he compared the stock market to a beauty contest where the winner is not the most beautiful contestant but the one whom the greatest number of people consider beautiful.[6]

While speculation can move a lot of money from one person's pocket to anoth-er's, it is not earned money in the economic sense. Therefore, we will not be concerned with it further in this chapter, but we will be giving it our due atten-tion in Chapter 4, Global Finance: Markets, Movers, and Motives.

Chapter 4 will also touch on the controversial phenomenon known as *share buybacks*, in which a public company spends its money buying back its stock instead of making other uses of the money, such as investing in new products, production equipment, or in people.

## How Changes in Factor Payments Change Society

We cannot stress enough the importance of factor payments, as they are the reality of any economy. They determine who gets the money, who gets more, and who gets less. And that is the central topic of this chapter.

For an illustration of these economic principles as work, let's look at a massive upheaval that occurred in the established social order a few centuries ago. There are central parallels with today's information economy, as we shall see.

In the feudal economy of the Middle Ages, the nobility (feudal lords) owned the land and could demand high rents for it, because productive land was scarce relative to the abundant human labor that was able and willing to work the land. Rent was high and wages were extremely low. In fact, in the feudal economy there were no wages. What happened when the Black Death wiped out much of the peasant workforce? The best-selling historian, Yuval Noah Harari, recounts the immense losses:

> The plague quickly spread all over Asia, Europe and North Africa, taking less than twenty years to reach the shores of the Atlantic Ocean. The plague peaked in the fourteenth century. Between 75 million and 200 million people died—more than a quarter of the population of Eurasia. In England, four out of ten people died, and the population dropped from a pre-plague high of 3.7 million people to a post-plague low of 2.2 million.[7]

How did this horrible human catastrophe affect wages and the structure of the economy? Clearly there was a massive decline in the supply of labor, so we would expect to see wages rise. There is indeed evidence that governments in both England and France tried to prevent wages from rising. The nobility felt that peasants were getting ideas above their station. However, the picture is clouded by the fact that prices rose between 1347 and 1351 due to a drop in supply—crops were not being harvested and fell victim to plagues of locusts and mice. Rising price levels effectively depressed real wages, despite the fall in the labor supply. Then in 1375 there was a bumper harvest. Crop prices plummeted and farming revenues fell. But due to another plague only a few years before, labor supply was tight. The peasants had the upper hand in negotiations, and feudal lords were in economic trouble. Some lords abandoned their properties. Others negotiated terms much more favorable to the workers. It was the beginning of the end for agrarian feudalism, which finally dissolved in the sixteenth century.[8]

Some believe that in today's information era, a new feudalism is arising. Blogger Zach Scott writes:

> In the common conception of feudalism, a relatively small rentier class (lords) uses a variety of subtle and overt political and economic systems to extract value from the daily

lives of the producer class (peasants), who generally have little choice or influence over the system. [Similarly today users] participate in platforms, often with only the barest knowledge of the data they surrender, and that data is then used to generate value exclusively for the platform owners. But there are far more parallels between our current digital ecosystem and feudal societies than can be described with broad strokes, and the commonalities are so striking that it could be argued that the digital ecosystem, and especially the social media ecosystem, constitutes a de facto feudal society.[9]

Clearly, the structure of society and the sociopolitical context can have a strong determinative effect on factor payments. Think of a simple, extremely autocratic system in which only the king is allowed to own land. All of his subjects have to work on his farms at minimal wages and buy everything they need from stores owned by the king. We shall discuss the sociopolitical context later in this chapter, as it has important implications for the debate on inequality.

## A Very Brief History of Economic Thought

As we have just discussed, major changes in factor payments relative to one another can change society in major and sometimes irreversible ways. This issue has therefore concerned economists for centuries and has led to the development of several economic theories.

It is beyond the scope of this book to provide the reader with a complete journey through the development of economic thought that brought us to where we are today—countless volumes have been written on it. Suffice it to say that classical economic thought followed a long arc—from Aristotle to the early Church to the earliest mercantilist traditions to Adam Smith to David Ricardo to John Stuart Mill to Karl Marx. The break between classical economics and the modern school was the Marginal Revolution, with thinkers like William Stanley Jevons (who brought mathematics to economics) and Francis Ysidro Edgeworth, who were followed by the Austrian School that emphasized utility; the Lausanne Collegiate School, with Léon Walras and Vilfredo Pareto, that was concerned with general equilibrium; and then the Cambridge School with Alfred Marshall, Arthur Cecil Pigou, and John Maynard Keynes (cited earlier for his profound insights on the history of money). In the twentieth century there was a continued shift in economics from a more philosophical social science to a more empirical social science; the number-crunching associated with the latter has been accompanied by the added pretensions of being a hard science, like physics. But economics remains a social science.

Post–World War II, prominent economists emerged, such as Paul Samuelson, John Kenneth Galbraith, and Milton Friedman, and more recently, Nobel Laureates such as Daniel Kahneman and Richard Tyler for their pioneering work in the relatively new field of behavioral economics, which ties human psychology to economic behavior. The list of Nobel Laureates[10] in Economic Sciences, and the particular research areas for which they were rewarded, provides an interesting view into the development of the "dismal science," as its practitioners endearingly call it.

This concludes our light-speed introduction to the history of economic theory. Let's now look at the history of the economies our theorists have tried to analyze and some of the insights they came to that will help us better understand the role and distribution of money in society.

## A Quick Tour Through Economic Epochs

In order to know where we are going, it helps to understand where we are now and how we got here. Having whetted our appetite for a bit of economic history with the discussion of the Black Plague earlier, we will now zoom out to look at the highest-level milestones of human economic achievement. See Figure 2.1.

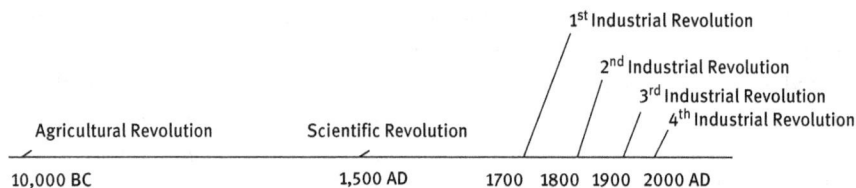

**Figure 2.1:** Transformative economic revolutions (Fig. Note 2.1).

Since we have already provided a history of money in the first chapter, we will now focus on the economic development of society and how that changed the distribution of money between parties.

### The Agricultural Revolution (10,000 BC) and the Invention of Money

During the Agricultural Revolution, humans transitioned from a roaming hunter-gatherer existence to domesticate plants and animals, and to live in permanent settlements.

Yuval Noah Harari describes this monumental transition in *Sapiens*, his book about human history:

> For 2.5 million years humans fed themselves by gathering plants and hunting animals that lived and bred without their intervention .... . All this changed about 10,000 years ago, when Sapiens began to devote almost all their time and effort to manipulating the lives of a few animal and plant species. From sunrise to sunset, humans sowed seeds, watered plants, plucked weeds from the ground and led sheep to prime pastures. This work, they thought, would provide them with more fruit, grain, and meat. It was a revolution in the way humans lived—the Agricultural Revolution.[11]

Only a few animal species were suitable for domestication, and we have not been able to add to that list for the last couple of thousand years. The same is largely true for plants—even today, more than 90 percent of the calories that feed the human race come from plants that were domesticated between 9,500 and 3,500 BC: wheat, rice, corn (called *maize* outside of the United States), potatoes, millet, and barley.

Most earlier scholars cast the Agricultural Revolution as a giant leap forward for humanity. But Harari provocatively calls it "history's biggest fraud"[12] for the following reason: There is no evidence that the Agricultural Revolution improved the human condition; on the contrary, it may have worsened it. Foraging humans depended for their survival on a broad and intimate knowledge of the plants they gathered and the animals they hunted. They had a varied and healthier diet. While the Agricultural Revolution enlarged the total food supply, it did not improve the human diet, nor did it allow humans more leisure. Humans were breaking their backs from dawn to dusk in the fields to cultivate wheat and to protect their crops against pests. The human body is optimized to climb trees and run after animals, not to stand bent over crops all day. Studies of ancient skeletons confirm a range of associated ailments such as slipped discs, arthritis, and hernias. Humans had to live in settlements close to their crops because their cultivation demanded so much time. Cultivating crops imposed village life on previously free-wandering humans.[13]

It might seem that humankind traded freedom for security, but growing a single crop did not give people economic security. Peasants who relied mainly on one crop to feed themselves were actually less secure in their food supply than hunter-gatherers who could thrive on a variety of foods. While village life brought some benefits, such as better protection against wild animals and the elements, it carried enormous, new risks. People were always just one crop failure away from starvation. Gathering together in close quarters also enabled diseases to spread much more quickly.

Harari does point to one collective yet highly questionable benefit. The Agricultural Revolution did allow the same size of land to support a larger number of humans, even though they were malnourished and had aching backs. As Harari concludes: "This is the essence of the Agricultural Revolution: the ability to keep more people alive under worse conditions."[14]

This would not be the last time we humans chose quantity over quality of life. It is a recurring theme in our economic development. But by the quantitative metric of human species success, rather than by the quality of life, the Agricultural Revolution was wildly successful. The world population in 10,000 BC is estimated to be somewhere between one and 10 million humans. By 1,000 BC the population had grown to 50 million, and by 500 BC it had grown to 100 million.[15]

With the success of the Agricultural Revolution came vast increases in the scale of production and commerce, and the need for new technologies to serve that growing economy and society. The first known money appeared around 3000 BC in ancient Sumeria, and it was intimately linked to the agrarian society it was invented to serve. It was denominated in fixed measures of barley grains measured out in standardized bowls. Each bowl measured out one sila of barley, which was the unit of money in ancient Sumeria. (Money was literally a measure, as it still is today.) The reason the first money had to be a commodity was because people had not yet been taught to trust the abstraction of money. Being paid two silas of barley for a day's labor was acceptable, because you could eat the barley if you wanted to instead of trading it. Little trust was required. The only thing you had to check was whether the measure was true or, in later cases, whether the scale was unbiased and the weights were true.

A big breakthrough came when people learned to trust money that had no intrinsic value. The first money of this kind, silver shekels (0.3 ounces of silver), appeared in ancient Mesopotamia in the middle of the third millennium BC. Silver is a precious metal today, but it had no inherent value at the time since it was inedible and was too soft to use as a tool. (It had some use in jewelry. But unlike gold, it tarnishes quickly.) Set weights of silver eventually gave way to coins. The first coins were struck around 640 BC by King Alyattes of Lydia in western Anatolia. Unlike pieces of metal, coins did not have to be weighed for each transaction, and the mark imprinted on them indicated that a political authority (i.e., the king or emperor) guaranteed the coin's value.[16]

As societies grew larger and more complex, the ability of the human mind to store and process information was exceeded by the sheer amount of data that society generated and needed to remember, particularly about transactions and taxes. This led to the advancement of two human activities we take for granted today: mathematics and writing. It is well known that money and numbers go hand in hand; the earliest counting systems started with the Ishango bone described in the previous chapter.[17] But it is less well known that money prompted another great human invention—that of *writing*, which first appeared in ancient

Sumeria somewhere between 3,500 BC and 3,000 BC. The earliest writing was limited to facts and figures. It was, in fact, bookkeeping of transactions. In modern technological terms, we could say that they had spreadsheets before they had word processors. The earliest scripts analyzed by archaeologists were recordings of sales and purchases of grain. In other words, our first writing systems were meant for bookkeeping, not storytelling. Writing followed money.

### The Scientific Revolution (1500 AD)

By 1500 AD the world population was somewhere between 400 and 500 million people.[18] Annual global GDP per capita (stated in 1990 dollars to account for inflation) was between $500 and $600.[19] That was not much higher than the global per capita income 1,500 years before. Per capita income was stuck between $400 and $500 for a millennium. However, 500 years later, in the year 2000, there were six billion people on the planet, with annual global GDP per capita (using 1990 dollars as the measure again) of $6,000.[20] That represents a ten-fold increase in average income per person in 500 years. What made that possible?

It was possible because about 500 years ago, humanity engaged in a Scientific Revolution that equipped us with the technological know-how and the scientific methods that, starting in the late eighteenth century, fueled four industrial revolutions which each boosted human productivity in previously unimaginable ways. Each industrial revolution built on those that came before it, and each was more consequential than the previous, transforming society along the way so that the world that existed in 1500 is now unrecognizable. Furthermore, the frequency of the industrial revolutions increased—while the first three came at roughly one-century intervals, the third and fourth were only a few years apart and happened during many of our lifetimes.

The first two industrial revolutions have been well-known history for a while, and the third had already been identified by other commentators. But we have Klaus Schwab, prominent founder and executive chairman of the World Economic Forum, to thank for announcing the fourth revolution in his eponymous book[21] and for making the distinction between the third and the fourth revolutions.[22]

### The First Industrial Revolution (Early Eighteenth to Early Nineteenth Century)

This revolution was enabled by the invention of the steam engine in 1698, which would eventually power factories and locomotives. The resulting mechanization of production (as we went from muscle power to machine power), and the ability to transport raw materials and finished goods via rail over land (previously only possible over the ocean or major inland waterways) irrevocably changed the world's economic, social, and physical landscapes.

### The Second Industrial Revolution (Late Nineteenth to Early Twentieth Century)

The major technologies enabling the Second Industrial Revolution were electricity, which eventually replaced most of steam power, and the assembly line. These two technologies combined to enable mass production in the late nineteenth and early twentieth centuries. The most famous pioneer of mass production was the car manufacturer, Henry Ford. Due to Ford's efforts, soon imitated by others, automobiles went from niche transport vehicles (a bit like all-electric cars today) that co-existed with horses and buggies for the first two decades of the twentieth century, to the dominant form of personal transport in the developed world by the 1930s (see Figure 2.2). To this day, the "buggy whip" remains a dominant symbol of obsolescence.

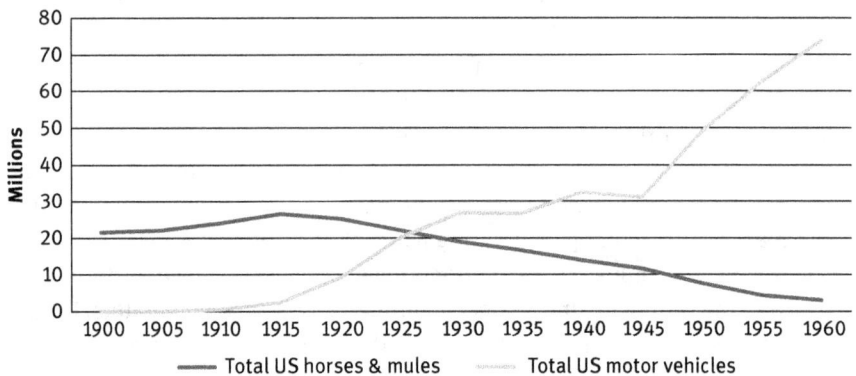

**Figure 2.2:** Replacement of horses by automobiles in the United States (Fig. Note 2.2).

The post–World War II automobile explosion became the second wave of this industrial revolution, defining a new way of living for much of the developed world and for the United States in particular, as newly mobile workers and their families moved from cities to suburbs.

### The Third Industrial Revolution (1960s to 1990s)

This revolution is usually called the Computer or Digital Revolution. It was spurred by the development of semiconductors: the transistor was invented at Bell Labs in 1948, with the first integrated circuits following about a decade later. In the 1960s came mainframes, and personal computing (Figure 2.3, licensed under CC BY-SA 3.0 U.S.) started in the 1970s, picking up speed in the 1980s. The 1990s saw the introduction and rapid adoption of the internet.

**Figure 2.3:** IBM Personal Computer Model 5150, launched in 1981 (Fig. Note 2.3).

### The Fourth Industrial Revolution (2000s to present)

According to Schwab,[23] the Fourth Industrial Revolution builds on the Digital Revolution as digital systems become "smart" and transform everything from smart factories with communication over the Internet of Things (IoT) to smart cars that can drive themselves. Everything will be connected through the IoT, just as everyone became connected through the original internet. But Schwab also includes technologies other than advanced robotics and artificial intelligence in the Fourth Industrial Revolution. They range from biotechnology such as gene sequencing and manipulation to materials technology like nanotechnology to quantum computing and renewable energy technologies.

## Revolutions Always Have Consequences

Our tour through economics epochs shows how one revolution had led to another. Now let us look at the long-term consequences of these various movements and, in particular, ask why it is that, despite progress, we still have a problem of global poverty.

Many people allow themselves the occasional minor fantasy that they may be descendants of royal blood or nobility. That is one reason why family-tree making (genealogy) and lately the accompanying DNA testing are popular. But if you were alive at any point more than a couple of centuries ago, the chances are probably more than 90 percent that you were a dirt-poor farm laborer. Depending on the sociopolitical structure of the country you were in, you were either a serf or peasant who had to serve some lord (which also entailed fighting in his wars), or you were a slightly more independent subsistence farmer. Feeding yourself and your family was your primary daily concern. Starvation was always but one failed harvest away, pestilence lurked around every corner, and the roads were not safe to travel. If you are reading these words, you can consider yourself extremely fortunate compared to the vast majority of humans who lived on this planet long before you.

### The Industrialization of Agriculture

Before the Industrial Revolutions mechanized it, farming was extremely inefficient. After industrialization (starting with the First Industrial Revolution and continuing through the others), a much smaller and continually shrinking number of farmers could feed a fast-growing number of factory and office workers in towns and cities. Today in the United States, only 2 percent of the population (working on about 2 million farms) feed not only themselves, but the entire population of the United States, and export over $130 billion worth of agricultural products to the rest of the world each year.[24]

If agriculture had not been industrialized in the rural areas, the Industrial Revolution could not have happened in the urban areas. Workers need to eat, and not enough people would have been able to work in the factories and offices without the food surplus produced for them by more labor-efficient farms.

In economic terms, this transition from subsistence farming to mechanized farming meant a huge increase in the factor payment to labor, otherwise known as wages. The agricultural value-added per laborer in the United States (what each farm laborer adds to the GNP) now exceeds $80,000 per year. Compare that to the poorest countries in sub-Saharan Africa, which have not yet made the transition to industrialized agriculture and are still stuck below $1,000 per laborer per year.[25]

While workers in agriculture and in any other industry are not paid their full value-add but only some portion of it (an important topic that we will get to soon), they benefit as long as they proportionally share in the productivity gains.

**Note 2.1 Some Are Left Behind by the Industrial Revolution**
Here we have our first explanation of why some people—in this case, farming communities in the developing world—have so little money compared to others. The first two Industrial Revolutions in agriculture (mechanization and electricity) have not reached them yet.

Furthermore, they too often lack the transportation and other infrastructure brought by the First Industrial Revolution that would allow them to get increased agricultural production to market, and they may lack the connective technology of subsequent revolutions. Today 1.1 billion people (14 percent of the world's population) still live without electricity.[26] Meanwhile, today's modern farmer in developed countries is fully current with the first two Industrial Revolutions, and is in the process of incorporating the last two.[27]

## The Industrialization of Production

For our impatient generation, spoiled by the pace of the Third and Fourth Industrial Revolutions, it is hard to comprehend how slow-moving the First Industrial Revolution was. It took a long time from the invention of the steam engine to its widespread productive use, and an even longer time to achieve a rise in productivity and living standards that would benefit society. It is estimated that the turning point in living standards was only reached by about 1830.

There was also a dark side to the Industrial Revolution. It was during this time that Europeans began working much longer hours in what the poet William Blake called the "dark satanic mills," commonly 3,200 hours per year for men, women, and children alike, often under atrocious conditions. In this First Industrial Revolution, European workers toiled about 50 percent more hours than their modern-day counterparts in the developing world.[28] The vast majority of us are indeed very fortunate to live in the current century.

A big reason for living standards not improving faster during the First Industrial Revolution, was the lagging effect of what economists call *Malthusian economics*. Robert Malthus was an English cleric who wrote an influential book, *An Essay on the Principle of Population* in 1798, opposing the optimism that prevailed due to the technological advancements of the First Industrial Revolution. Malthus made the following observation: An increase to the food production of a nation will only lead to a temporary increase in well-being, because it will lead to population growth, which will restore the original per capita food production. In other words, the more food we produce, the more mouths there will be to feed. This rather pessimistic view of humanity's future is called the *Malthusian trap*. Malthusian views can be found in art and literature from Charles Dickens to dystopian modern science fiction and video games.[29] Today, economic scholars of the First Industrial Revolution frame it not so much as a technological revolution but as a societal revolution during which society finally broke out of the Malthusian trap. Again, we see that economics is a social science, and the history of economics is the history of human progress.

How did industrializing society break out of the Malthusian trap? Until the eve of the First Industrial Revolution in Britain, it did not look like it would. Before the late eighteenth century there was a period of stagnation in per capita incomes. The technological progress led to increased population rather than improved standards of living. But then, with the onset of what is called the Great Divergence around 1760, the British economy started the transformation to the post-Malthusian age during which technological progress outpaced the drag of population growth. Economic historians still argue about which economic models can explain this transition, but most point to a growth in innovative activity as the most important force in the explosion of productivity that propelled society out of the Malthusian trap.[30] Most of their analyses are based on the foundation laid by Joseph Schumpeter, who was the first economist to bring the process of innovation into rigorous economic thought. Setting the human mind free to apply the new scientific knowledge yielded by the Scientific Revolution, in innovations that benefited society, is what finally allowed us to thrive.

**Note 2.2 Technological Innovation Increases Human Productivity**
Here we have our second explanation for why some people have more money than others: Scientific knowledge combining with the power of human ideas increase human productivity to levels that pay not only for population growth, but create excess value for society to become rich and reinvest in itself. The more innovative a society is, the wealthier it will tend to be. The larger the role that particular individuals play in those innovative activities, the more money they will make.

However, as we shall see in our third explanation, technological innovation also has a dark side: It may decrease the relative wages of those workers associated with the older technologies that have become less important to the growth of the economy.

## The Laborer's Wages

Adam Smith published his famous book, known for short as the *Wealth of Nations*, in 1776. It was published the same year as the American Revolution, during the early years of the First Industrial Revolution in Britain. Smith had extensively researched the writings of others and conducted his own primary research (which included several years of factory observations) to write this book, which actually contains five books. In it, Smith defined the *free-market system*, which comprises key elements that we now take for granted, such as:

- **Specialization.** Instead of one worker making the whole product, the production steps are broken up, with workers specializing in each step and sequentially adding value. (Smith was intrigued by his observation of a pin factory, which showed him how much productivity could be gained by specialization.)
- **Competition.** Sellers of goods need to compete for the business of buyers looking for the best price.
- **The law of supply and demand.** Buyers will bid up the price of a product if it is scarce and they have high demand for it. The higher price will induce sellers to produce and sell more of the product. Conversely, when there is an oversupply, factory owners will have to drop their prices to attract more buyers, at the same time decreasing their production of the product.

Smith's ideas formed the cornerstone of what we would refer to today as the classical school of economics. His views on how workers earn a living in a new system of specialized labor have influenced us to this day and have provided us with a key rationale for using money—since workers are now specialized, each of them is unable to supply themselves through the fruits of their own labor. Every worker needs things produced by the labor of others. Every person thus becomes a merchant; people exchange their labor for items, thus acquiring over time all the other things they need to live. This calls for a medium of exchange (money) to manage all these exchanges. Bartering is impractical because our needs are too numerous and varied.

### The Labor Theory of Value (LTV)

While all this makes perfect sense to anyone who grew up in the capitalist system, it does not yet tell us what the exchange value of a good ought to be. For that, Smith developed the *labor theory of value* (also known to economists by its acronym, LTV), which is that the "real" value of anything must be assessed in terms of the labor required to produce it. It is explained as follows by Smith:

> The value of any commodity, therefore, to the person who possesses it, and who means not to use or consume it himself, but to exchange it for other commodities, is equal to the quantity of labour which it enables him to purchase or command.
>
> Labour therefore, is the real measure of the exchangeable value of all commodities. The real price of every thing, what every thing really costs to the man who wants to acquire it, is the toil and trouble of acquiring it. What every thing is really worth to the man who has acquired it and who wants to dispose of it, or exchange it for something else, is the toil and trouble which it can save to himself, and which it can impose upon other people. What is bought with money, or with goods, is purchased by labor, as much as what we acquire by the toil of our own body. That money, or those goods, indeed, save us this toil. They contain the value of a certain quantity of labor, which we exchange for what is supposed at the time to contain the value of an equal quantity. Labor was the first price, the original purchase money that was paid for all things.[31]

But how is the real value then determined in practice? Smith went on to explain that while equal quantities of labor always have the same value in this system, the nominal price in terms of money can vary as the value of money changes.

So Adam Smith, a classic proponent of the free-market system, articulated the labor theory of value. In what is in hindsight an ironic twist, Karl Marx adopted the LTV a century later, though he never called it that. The LTV is central to the Marxist philosophy—that workers are exploited by their capitalist bosses. Marxists reason that laborers work for part of the day to add the value that covers their wages, and the remainder of the day to enrich the capitalists who employ them.

In fairness to Smith, that is not exactly what he had in mind. Smith's idea of price or value in exchange was based on the labor that someone was willing to *expend* to acquire a product. In this, Smith anticipated the more nuanced analysis of value by later classical economists like David Ricardo. For example, you may be willing to spend three months' wages to buy a certain car that you desire. But you are not going to spend that much to buy an undesirable vehicle, no matter how hard the factory workers toiled to make that vehicle. The latter is an illustration of what is called the *subjective theory of value*.

### The Utility Theory

For all but those in the Marxist school, the labor theory of value was replaced in the early nineteenth century by the utility theory, expounded by William Stanley Jevons. The *utility theory* acknowledges that there is no intrinsic monetary value in anything but the value that we humans assign to it based on our current needs and wants. The utility theory explains why a glass of tap water in a restaurant is expected to be free (at least in North America), while a person dying of thirst in the middle of the desert would give all the money in their wallet to buy that same quantity of water. Jevons went on to craft a theory of exchange that fits on top of his theory of value.

In the simplest terms, the value of anything is determined by the amount of money someone is willing to pay for it. If we add the element of competition and the laws of supply and demand, it follows that when many sellers compete to provide a good or service, buyers will take advantage of that competition to drive down the price of the good or service they are buying.[32]

Businesses understand this effect very well, and are always trying to avoid the "commoditization" of their products, where their products as seen as the same as those provided by the competition. They will try to add features, however small, to convince potential customers that their product is better and deserving of a higher price. This is called *product differentiation*. Take a consumer packaged good (CPG) like toothpaste. Even if you like to buy the branded product like Colgate or Crest, you will always pay less for their regular version, rather than the new-and-improved version with special ingredients X or Y. That is because the former is more of a commodity, and the latter is more differentiated—at least for a short while, until competitors imitate it. CPG companies make most of their profit from the latter, which explains their constant tinkering with packaging, features, and ingredients.[33]

The extreme case of differentiation is a *monopoly*: when a supplier sells a product for which there is no apparent substitute, and when it is very hard for other suppliers to enter that market. If you were a monopoly supplier, you may think that you could charge whatever you like for it. But if you set your price too high, no one may want to buy what you are selling, and the higher your price, the less you will sell. Think of ticket prices to a unique, once-in-a-lifetime show. The ticket prices may be high because of the monopoly effect, but there is clearly a maximum, as it's likely that no one would pay a million dollars to see it. Even monopolies have their limitations and cannot make unlimited revenue or profit. In fact, microeconomic theory tells us that monopolists can determine either how much they want to sell, or the price at which they want to sell, but not both. The price of a monopoly good is determined by the buyer demand and the pricing strategy of the monopolist, who presumably will want to maximize profits.[34] For most monopolies, the selling price will be higher than in pure competition, but the quantity sold (and produced) will be lower than it would be under pure competition. The latter point is why it is often argued that monopolies hold back economic growth.

If you are a worker who earns wages for a living and you hope to make more money that way, you will have similar considerations. First, you need to find a line of work in which there is a high economic demand. That means you cannot look only at how many positions are available and how many other workers you will be competing with, but also at how much employers are willing to pay for that kind of work. Second, you need to continuously differentiate yourself as much as possible by acquiring and improving the most in-demand skills in your chosen profession.

It is well known that earnings rise and the unemployment rate drops by level of educational achievement. In the United States in 2018 the unemployment rate for people with professional degrees was only 1.5 percent, while the rate for people with only a high school diploma was 4.1 percent. Median weekly earnings for professionals was $1,884 compared to only $730 for those with only a high school diploma.[35] This relationship is present across the spectrum of educational achievement, with more education associated with higher earnings and lower unemployment.

> **Note 2.3 Skills Supply and Demand Affects Wages**
> Here we have our third explanation of why some people—in this case, wage-earning workers—make more money than others. In a free market for labor, those with skills which are both scarce and in high demand in the labor force will generally make more money than those who have skills that are plentiful and in low demand.[36] Compounding this effect is the general (beyond labor) free market, which favors goods and services that are scarce and in high demand, benefiting all whose income is associated with the sales of these goods and services (whether as wage earners, advisors, or investors).

In this regard, let's pause for a moment to reflect on the importance of pricing in the free market, which we know almost too well. In a free-market society, we let the money price of a good or service communicate the value of that good or service to everyone concerned. Price thus can be considered a piece of information needed by all market participants. It has proven to be an efficient coordination mechanism, as it is watched by both buyers and sellers. It also allows for decentralization of production decisions, and for willing buyers and sellers to exchange value. The market price is what makes Smith's invisible hand work as if by magic.

The price concept is not without its flaws and omissions, as we will see later in this chapter. Sometimes, for example, it fails to capture information about all the costs and benefits associated with the production and consumption of a good. Economists speak of *market failure* when they describe situations in which inefficient allocations of goods and services happen in ostensibly free-market systems. Market failures result in net social welfare losses, and these usually need to be remedied by society, with people acting collectively through government structures.

## The Sociopolitical Context for Making Money

We have discussed all the textbook ways in which factor payments determine who makes more or less money. But we would be remiss if we did not also refer to the sociopolitical context which, for most of history, has had a larger influence on determining who is poor and who is rich. Inequality has been a constant companion in the human journey. Examining the sociopolitical context can go far in explaining the value of factor payments and to whom they may flow.

There is much talk today of wealth concentration in the hands of the "1 percent." Have the rich been getting richer, or is this normal? Has this been the dominant economic trend in human history? And what has led to reductions or increases in inequality? These are some of the questions Walter Scheidel covers in *The Great Leveler*,[37] his survey of inequality through the ages until the present day.

Piecing together data on relative wealth from archaeological and written records, Scheidel shows that unequal shares of wealth go back at least to the early agricultural settlements that existed between 6000 and 4000 BC, and that they spanned the globe. For example, burial sites from ancient Mesopotamia have graves for children that can only be explained by family wealth, not by personal achievement.

Why would agriculture result in increased social stratification? It's because crops are suitable for storage, which makes it easier for elites to appropriate surplus food resources. All premodern states, as well as the vast premodern empires like the Roman Empire and Han dynasty, exhibited great inequality between the ruling elites and the masses. For example, Scheidel assesses the degree of inequality in ancient Rome as follows:

> At the peak of its development in the mid-second century CE, an empire of some 70 million people generated an annual GDP of close to the equivalent of 50 million tons of wheat, or approaching 20 billion sesterces. The corresponding mean per capita GDP of $800 in 1990 International Dollars appears plausible in relation to other premodern economies. According to my own reconstruction, the households of some 600 senators, 20,000 or more knights, 130,000 decurions, and another 65,000 to 130,000 unranked wealthy families added up to a total of a quarter of a million households having an aggregate income of 3 billion to 5 billion sesterces. In this scenario, about 1.5 percent of all households captured between a sixth and close to a third of total output.[38]

The 1 percent has indeed been with us for a long time.

Access to political power provides economic rents (i.e., the ability to make more money) in itself. It is the judgment of historians that the Roman aristocrats of the first and second centuries BC were far too rich to have accumulated their wealth through farming or commercial activity alone. As Scheidel says:

> The more that personal fortunes depended on access to political rents, the more income from labor—at least if we can define corruption, embezzlement, extortion, military plunder, vying for benefactions, and taking over the assets of rivals as forms of labor—would have mattered than it did for entrepreneurial or rentier investors of capital in more orderly and pacified societies.[39]

A favorite mechanism whereby kings and emperors through the ages awarded their associates was by means of land grants. Such estates then became family property, which got passed on from generation to generation, perpetuating and reinforcing inequality. While the transfer mechanisms may be different today, few would doubt that the politically well-connected are able to turn those connections into ways of making more money pretty much anywhere, whether in the present-day United States, China, or South Africa.

---

**Note 2.4 The Economic Advantage of Power and Connections**
Here we have our fourth explanation as to why some people make more money than others. The well-connected in society always find ways of turning their political power, or their close proximity to those in power, into economic power. Sometimes these gains are overtly corrupt in nature, but in most developed economies the gains are made perfectly legally within the prevailing rules and laws of that society. The rich also work very hard to transfer their privileges to the next generation, and to pass on their accumulated wealth from generation to generation—for example, by lobbying against inheritance taxes, or simply making sure that their children benefit from the personal networks they built up.

---

Scheidel concludes that increases in inequality were driven primarily by technology, economic development, and state formation. But his most unsettling conclusion is that leveling (a reduction in inequality) over all of human history only happened when there were violent shocks to the system that at least temporarily slowed or reversed the concentration of wealth due to the accumulation of capital and political power. He classifies these violent shocks into four categories, the "Four Horsemen," which are: transformative revolution, mass-mobilization warfare, civil war, and plagues. According to this theory, the lowering of inequality in the United States after the Gilded Era of the 1920s and the Great Depression was due to the mass mobilization warfare of World War II and its aftermath. Since the 1970s, inequality has been on the rise again as the mid-twentieth century forces receded and the long-term trend reasserted itself.

But economic trends—even long-term trends—are not inevitabilities. Nor are they laws of physics, like gravity, that have to be obeyed. The degree of inequality in a society reflects the cumulative political and economic choices which that society made over time. Countries with otherwise very similar types of economies and cultures can show quite different patterns. For example, between 1980 and 2007 (i.e., until just before the Great Recession) the share of the top 1 percent rose by about 135 percent in the United States and the United Kingdom, but only by 76 percent in Canada and by 39 percent in New Zealand.[40]

## The Current Distribution of Money in the World

As we have seen, money has always been unevenly distributed through history. Our focus here will be on money's distribution during modern times, particularly in the last few decades.

The current situation is one of contrasts. Proponents of different policies have a way of picking their preferred facts, but it is not acknowledged often enough that a number of statements which seemingly tell different stories could be true at the same time. The following all apply to the last few decades:

- Hundreds of millions were lifted out of poverty in the developing world, particularly in large fast-emerging markets like China, growing the size of the global middle-class.
- Middle-class wages in developed economies such as the United States have stagnated since the early 1970s.
- The rate of wealth accumulation at the top exceeded that at the middle and bottom, resulting in a higher concentration of wealth at the top.
- Low-income jobs are growing faster than middle-income jobs.

What is the explanation for the above? Which forces are at work?

### Larger Pie, More for the Many

Economists use gross domestic product (GDP) as a way to measure the total output of an economy. It is the sum of all consumer spending, investment, net inventory changes, government purchases, and net exports. The world economy has grown rapidly over the last few decades, from just over $1 trillion in 1960 to over $80 trillion in 2017. (At a global level, there are no net exports.)

Economic growth outpaced population growth over the same period, with the result that GDP per capita (per person) grew robustly as well, from $450 in 1960 to $10,700 in 2017 (see Figure 2.4). This seems to be a rosy picture, and in aggregate terms it certainly is. But it does not provide information about those who have been left behind by this growth in the economy, nor those who, as of late, have been going backward.

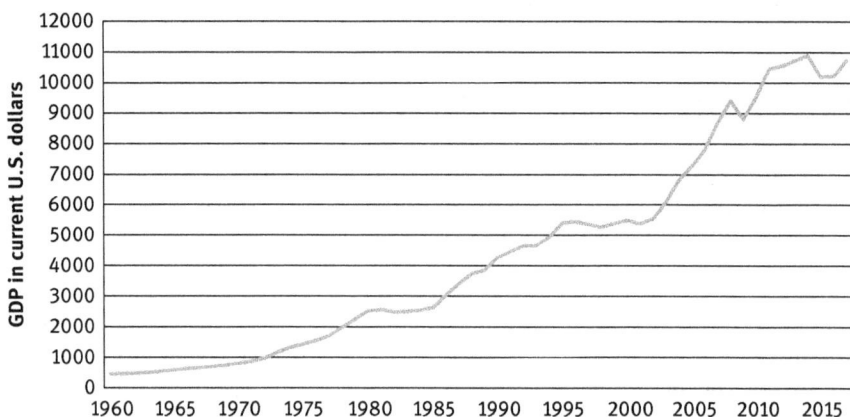

**Figure 2.4:** World GDP per capita 1960–2017 (Fig. Note 2.4).

According to most analyses, the percentage of people in the world living in extreme poverty has been on a steady decline in the last couple of decades. The latest World Bank estimates[41] show that the number of people who live below the extreme poverty measure of $1.90 a day (in purchasing power parity 1990 dollars) has steadily dropped from 35.9 percent in 1990 to 10.0 percent in 2015. This is largely due to impressive progress in the East Asia and Pacific regions (down to 2.3 percent) and South Asia (percent unavailable), where economic growth has also been shared among the population. Sub-Saharan Africa has the highest remaining concentration—over 40 percent—of extremely poor people. The World Bank, which itself has been instrumental in reducing poverty through developmental loans and other means, has the stated goal of all but eliminating extreme poverty in the world by 2030—which means reducing it to less than 3 percent—and has reported that this is on-schedule, given recent estimates for 2018.

In September 2018, the Brookings Institution announced a global tipping point that, for the first time since the Agricultural Revolution, the majority of humans are no longer poor.[42] By their calculations, a little over 50 percent of the world population, or 3.8 billion people, now live in households with sufficient income to be classified as middle- or upper-class. The Brookings definition of the middle class is globalized, comprising households spending $11 to $110 per day per person in 2011 purchasing power parity. In macro terms, this is a tremendous achievement for humanity as a whole, with much to be optimistic about. The future projection from the same report is for robust middle-class growth: 4 billion people will be classified as middle-class by the end of 2020, with a predicted 5.3 billion people by 2030. By 2030, the vulnerable group will have shrunk by 900 million people.

In terms of total amounts of money to spend, the middle class dominates. While the rich have more money, there are relatively few of them, and while the poor are many, they have little to spend. That is why the emergence of a middle class with disposable income is considered to be a robust metric of economic progress. Brookings[43] summarizes the breakdown of global demand (money being spent) as follows: Private households account for about half of global demand, with investment and government consumption each being about a quarter. Of household demand, two-thirds come from the middle class. That is why most businesses target the middle class—it is where the lion's share of the money is.

### Larger Pie, More for the Few

While GDP per capita is a good average measure of economic prosperity, it can disguise inequality. For example, imagine two small islands, each with a population of 100 people. Both islands have an identical annual GDP of $5 million each and therefore a GDP per capita of $50,000. However, on Island A there is a society with 10 nobles making $4 million of the total $5 million—that is, $400,000 each. This leaves only $1 million for all the 90 other inhabitants, who each will make $11,111 per year on average. On Island B, on the other hand, there is an idealistic egalitarian society, with everyone sharing equally in the income, allowing each person to make $50,000 per year.[44]

On which island would you rather live? Well, it partly depends where you think you will end up in society. If, for example, you think you would be selected and deserving to be one of the nobility, you would prefer Island A. It also depends on your sense of fairness versus your views on human failings like "laziness" and "free-riding." Maybe you think not everyone contributes enough to share equally in the spoils. Or you may be concerned that any level of perfect equality can only be achieved by some form of coercion, like under a communist system. These two island systems represent the extreme ends of an ongoing ideological debate, with most of us probably preferring to have something in between the two extremes—a system in which exceptional talent and extra effort are still rewarded, but there is also economic justice (or at least some basic safety net for everyone) for those who do not have all the opportunities.

For us, the analysis gets much more interesting when we change the discussion from the normative—asking how superior individual talent and work ethics makes some more deserving of a larger piece of the pie—to the positive: asking which economic forces and major trends might lead different members of society to share more or less in the growth of the economy regardless of their personal efforts. This takes us back to the discussion on factor payments we had earlier in this chapter. We have already seen how the Black Death ultimately led to the demise of the feudal system in Europe, empowering workers and tipping the scales from the aristocracy to workers.

In parts of the world such as China and other parts of Asia where we have seen rapid industrialization coupled with a rising middle class over the last few decades, we are seeing a repeat of the transition the major developed economies in the west went through a century or so ago, with similar effects. People have moved en masse from the farms to the factories and then to offices in a rapid wave of urbanization. But while a growing and thriving middle class has now arisen in these rapidly emerging countries (China in particular), effectively catching up with the West, the effect on the majority of workers in the already developed economies has been less favorable. Many workers in traditionally wealthy countries feel pinched by the twin forces of globalization and automation.

There are some interesting parallels between what happened in the First and Second Industrial Revolutions a century or more ago and what is happening today. Who do you think sounded the following alarm in a 2018 speech?

> Marx and Engels may again become relevant . . . . The benefits, from a worker's perspective, from the first industrial revolution, which began in the latter half of the 18th century, were not felt fully in productivity and wages until the latter half of the 19th century. If you substitute platforms for textile mills, machine learning for steam engines, Twitter for the telegraph, you have exactly the same dynamics as existed 150 years ago—when Karl Marx was scribbling the Communist Manifesto.[45]

If you guessed some radical left-winger or neo-Marxist, you guessed wrong. It was Mark Carney, Governor of the Bank of England, speaking to a business audience at the Canada Growth Summit in April 2018. Carney was clearly not advocating for Marxism, but warning against a set of economic conditions which could make Marxism attractive again for those who feel disadvantaged and left out by the current system.

The First and Second Industrial Revolutions did indeed lead to a surge in productivity and production, but workers who were being substituted by machines did not see their wages rise for decades. Many believe the economic upheavals caused by these Industrial Revolutions led to both the left- and right-wing extremism of the late nineteenth and early twentieth centuries, which gave us militant ideologies like Marxism, Fascism, and Nazism, spawning many conflicts, including two World Wars. In his speech, Carney went on to talk about the "hollowing out" in the middle of the job market as computers are taking over the work of mid-level workers[46] who are the core of the middle class.

The First and Second Industrial Revolutions caused a mass migration from farms to cities, as laborers ran out of work on farms due to farm mechanization and moved to find work in the new factories located in cities. (We could see a replay of this effect in a fast-industrializing China over the past few decades.)

The spoils of the Third and Fourth Industrial Revolutions have also not been evenly distributed geographically. The increasing income stratification we are seeing is being accompanied and amplified by stark regional differences in average income, salaries and property values.

An extensive recent analysis of U.S. residential land values published in a recent Federal Housing Finance Agency working paper[47] casts light on regional disparities. Property values reflect the desirability of the location as well as the ability to pay of those who want to live there. The distribution of land wealth is very unequal—an acre of land in Brooklyn Heights, New York costs $41 million while an acre of land in Yale, Arkansas costs only $5,300—but the growth in value at the high end also exceeds the growth at the low end, meaning that the gap is growing. These land-value disparities reflect the differences in economic situations between dense, wealthy coastal areas such as San Francisco, Seattle, Washington D.C., and New York, and the inland towns in the United States.

But we should not only be concerned with geographic disparities in income between states. Such disparities can also be seen within states. A recent report[48] by the Economic Policy Institute (EPI) states that from 2009 to 2015, the incomes of the top 1 percent grew faster than the incomes of the bottom 99 percent in 43 states and the District of Columbia. In 2015, a family in the top 1 percent nationally received, on average, 26.3 times as much income as a family in the bottom 99 percent.

Recent data from the U.S. Bureau of Economic Analysis (BEA) highlight the wide range of per capita personal incomes across counties in the United States, and the high concentration of income in a few counties:

In 2017, it ranged from $11,937 in Issaquena County, Mississippi to $233,860 in Teton County, Wyoming. Per capita personal income exceeded $100,000 in 12 counties: Teton,

Wyoming; New York, New York; Pitkin, Colorado; Bristol Bay, Alaska; Marin, California; Summit, Utah; San Francisco, California; Nantucket, Massachusetts; San Mateo, California; Fairfield, Connecticut; Blaine, Idaho; and Westchester, New York.[49]

We are facing a significant urban versus rural split in incomes, in which the gains of the knowledge economy accrue to professional and knowledge workers concentrated in large urban centers, while manufacturing in smaller towns and cities are on a perennial decline at least in developed nations.

## Corporations Are Unequal Too

While we are mostly concerned with inequality among people, our discussion would be incomplete without pointing out that there is significant inequality in the corporate world as well. And this inequality does affect workers. Those who are in richer companies and in industries that are doing well economically will generally be doing well themselves. A recent analysis of 5,750 of the world's largest companies by the McKinsey Global Institute shows that inequality is a stark reality in the corporate world: The top 10 percent of "superstar" companies capture 80 percent of the *economic profit*[50] while the bottom 10 percent destroy as much economic value as the top 10 percent create.[51] The vast majority of companies in the middle create near zero economic profit. This distribution has become more skewed, as today's superstar companies are making 1.6 times the economic profits of the superstars of 20 years ago.

Another important insight from the McKinsey analysis is that 70 percent of the worldwide growth in GDP came from only five superstar activities: the first is the internet, media, and software. The second is pharmaceuticals and medical products. The third is financial services such as banking, credit, insurance, and asset management. The fourth is professional services such as R&D, management, and other high-skilled services. The fifth is real estate. If you are making your money in one of these superstar activities, chances are higher that you will be doing well. If not, you have a much steeper hill to climb.

A related concern is the degree to which the largest superstar industry is dominated by only a handful of players. Lately, there has been increased public discussion on whether today's technology industry behemoths such as Apple, Alibaba, Microsoft, Google, Facebook, and Amazon are enjoying outsize profits due to entrenched leading positions in the industry and the difficulty for other companies to effectively challenge them. In the United States, some are calling for the breakup of these companies on antitrust grounds, similar to how AT&T Corporation (the so-called Bell System) was broken up in 1982 to increase competition in the U.S. telecommunications industry. At the start of the previous century, the United States broke up major monopolies in the railway and energy sectors. There is indeed historical precedent for government action to increase competition in industries that have become dominated by large companies who make outsized profits.

### Today's Face-Off: Computers versus Humans

One of the most remarkable aspects of the last two industrial revolutions is the breathtaking pace at which they spread. Although, as mentioned earlier, the various revolutions still have not reached the entire planet. Yet the spread of these revolutions, particularly the latest ones, is vast. Three quarters of U.S. adults[52] carry smartphones, a technology introduced little over a decade ago. In total, 95 percent of U.S. adults have either a smartphone or at least a basic cell phone, a technology that isn't even 40 years old. But the effect of mobile phones on the rest of the world, particularly the developing world, is even more transformative. According to a recent Pew Research Center survey,[53] 83 percent of adults in emerging economies now own a mobile phone, while 45 percent own a smartphone, and 60 percent use the internet. The GSMA, an industry association of mobile-phone operators worldwide, predicts that 5 billion people will use the mobile internet by 2025, up from 3.3 billion people in 2017.[54]

What forces have been unleashed by this, the Fourth Industrial Revolution?

Economists—such as David Autor at the Massachusetts Institute of Technology—have done a lot of analysis of employment trends over the last decade, particularly with reference to the downward pressure of automation on workers' wages.[55] What they found is that high-end jobs like professional, creative, and managerial positions are growing, as are low-paying, poor-quality jobs are the bottom-end of the wage spectrum, which may sound surprising, as we would think of machines as replacing lower-level workers first. Where automation is doing most of its damage, and where many jobs are already stagnant or on the decline, is in the middle of the spectrum, which explains the hollowing out of the middle class that Carney spoke about. The term for this divergent trend is *job polarization*. What it means is that routine jobs in the middle are shrinking while high-end, non-routine jobs are growing strongly and low-end, non-routine jobs are growing mildly in this age of automation and AI.

In a recent paper,[56] Autor finds continued evidence for a fall in real wages for non-college-educated workers. An additional finding is that urban non-college-educated workers currently perform "substantially less skilled work than in prior decades." This de-skilling is the direct consequence of automation.

Autor's analysis divides workers into three broad clusters: manual and service occupations ("low" skill); production, office, and sales occupations ("middle" skill); and professional, technical, and managerial occupations ("high" skill). He finds a major decline in middle-skill employment, a slight decline in low-skill employment, and a sharp rise in high-skill employment between 1970 and 2016.

A few years ago, Maximiliano Dvorkin, an economist at the Federal Reserve Bank of St. Louis, did an analysis to illustrate these trends. Figure 2.5 replicates Dvorkin's original analysis with the latest data from the U.S. Bureau of Labor Statistics.[57]

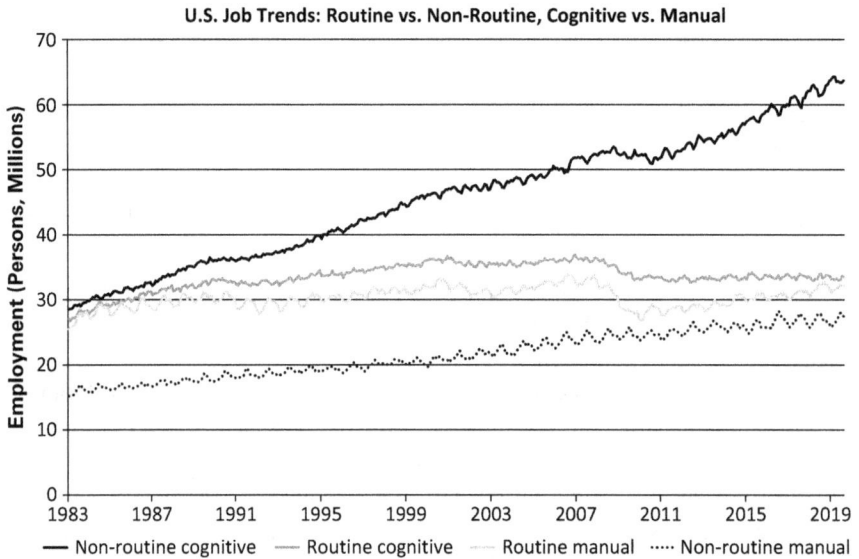

**U.S. Job Trends: Routine vs. Non-Routine, Cognitive vs. Manual**

—— Non-routine cognitive ——— Routine cognitive ——— Routine manual ····· Non-routine manual

**Figure 2.5:** Jobs involving routine tasks aren't growing (Fig note. 2.5).

The disappearing middle-class jobs are routine in either manual work content, like factory work, or routine in cognitive work content, like administrative or sales work. On the bottom end of the pay scale, low-paying, non-routine jobs like home healthcare workers are still growing. (The growth in non-routine, manual jobs is not necessarily a positive, as these are the lowest paid jobs.) But automation is eating previously decent-paying, routine work, and thereby the livelihoods of the middle class and opportunities for people to advance into the middle class. The divergence in employment growth from routine cognitive and manual work started in the late 1980s. These categories were also hardest hit during the Great Recession of 2008. Subsequently, it looks like routine, cognitive employment has been stagnant, while routine, manual employment has picked up a little bit. Many routine, cognitive jobs such as clerical or sales jobs have been permanently eliminated by automation, while some routine manual work will still follow the economic cycle up as, for example, home construction activity picks up.

The current low unemployment rate in the United States does not mean that everyone is economically fine. About 40 million out of 320 million U.S. citizens live below the official poverty margin, according to the U.S. Census Bureau.[58] And according to a recent consumer survey,[59] 39 million Americans (about 15 percent of the adult population) cannot afford a summer vacation this year. Another survey[60] found that only 40 percent of Americans would have enough money on hand in savings to pay for an unexpected $1,000 expense, such as an emergency room visit or car repair. This suggests an unequal distribution of wealth and income, with the bottom barely scraping by.

The most widely-used measure of inequality is the *Gini index* (also called the *Gini coefficient*). It combines the details on the share of wealth distribution into a single number, ranging from 0 (perfect equality) to 100 (extreme inequality, in which one segment takes all the income). The Gini index confirms the rise of inequality in the United States, as shown by an increase from 37.5 in in 1985 to 41.5 in 2016.[61]

The so-called *Great Gatsby Curve*[62] pioneered by Alan Krueger shows the relationship between inequality (represented by the Gini coefficient) and the ability of people to pass on their money-making proficiency to the next generation, called *intergenerational earnings mobility*. The Great Gatsby Curve can, most notably in our supposedly meritocratic world, be used to show that the increasing return on an investment in higher education leads to lower intergenerational social mobility.[63] That is because the rich can afford to prepare and send their children to expensive colleges, and the poor cannot.

A perhaps more intuitive way to look at inequality is to simply track the share of income by the top 1 percent over time. As can be seen in Figure 2.6 (source: World Inequality Database), this share was at its lowest point in the middle of the twentieth century after declining from its heights during the Roaring Twenties and subsequent Great Depression in the 1930s. It declined sharply during World War II and kept declining into the 1970s. But the share of the 1 percent has edged back up again since the late 1970s. It is now nearly back to its peak a century ago.

A recent OECD report[64] provides evidence that the middle class is losing ground worldwide. The OECD defines the middle class in any country as those whose incomes fall within 75 to 200 percent of the median. For example, in the United States that would be a single-person income of between $23,400

**Income share of the top 1 percent in the United States over a century**

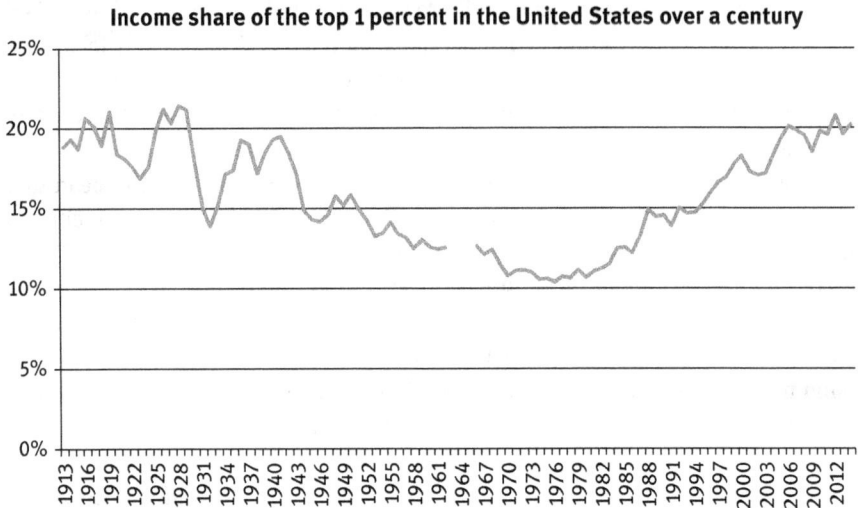

**Figure 2.6:** Pre-tax national income share of the top 1 percent from 1913 to 2013 (Fig. Note 2.6).

and $62,400. There are multiple elements to the decline: First, the proportion of people in the middle class in OECD countries has declined from 64 to 61 percent in the last 30 years. (In the United States, only 50 percent are now in the middle class.) Second, and more important, the incomes of those in the middle class have declined relative to the richest group. Third, fewer people in their twenties are now in the middle class—68 percent of Baby Boomers were middle-class during their twenties, declining to 64 percent of Generation X, and then to only 60 percent of Millennials. Lastly, rising expenditures associated with a middle-class lifestyle, particularly the costs of buying a house, have far outpaced the growth of middle-class incomes over the last two decades. It is no wonder that the middle class is feeling squeezed—they are being squeezed.

Remember that the middle class is where the bulk of the money is made and spent. Any significant trend like this that squeezes the middle class will have a profound effect on society.

But we need to be careful when we talk about the situation of the middle class versus the rich. We may be oversimplifying. A number of recent analyses have suggested that the *upper-middle class* has been growing strongly and is doing quite well. In fact, the upper-middle class seems to be closer to sharing the fortunes of the rich than the fortunes of the middle class below it. A 2016 study by Stephen Rose, an economist at the Urban Institute, found that the upper-middle class has expanded from about 12 percent of the population in

1979 to a new record of almost 30 percent as of 2014. (Rose defined the upper-middle class as any household earning $100,000 to $350,000 for a family of three: at least double the U.S. median household income and about five times the poverty level.) A stricter definition of the upper-middle class as the top 20 percent in a study[65] by Richard Reeves of the Brookings Institute also shows much stronger income growth for this segment over the last few decades.

Writing in *The Atlantic*, Matthew Stewart talks about a "A New American Aristocracy," a segment which he constructed by combining the top of the upper-middle class and the bottom of the upper class into a "9.9 percent" (just below the very top 0.1 percent).[66] This segment of the population is doing far better than all the segments below them. According to Stewart, people in this group are not the flamboyant rich, but the most successful cohorts of the professional class who believe that they have achieved their station in life through meritocracy, and yet are doing everything they can to pass their status down to their children.

An aristocracy does imply a certain permanence, but other research shows how hard it is to stay within the top 20 percent of earners. In a longitudinal study that tracked more than 18,000 Americans from 1968 to 2011, Hirschl and Rank[67] found that 70 percent of the population made it into the top 20 percent of earners for at least one year, but only about 21 percent remained there for ten consecutive years. Success can be fleeting.

Is the discontent we have seen in recent years in major, developed economies such as the United States, United Kingdom, and France due to a problem in the Fourth Industrial Revolution that we have seen in the first two Industrial Revolutions—namely, the juxtaposition of increased productivity and stagnant wage growth? Let's look at what the data tell us on the growth of productivity and real wages over the last few decades.

The Economic Policy Institute has done exactly such an analysis for the United States, using U.S. government data. It shows that while productivity and wages grew in sync between 1948 and 1973, the gap between productivity and a typical worker's compensation has opened up dramatically since 1973, as can be seen in Figure 2.7 (source: EPI analysis). Between 1948 and 1973, productivity increased 95.7 percent and hourly compensation increased by 90.9 percent. From 1973 to 2017, productivity rose a further 77.0 percent, but hourly compensation only 12.4 percent. That means productivity has grown more than six times as fast as wages during this period.

What could be the cause for this disparity? The French economist, Thomas Piketty, wrote a voluminous, much-discussed 2013 book titled *Capital in the Twenty-First Century*, with the English translation published in 2014.[68] Piketty extensively analyzed the evolution of income and wealth over the past 300

**Cummulative percentage growth in productivity and hourly compensation, 1948 - 2017**

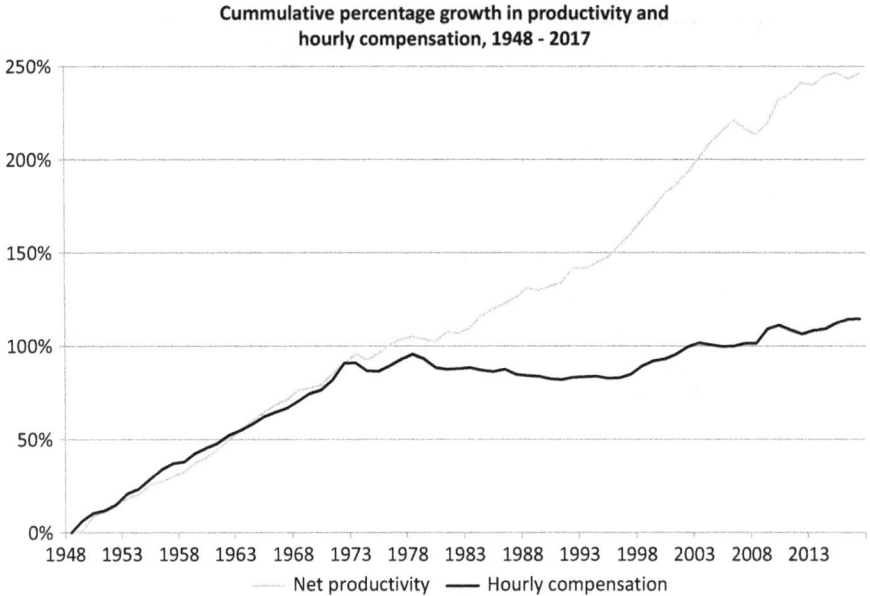

**Figure 2.7:** Productivity growth and hourly compensation growth, 1948–2017 (Fig. Note 2.7).

years, with a focus on Europe and America. He showed that the period from about 1914 to the 1970s was a historical outlier in which both income inequality and the stock of wealth (relative to annual national income) fell sharply. However, since the 1970s both wealth and income gaps have been rising back toward their pre-twentieth-century norms.

Piketty came up with a theory as to why capitalism leads to these unequal results most of the time, concluding that there is a natural tendency for the rate of return on capital to exceed the rate of growth of the economy. The two world wars, the Great Depression, and high taxes during the first few decades after the end of World War II reduced the return on wealth during the twentieth century until the early seventies. But now that these events have receded, wealth is apparently exerting its power again.

---

**Note 2.5 The Long-run Advantages of Capital**
Here we have our last explanation of why some people—in this case, owners of capital—make more money than others. There seems to be a long-term economic trend that we are reverting to again, whereby the factor payment to capital increases faster than the rate at which the economy grows.

Piketty's conclusion—his suggestion for redistributive action to be taken—led him to be called a "modern Marx" by the free-market orientated *Economist* newspaper: Assuming that the *concentration of wealth* is inevitable and has to be remedied, Piketty suggests a tax regime that would redistribute wealthy to correct for the natural trend.[69] Though there are many others who have criticized Piketty's policy prescriptions, there is a general respect for his exhaustive analysis of the data and his contribution to the analysis of unequal wealth accumulation.

If you want to get a more intuitive feel for how the return on capital may keep exceeding the return on labor, do the following thought experiment: Imagine a future—maybe 100 years from now—where all jobs are performed by intelligent machines. No wages are paid to any human laborer, because human labor is no longer needed. Then all the money that laborers would previously have made will go to the owners of the machines, the owners of the workerless factories where machines make machines, and those who hold the intellectual property rights to the technologies in the machines. Wages will be zero, and the rate of return on capital will be extremely high. What will become of laborers? If we are not careful in managing the transition to such a workerless economy, the lack of sufficient wage income to invest in the ownership of financial capital, and the lack of skills to create intellectual capital, will exclude and impoverish large parts of the population. Many people are concerned that we may be headed to such a future, and some are proposing a Universal Basic Income or Citizen's Dividend so that every citizen may receive a guaranteed, unconditional minimum income every month that will cushion the blow of jobs lost due to automation.

A last point on the growth on inequality concerns the ability of one generation to pass on its gains to the next generation. This is known by economists as *intergenerational wealth transfer*. Piketty also analyzed that for France, for which detailed data are available. He found that as long as wealth is concentrated (as currently reflected by rising inequality) and the return on capital is high enough, wealth will become self-perpetuating across generations.

## The Pain and Gain of Redistribution

The response to Piketty is a good segue to our final section in this chapter. People generally do not like to part with their money or their privileges. We tend to be quite fond of both and, as we do, it doesn't take us long to believe that we fully deserve both. If you have flown business class for a year, it is quite a shock to go back to economy class.

Who do you think said the following—maybe Karl Marx or Friedrich Engels?

No society can surely be flourishing and happy, of which the far greater part of the members are poor and miserable. It is but equity, besides, that they who feed, clothe and lodge the whole body of the people, should have such a share of the produce of their own labor as to be themselves tolerably well fed, clothed and lodged.

No, it was Adam Smith in his bible of free-market capitalism.[70] Adam Smith was a moral philosopher long before he was considered to be an economist. Economics as a subject did not even exist at Smith's time. At the same time that Smith commented on the marvels of the invisible hand, he was concerned about the welfare of the people. We will do well to take heed of Smith's philosophical example, to keep both concepts in our mind all the time, and to balance them when they seem to be in conflict.

In this book, public policy is out of scope. However, the mechanisms that society sets up through its governing structures to pay for the common welfare and to provide safety nets for the vulnerable, clearly redistribute large amounts of money from some to others. In any advanced, modern state—even one like the United States, which tends to be more aggressively free-market than, say, the social democracies of Europe—we all give and we all take to a larger extent than we sometimes realize. We all pay taxes (even the indigent pay sales taxes, and low wage workers pay payroll taxes) and we all benefit from public roads, national security spending, education, social security, and other public goods.

With so much money passing through the public purse, what economists somewhat awkwardly call *rent-seeking* is going on all the time. Rent-seeking is a technical term, and should not be seen as necessarily pejorative. Rent-seeking is simply when people and organizations try to gain benefits for themselves through political action, typically to get a larger share of government spending for themselves, or to pay less into the treasury. For example, a company or industry advocating for additional subsidies is engaging in rent-seeking behavior. Retired people who lobby for higher social security benefits are similarly engaging in rent-seeking behavior.

Rent-seeking is as old as our government institutions. The Roman Senate was constantly petitioned for more money—for example, for additional benefits for retired legionnaires and other patronages. The First Triumvirate—between the ambitious future emperor Julius Caesar, the wealthy Crassus, and the wily general Pompeii—was an alliance of convenience formed precisely for this purpose. Half a millennium before, Caesar, King Cyrus of Persia, gave the Jews exiled in Babylonia both permission and money to return to Jerusalem and rebuild the temple.[71] As long as the government has money, people and corporations will knock on its door for chunks of it, or try to persuade the government to take less from them in taxes. Not all of that is bad, nor is all of that good, but the allocations that the government makes will always have consequences.

During our time, the increasingly unequal distribution of money between the top, middle, and bottom of the income and wealth spectrum has led to a timely debate about what new mechanisms may be needed to support people whose jobs are being taken over by machines, and what a fair tax burden for the wealthy is. All of these issues have significant money implications. Ultimately, personal wealth (or the lack of it) is the reason we all care about the topics in the remainder of this book: the creation of money and credit, markets and their madness, the technology of money, and the future of it all. The better we understand these subjects, the closer we will be to mastering this curious social technology we call money.

Part II: **Central Banks and Global Finance**

# Chapter 3
# Fiat Currency and Credit: How Banks and Treasuries Create and Control Money

*Money is the most powerful and useful tool that macroeconomic policymakers have.*
—Paul Samuelson and William Nordhaus, *Economics*, 1985

This chapter answers a fundamental question: How do banks and treasuries create and control the money? As we shall see, these institutions, separately or jointly, have many roles, including:
- Extending credit
- Printing fiat currency
- Setting monetary and economic policy

We will delve into each of these, but first, here is a brief and telling history of a particularly important kind of bank—namely, one entrusted with the capital of a sovereign nation, or the so-called central bank.[1]

## Early Central Banks

The most famous central bank of all time is surely the Bank of England, founded through a unique partnership of the public and private sectors. Granted a royal charter in 1694,[2] its earliest stockholders came from a variety of backgrounds. The opening ledger for the bank shows a purchase of shares for £10,000 from King William and Queen Mary, but on the same page is a purchase from a citizen for £25. The first stockholders were primarily from the "trades and professions, including carpenters and grocers, merchants, doctors, knights and royalty," according to the bank's website.[3] A pamphlet by a founder[4] described a wide range of views on the bank—from those fearing royal power[5] to those fearing popular revolution.[6] As it turned out, it was a little of both.

This innovative bank was the first to launch a system for bills of exchange for use by the mercantile class. This was not merely a major monetary innovation —it also had political implications.

For the first time in recorded history, this bank enabled a gathering of significant sums of private money beyond the sovereign's jurisdiction. The significance of this moment in history was well-documented by Charles-Louis de Secondat, Baron de Montesquieu, who famously said of the bank that "in this manner we

https://doi.org/10.1515/9781547401116-003

owe ... to the avarice of rulers the establishment of a contrivance which some-how lifts commerce right out of their grip." And even more daringly, the bank's bills had no precious metal backing. This could have been an end-run against the state similar to that envisaged by the founders of bitcoin today.

How did it happen? The English crown was deeply in debt, and had trouble borrowing because of its previous defaults and lack of creditworthiness. These monetary developments came in the context of the English Restoration, and the subsequent ascent of William of Orange to the throne as William III. William desperately needed money to pursue his military campaigns, so he allowed the bank to operate and indeed was its founding customer.

Over time, however, despite its potential for economic independence, the bank succumbed to the royal influence. The bank's early and continuing focus on funding the crown, noted one early historian, was "brought about not by the demands of trade and commerce, but by those of the Government."[7] In the end, the bank was nationalized. As we shall see throughout this book, the source of monetary innovation typically occurs outside of the established system and then gets co-opted. There are already signs that this may happen to cryptocurrencies, today's "rebel money," which we discuss in depth in Chapter 6.

While Holland and Sweden had older central banks (dating to 1609 and 1668, respectively), the novelty of the Bank of England was the private-public partnership. It was established to raise money for the crown, and so the neces-sary capital to lend against had to come from the private sector. The deal was that in return for funding the crown by means of loans, the bank was delegated the sovereign right to issue notes—that is, money.

Of course, private money has its own flaws: shallow liquidity (compared to a government printing press); risk of issuer default; and reliance on self-regulation by a small, tightly-connected group of elite participants that may lose the confidence of the people.

Fast-forward a century and we see this vulnerability at play in the early days of the United States. Thomas Jefferson wrote in a letter to John Wayne Eppes in 1813 that "bank-paper must be suppressed, and the circulating medium must be restored to the nation to whom it belongs." Three years later, he wrote to John Taylor of his belief that "banking establishments are more dangerous than stand-ing armies and that the principle of spending money to be paid by posterity, under the name of funding, is but swindling futurity on a large scale."[8]

In the United States, founders established the Bank of the United States in 1791, closed it in 1811, and reopened it in 1816 to 1836, and then went through a "free banking" era from 1837 to 1863, followed by "national banking" from 1863 to 1913, before finally establishing the Federal Reserve in 1913. This cen-tral banking system has three important features: a central governing board—

the Federal Reserve Board of Governors; a decentralized operating structure of twelve regional Federal Reserve Banks; and a blend of public and private characteristics.[9]

In Asia, central banks arrived relatively late on the scene compared to the West. In Japan, the first central bank was founded in 1882 under the Bank of Japan Act of that year. The catalyst for this event was the *New Currency Act* of Meiji 4 (1871), which replaced the unique currencies of fiefdoms with a central currency, the yen.[10] China followed suit a generation later. China's first central bank was established in 1905 as the Bank of the Board of Revenue or Treasury Bank (大清户部銀行). Three years later, its name was changed to the Daquing or Great Qing Government Bank (大清銀行).[11] The Da Qing Bank's note was granted exclusive privilege to be used in all public and private fund transfers, displacing all previous currency. It was also given exclusive privilege to run the state treasury. Renamed Bank of China in 1911, during the revolution that overthrew the Qing Imperial Dynasty, it continues today.

In other countries, original central banks have continued in operation, even as those in Europe joined the European monetary system, founded in 1999, and continuing today as the European System of Central Banks (ESCB), comprising the European Central Bank (ECB) the national central banks of all EU Member States. The ESCB includes both those countries that have adopted the euro, called Eurosystem, and those maintaining national currencies outside that system.[12]

There are ten central banks operating today that have survived the vicissitudes of economics for more than 200 years. All of them are located in Europe and, with the exception of the Bank of England, are part of the ESCB. Five of them have switched from national currency to the euro (Austria, Finland, France, the Netherlands, and Spain), while five continue to use their own currency (Denmark, England, Norway, Scotland, and Sweden).

- We will start with one that dates back to 1609–*De Nederlandsche Bank* in the Netherlands. This bank traces back to the original Bank of Amsterdam, which was founded to clear up the uncertainty surrounding too many types of coins in circulation—including some of dubious value. It was eventually chartered in 1814 by King William I and today is part of the ESCB.
- *Sveriges Riksbank*,[13] or the *Riksbank*, founded in Sweden in 1668, sets monetary policy to "ensure that money retains its value and that payments can be made safely and efficiently." It also issues banknotes (paper currency) and coins.
- *Bank of England*,[14] mentioned earlier as established in 1694, currently has three main missions: It sets interest rates, ensures financial stability, and regulates banks and insurance companies.

- *Bank of Scotland*,[15] founded by an Act of the Scottish Parliament in 1695, operates as a retail and commercial bank. It is empowered by the Scottish parliament to issue currency.
- *Banco de España*[16] came into existence in 1782 and was decreed by King Carlos III. In addition to fulfilling the functions of a modern central bank, it also helps to preserve Spain's cultural heritage by maintaining an art collection.[17]
- *Banque de France*,[18] in operation since 1800, is now part of the Eurosystem. Its three main missions are monetary strategy, financial stability, and the provision of economic services. It is the largest printer of euro notes.[19] This bank pulled off one of the most ambitious policy changes in the history of money, when it declared in January 1960 that henceforth that every 100 francs would be worth 1 nouveau (new) franc. For years afterward, the older generations were still speaking in thousands when buying daily groceries, but the policy prevailed, showing that as an innovation money is hardly a fixed concept.
- *Norges Bank*,[20] founded in 1816 in Norway, has several core responsibilities that include promoting price stability through monetary policy, contributing to efficient financial infrastructures and payment systems, and managing the portfolios of one of the government's sovereign wealth funds: the Government Pension Fund Global, also known as the Oil Fund, as its base capital comes from petroleum revenue accruing to the government.[21] This fund operates for the benefit of all Norwegian people via government programs as needed.
- *Danmarks NationalBank*, the central bank of Denmark, was founded in 1818 and focuses on ensuring stable prices, safe payments, and a stable financial system. The Danish currency is the *krone* (meaning crown), first introduced in 1875.
- *Bank of Finland*, founded in 1819, has as its goal "keeping the financial system stable and secure while fostering and easing the flow of cash."[22]

**Note 3.1 Social purpose of sovereign wealth funds**
Serving a broad public purpose is not unusual for sovereign wealth funds, which are owned and directed by national treasuries, not central banks.[23] What sets Norway apart is its use of profits from a key nationalized industry to accomplish what amounts to income redistribution. Oesterreichische Nationalbank (OeNB), the central bank of Austria, founded in 1816, uses the Euro. Like many central banks, it is involved in cash management, monetary policy, financial stability, statistics, and payments, but it also has a broader social purpose. As its website states, "An organization committed to diversity and sustainability, the OeNB also promotes the sciences and research, and it supports cultural activities."[24]

## Central Banks Founded in the Modern Era

Now let's take a few examples of central monetary authorities (banks and/or treasuries) noting total central bank assets[25]:

*Europe ($5.3 trillion in assets).* The *European Central Bank* has the exclusive right to authorize the issue of banknotes in the Community. As mentioned earlier, it is part of a European System of Central Banks that serves all of the central banks in the region, including those that have preserved their national currency.

*China ($5.3 trillion in assets).* In the People's Republic of China, the *People's Bank* has a mission to "prevent and mitigate financial risks, and maintain financial stability."[26] It includes a China Investment Corporation, which was created in 2007 in order to manage China's foreign exchange reserves. Primary responsibility for bank supervision rests with the government. The Ministry of Finance for China has attributes of both a treasury and a central banking system. It administers macroeconomic policies and the national annual budget, functions generally associated with treasuries.[27] It also handles fiscal policy, economic regulations and government expenditures for the state. In addition, it publishes annual macroeconomic data on aspects of China's economy, including economic growth rates, central government debt, and borrowing.

*Japan ($5.2 trillion in assets).* As the central bank of Japan, the Bank of Japan Act sets the bank's objectives "to issue banknotes and to carry out currency and monetary control" and "to ensure smooth settlement of funds among banks and other financial institutions, thereby contributing to the maintenance of stability of the financial system." Japan also has a Ministry of Finance that includes a Financial Bureau that administers the treasury system, manages government debt, issues coins, and oversees the Bank of Japan, among other functions.[28]

*United States ($3.8 trillion in assets).*[29] In the United States, the central bank function is performed by the aforementioned *Federal Reserve System*, nicknamed the "Fed," composed of twelve regional banks overseen by a board. It works in tandem with the U.S. Treasury, which has broad powers to advise the nation on domestic and international financial, monetary, economic, trade, and tax policy. The Treasury also has a minor supervisory role, overseeing national banks and thrift institutions. (Most U.S. banks are state-chartered banks supervised by the Federal Deposit Insurance Corporation (FDIC), which also insures their deposits.) The U.S. Treasury also does fraud investigations involving treasury instruments,[30] and devotes resources to prosecuting counterfeiters and forgers—a reminder that our world is not yet cashless. Most other financial crime-solving in the United States is led by the Federal Bureau of Investigation (FBI), which supports the Treasury's role at the Financial Action Task Force (FATF), the inter-governmental body responsible for developing and promoting policies to protect the global financial system against money laundering and other threats (for more on FATF's global role, see Chapter 4).[31]

*Germany ($2 trillion in assets).*[32] The central bank of Germany is the *Deutsche Bundesbank* (not to be confused with the privately-owned DeutscheBank). In its mission statement it describes itself as an integral part of the Eurosystem, which groups together the European Central Bank and the national central banks of all countries that have adopted the euro.[33] Finally, banking supervision and foreign reserves are also part of its mission.[34] Germany also has a Federal Ministry of Finance that is responsible for all aspects of German fiscal and tax policy and determines the broad outline of budgetary policy.[35]

The next two largest central banks are those of France and the United Kingdom, described earlier as some of the world's oldest banks.

**Note 3.2 Regional Associations of Central Banks**

National central banks do not operate in isolation. They often join forces with others in their regions or even worldwide.[36] The leading regional associations cover most of the world's seven continents.[37]

- **Africa.** In this region, the *Association of African Central Banks* is engaged in co-operation in the monetary, banking, and financial spheres; forming guidelines for cross-border agreements; and strengthening price stability and financial stability.[38] The association also considers the role of relevant international economic and financial institutions in the African region, and, more ambitiously, envisions a single currency and a common central bank in Africa.[39] In addition, within Africa there is a Bank of Central African States (Banque des états de l'Afrique Centrale)[40] and a Central Bank of West African States.[41]
- **Latin America.** An important organization here is the *Economic Commission for Latin America and the Caribbean*[42] (Spanish name is the *Comisión Económica para América Latina y el Caribe*). Founded in 1948 under the auspices of the United Nations, it has a broad economic agenda that includes central banks. In addition, the region hosts the Association of Supervisors of Banks of the Americas,[43] which strives to strengthen bank regulation and supervision as well as financial system stability in the region.
- **Europe.** The 28 members of the European Union have a general *European Central Banking System* that enables participation by central banks in all of the 28 countries in the European Union. Within this structure there is a Eurosystem that hosts a European Central Bank for the 19 countries that have adopted the Euro as their currency.[44] The capital for the European Central Bank comes from these 19 banks. Countries contribute capital based on their populations.[45]

As we can see from the above thumbnail sketches, central banks fulfill a variety of roles, including provision of credit, provision of tangible currency (printing money, minting coins), and setting of monetary policy.[46] These are considered the core functions of a modern central bank. The remainder of this chapter will focus on these three functions, with apologies for brevity. The subject of monetary policy alone could file a tome.

## Credit and the Creation of Money

No aspect of money is more fundamental than credit, a concept traceable to the very origin of money, as noted in Chapter 1. When we credit someone or something—whether we are making an accounting entry, offering praise, acknowledging an effort, or simply extending good will—we are exercising the human faculty of trust. And when we receive credit, we benefit from that trust. (See Note 3.3.)

---

**Note 3.3 Definition of *credit* in English: credit**
**NOUN** 1 *mass noun* The ability of a customer to obtain goods or services before payment, based on the trust that payment will be made in the future.
  Source: Oxford University Press February 2019 (online dictionary)[47]

---

In the most typical modern-day scenario, the main creator and controller of money is a central governmental authority known as a central bank and/or treasury that issue fiat currency. But money is not just the creation of major governmental arms. Any credit-creating institution can bring money into being.

By extending credit, an entity—be it a government, a bank, or a company extending credit to customers—can literally "create" money. Of these three sources, banks are the most important and the main subject of this chapter. Although the ultimate endorsers of money are the national governments that charter the banks, and many financial companies imitate them, banks play arguably the most important role in the creation and control of money. For governments and companies, money is a means to an end; for banks, money is their very raison d'etre.

How, then, can a bank create money? Looking closely at any bank loan is instructive. In the process of making loaned money available in a borrower's bank account, a bank makes the typical double entry required under accounting rules. The bank records the loan by increasing a current asset such as Loans Receivable and increasing a current liability such as Customer Demand Deposits.[48] However, *the bank does not actually physically transfer the money away from other internal or external accounts*; rather, it credits the borrower's account with a deposit, although no such *deposit* has taken place—no corresponding *deposit* has been made elsewhere. In this sense, a bank literally credits money out of nothing when it extends what is called a bank loan. The bank does not loan any existing money, but instead creates new money.[49]

Some believe that banks can create credit only because they keep fractional reserves to fulfill their financial obligations (the *fractional reserve* theory). Others see banks as merely financial intermediaries, with no active monetary role themselves (the *financial intermediation* theory). But both of those theories betray our all-too human tendency to believe that money is concrete. This is not always the case. Bank reserves, an amount they must have on hand as a buffer against the risk of bad loans, are at least partly intangible. (The actual physical currency may not in fact be in residence in the bank claiming it—a lesson learned during runs on banks, discussed later in this chapter.) Reserves are only held by the bank because of prudence, or regulatory requirement. The reserves are not necessary to create the loan. And if banks are only intermediaries with no real deposits on which to base credit, then that raises the question of where credit comes from—the answer is that it comes from banks themselves.

**Note 3.4 Money Creation Theory Tested**

Researcher Richard Werner decided to test the money-creation hypothesis by examining what exactly happened inside a bank during the process of granting a bank loan. In a case study involving an actual loan application, which he filmed, he found that once all the necessary bank credit procedures had been undertaken and loan documents were signed that the borrower's current account was credited with the amount of the loan. (His research papers shows exactly what happened with the internal accounting.) The researcher asked a two-part question.

In order to book the borrower's loan principal into the borrower's bank account:
- Did the bank actually withdraw this same amount from another account? Or
- Did the money come from nothing more than the creation of credit (the *credit creation theory*)?

Werner found that the first scenario did not occur, but the second one did. If the first had happened, there would have been a reduction of equal value in the balance of another entity—either drawing down reserves (as the *fractional reserve theory* maintains) or other funds (as the *financial intermediation theory* maintains). As a result, he found that the *credit theory of banking*, is more realistic than the two other more dominant theories.

He illustrated it by showing this as the accounting record kept:

**Table 3.1:** Account changes due to bank loan (*credit creation theory*).

| Assets | | Liabilities | |
| --- | --- | --- | --- |
| Loans and investments + € 200 | | Deposits (borrower's A/C) + € 200 | |
| Total | + € 200 | Total | + € 200 |

Werner explains: "When extending bank credit, banks create an imaginary deposit by recording the loan amount in the borrower's account, although no new deposit has taken place (credit creation out of nothing)."[50]

## Bank Runs

Bank runs reveal the painful lesson that just because an account shows an amount of money as of a certain date, this does not mean the money is actually there to be withdrawn. But long before the run happens, trust is broken. People lose faith that that banks will give them back their money. So they panic and try to draw money out of their bank accounts—en masse. In bank runs of the past, depositors would line up and physically remove money. In today's digital runs, they request that it moves to another account.[51] Either way, the bank that holds the money—particularly a line of credit created out of nothing more than the borrower's good financial reputation—may be asked to provide more than it has in store.

In his most recent book about money,[52] Dartmouth professor Charles Wheelan shows how credit can inflate money supply in a way that can link the concepts of credit to money supply to show how trust can be misplaced. "I have $10,000. You have nothing. I deposit $10,000 into the bank. The bank loans you $9,000. Money supply has gone from $10,000 to $19,000. The only problem is when I want my money back and *you can't pay it*."

## Toxic Collateral

"*You can't pay it*" is never a good situation. In fact, inability to pay debts when they fall due is a commonly accepted definition of insolvency,[53] and was at the root of the 2008 to 2009 financial crisis. This crisis certainly was triggered by absence of cash on hand when lenders called their loans. It was also caused in part by a rise in interest rates from June 2004 to June 2006, which made it difficult for holders of variable-interest-rate mortgages—which were borrowed at low rates and repaid at rising rates—to make their monthly payments, leading to mortgage defaults in 2007.[54] For banks, interest-rate risk is a fact of life, and it can work conversely for them when, in contrast to the example above, banks find themselves accepting low fixed-rate payments in a time of ever-higher interest rates.[55]

But at a deeper level, the last decade's financial crisis was based on an essential aspect of credit, namely collateral—in this case, the collateral contained in mortgage-backed securities.

By its very nature, mortgage lending involves collateral—namely, real estate. But when the loan itself becomes securitized, the collateral is once removed from the source. If a person of low creditworthiness is granted a mortgage and then defaults, the bank can seize the building. But if that same mortgage is pooled with others like it to back a bond offering,[56] the entire structure can collapse. This in turn can harm housing markets and bond markets, with repercussions in the stock market as well, as the world saw a decade ago. In that crisis, the financial engineers got too clever with the instruments they created, and the traders did not heed the conditions attached to the instruments they happily traded.

Bundled mortgages were supposed to diversify the risk (because there would be creditworthy borrowers along with risky ones), but instead many mortgages in a bundle defaulted, pulling down the whole market. There was a systemic risk that could not be diversified away. What if all housing prices stopped rising and declined? Many hard-pressed homeowners who realized they were underwater (mortgage debt exceeding house valuation) walked away from their houses and their loans. The housing market was overvalued, in bubble territory, just waiting for something to deflate it. Many homeowners were in debt up to their ears, especially in the so-called subprime market of the least creditworthy borrowers. The first wave of defaults caused house prices to tumble, which led to even more mortgage defaults, and so on. This kind of "positive feedback" poses danger for any economic system, as we shall see in the next chapter on global finance. With too many mortgages in default at the same time, the diversification of risk could not protect against this systemic effect.

As summarized by the report of the Financial Crisis Inquiry Commission in the United States, "There was an explosion in risky subprime lending and securitization, an unsustainable rise in housing prices, widespread reports of egregious and predatory lending practices, dramatic increases in household mortgage debt, and exponential growth in financial firms' trading activities, unregulated derivatives, and short-term 'repo' lending markets, among many other red flags."[57] The government report goes on to say that the red flags went unheeded. "The captains of finance and the public stewards of our financial system ignored warnings and failed to question, understand, and manage evolving risks within a system essential to the well-being of the American public."[58] A report from the U.S. Department of Treasury adds technical detail, laying the blame for the crisis not so much on inattentive stewards as on the features intrinsic to mortgage instruments of the era, such as teaser rates, prepayment penalties, and interest-only repayment options.[59] Taken together, these were innovations. Indeed, an upbeat Fed paper published in 2006 before the crisis about these many features was titled, "Mortgage Innovation and Consumer Choice."[60] This goes to show that not all innovation in the history of money brings progress—sometimes it backfires. In the next chapter we will read about some financial bubbles that began as innovative ideas.

### Commercial Credit Rating Agencies: Scorekeepers for Bonds and Other Securities

At the institutional level, a government or a company can raise money by issuing a debt security known as a bond, as explained in the next chapter's discussion of markets (as bonds are traded in bond markets). Typical bond offerings do not come with any collateral; if the bond issuer defaults, the bondholders may or may not get back the value of their principal.

When extending loans to companies or governments or buying their bonds, lenders look to credit ratings given by the leaders in a highly concentrated industry niche. Moody's Investors Service and Standard and Poor's (S&P) together control some 80 percent of the global market for credit rating services, and Fitch Ratings controls about 15 percent. They all use A, B, and C ratings, with some adding D for default. AAA + is the highest rating (typically reserved for sovereign debt[61] from the most creditworthy countries), with D being the lowest. While each rating agency has its own way of rating, most give highest marks to people who are good at handling credit.

The credit rating of a country or company directly affects the interest rate at which it is able to borrow money in the market. The lower the credit rating, the higher the interest rate. Large institutional investors who buy bonds, like pension funds, typically have limits on the lowest credit ratings they may invest in. These limits vary by institution and may change over time. Countries or companies that fall below this threshold find it difficult to borrow unless they can put up collateral, and even then their choice of lenders will be limited.

Not surprisingly, the main commercial credit rating agencies for business came under criticism for their role in the financial crisis of 2008 to 2009. At the time, they were issuing credit ratings without much oversight. In some cases, conflicts of interest caused rating inflation. Following the financial crisis, regulators in the United States put new restrictions on some credit rating firms to eliminate conflicts of interest, and established an Office of Credit Ratings at the Securities and

Exchange Commission to ensure compliance with Dodd-Frank rules.[62] The blame game, however, has been mixed from the beginning. While the main text of the official U.S. government report blamed the big three for contributing to the financial crisis, the minority report appended to the end of the report blames government policy—a view many economists share, according to one recent survey.[63]

### Consumer Credit: Borrowing Behavior as Invisible "Collateral"

Clearly, having quality collateral is key to lending and securitization. When banks extend credit to a borrower, the debtor's obligation may be secured by collateral. Such loans, called collateralized or secured loans, are considered to have lower risk than unsecured or uncollateralized loans. In an unsecured loan, line of credit, or credit card approval, the lender cannot fall back on collateral, so it must rely on the creditworthiness of the individual borrower. (Also, generally speaking, noncollateralized loans carry higher interest rates, since lenders have less recourse upon default.)

When lending to an individual, the lender will typically rely on the three-digit score(s) given by one or more of the consumer credit bureaus: Equifax, Experian, or TransUnion, complemented by a score issued by the Fair Isaac Corporation (FICO) (see Note 3.5). FICO scores fall in the following ranges: 300–579 (the very poor rating of 16 percent of consumers), 580–669 (the fair rating accorded to 18 percent); 670–739 (good, the scores of 21 percent); 740–799 (very good, a score enjoyed by 25 percent); and exceptional (a distinction achieve by the most creditworthy 20 percent). So, scores range from 300 to 850. Generally, a FICO Score above 670 is considered a good credit score on these models, and a score above 800 is usually perceived to be exceptional.[64] The average FICO score is 704. Not surprisingly, given the importance of credit ratings, consumer credit is a highly regulated area.[65] As for institutions, when lending to an institution or preparing to buy or sell a bond offering, a bank will consider the letter grade given by the credit rating agencies: Fitch, Moody's, and Standard and Poor's.

> **Note 3.5 Leading Consumer Credit Agencies: FICO and the Big Three**
>
> Consumers around the globe can choose from among a variety of consumer credit agencies—from Chengxin in China, to CRIF in Italy, to CreditInfo in Iceland.[66] The most dominant names in the consumer credit worldwide, however, are Experian, Equifax, and TransUnion.[67]
>
> **FICO** (San Jose, California). The Fair Isaac Corporation (formerly Fair, Isaac, and Company) introduced the first general-purpose credit score in 1989. Known as the FICO score, it filters through information in multiple credit reports to calculate a score. According to one source (CreditKarma), factors considered are payment history (35%), amounts owed (30%), length of credit history (15%), amount of new credit (10%), and mix of credit (10%).[68] The ideal

borrower has a long payment history, owes very little currently, has not taken out much recent credit, and has taken on a variety of types of credit in the past. Consumers who have never borrowed will have a low FICO score even if they have a high income and cash in the bank. The astute lender will also consider these factors along with the FICO score.

The company offers 28 unique scores that are optimized for various credit card, mortgage, and auto lending decisions.

**Experian** (Dublin, Ireland). This company collects and manages data used by lenders to make credit decisions. With 16,000 employees worldwide, it is the largest credit score-keeper. It operates 18 consumer credit bureaus and 11 business credit bureaus.[69]

**Equifax** (Atlanta, GA). Equifax also collects information and issues a score. With 10,400 employees, it is also a dominant player. Its common stock is traded on the New York Stock Exchange (NYSE) under the symbol EFX.[70] In fiscal 2017, Equifax experienced a cybersecurity incident following a criminal attack on its systems that involved the theft of certain personally identifiable information of consumers in Canada, the UK, and the U.S. Following the incident, Equifax strengthened its cybersecurity protocols.

**TransUnion** (Chicago, IL). This scorekeeper is a publicly held company based in Chicago with some 4,600 employees. In addition to traditional credit rating services, it has created a service, CreditVision®, which allows customers to reliably score 26 million U.S. consumers who otherwise would have no credit score.[71]

These three credit-reporting agencies have teamed up to create the independently managed firm VantageScore Solutions, which recently released the fourth and latest version of its credit scoring model, the VantageScore 4.0.

The higher a consumer's credit score is, the better the chance the borrower has to get a high credit limit and/or a lower rate of interest on debt—be it for a mortgage, student loan, auto loan, credit card, or home equity line of credit. One obvious consideration for the consumer credit bureaus is the amount and type of debt a consumer already has compared to national averages. In the U.S., the total amount of consumer debt is $13.67 trillion, of which $9.2 trillion is in mortgages and the remaining $4 trillion-plus in other kinds of debt—namely $1.49 trillion in student debt,[72] $1.28 trillion in auto loans,[73] $800 billion-plus in credit card debt,[74] and $500 billion-plus in home equity lines of credit.[75]

Consumer credit scores are very important to consumers in today's economy. They are not only used by the financial industry to determine whether to extend credit to a consumer and on what terms, but they are also used for other purposes, like in background checks by prospective employers. This means that some people are being judged by their score, as if a low score reflects poorly on their character. But a low score may simply mean that a person has chosen not to take out credit. Or it may be an error—the case for one in five consumers, said a 2012 report from the Federal Trade Commission.[76] As a recent article in the Atlanta Journal and Constitution reported: "Credit Errors Upend Lives of Thousands of Consumers."[77]

Some countries have passed laws to protect consumers, such as the Fair Credit Reporting Act in the United States, which requires employers to obtain permission before pulling a score, and the Credit Rating Agency, which increases the transparency and accountability of credit rating agencies.[78]

## Non-bank Financial Intermediation

Banks are not the only institutions issuing credit. Worldwide, there is a broad sector called "non-bank financial intermediation."[79] The share of global financial assets held by this sector has been increasing and now stands at 48.2 percent, according to the Financial Stability Board, a global watchdog established after the financial crisis.[80] In the United States, this sector is called *non-bank banking*, a term that replaced a previous somewhat pejorative term, *shadow banking*.[81] Although they have only 10 percent of market share for loan origination in the U.S., non-bank lenders have increased their market share from 2 percent just a half a decade ago[82] And in the mortgage space, non-banks are dominant.[83]

Overall, non-bank lenders have been blamed for contributing to the 2008 to 2009 financial crisis as well.[84] Their low capital requirements enabled too much risk-taking, and ultimately caused them to go into receivership (bankruptcy) and getting a bailout, adding more stress to the financial system.

## College Loans: Financial Slavery vs. Financial Freedom

Around the world, students are borrowing money to finance their education. According to one global lender, SoFi, average student debt in the United Kingdom is $30,800. Other high-debt countries include the United States ($30,000), Australia ($22,000), and Canada ($20,000).[85] Sometimes when credit is extended, the borrower experiences a sense of being enslaved by debt. So any lender that provides student loans, can be perceived in a negative light.

This is the case for recent college graduate Alyea Pierce. Finding herself $47,000 in debt due to student loans and realizing that it could take her nearly a lifetime to pay it off, Alyea wrote a play for the New York Fringe Festival called "Financial Slavery: The College Debt Sentence." The central image of the play is credit as a slave ship and creditors as slave masters. She told the *Guardian* newspaper that while some audience members felt that the comparison went too far, she stood by her words because "when researching and receiving stories from people about their student loan journey, the language used were feelings of feeling trapped, locked in chains, heavy, and too much weight."[86] Financial slavery has also been the subject of a lecture at Princeton University by Rev. Dr. DeForest "Buster" Soaries, Senior Pastor of First Baptist Church of Lincoln Gardens, New Jersey.[87] There have also been a number of self-help financial books that have this theme, including *DFree: Breaking Free from Financial Slavery* by Rev. Soaries,[88] and *Debt is Slavery* by Michael Mihalik.[89]

There is a counterargument that says that college graduates, far from being slaves, have greater financial freedom. As mentioned in Chapter 2, median weekly earnings for degreed professionals was $1,884 compared to only $730 for those with only a high school diploma.[90] An early study showed that college graduates earn an average of $1,200 per week versus high school graduates' $700 per week, proving that "education pays."[91] So the question is really: Which is higher, the additional income that a college degree can bring? Or the principal and interest payments involved with repaying loan over time Each case is different but clearly in many cases, college does pay.

### High-Interest Loans

Consumers who have poor credit ratings get shut out of the conventional financial industry. Unable to borrow money from banks or credit cards companies, they have to resort to companies who specialize in lending to risky borrowers. But such loans come at a very high price, with annual interest rates above 30 percent and as high as hundreds of percent. They find themselves in a never-ending spiral of indebtedness, borrowing at usurious interest rates today to pay off debts they made last week or last month, signing over future paychecks or car titles to these lenders.

Lending money to desperate people is clearly very lucrative for the lenders. This payday-lending industry is estimated to be as large as $90 billion in the United States alone.[92] In some lower-income areas, it is common to see payday loan stores lit up at night. (See Figure 3.1, licensed under Creative Commons attribution.) Lenders claim that they provide a valuable service by loaning money to high-risk borrowers who would otherwise be unable to borrow any money. Borrowers often complain about misleading fine print and onerous conditions.

## Fiat Currency

So far in this chapter we have looked at the role of central banks and how they can create and control credit. And we have also seen the downside of credit.

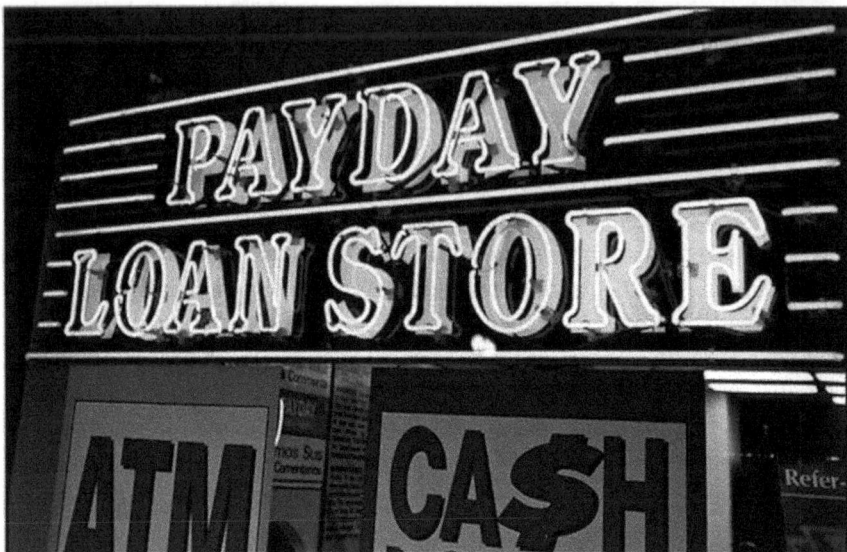

**Figure 3.1:** Neon sign for a payday loan store (Fig. Note 3.1).

Now we take a closer look at how government can get involved in producing money out of nothing—so-called fiat currency.

Each sovereign country is responsible for both fiscal and monetary policy, which are typically executed through treasury and central banking operations respectively.

Treasuries are closely aligned with government operations. Sovereign nations have always had a treasury function to levy taxes, issue debt, and to make expenditures from resulting funds. Even in countries where the roles of the treasury and the central bank intersect, taxation is reserved for treasuries, not central banks, to levy taxes.

In addition to national treasuries for collecting money via taxes, however, many nations have instituted central banks for storing it and replenishing its supply by printing more of it. One of the core functions of a central bank is to issue *tangible* (token) money—bank notes and coins—or to direct its issuance (as when the Fed guides the Treasury on how many bills to print in what denomination).

In addition, countries with their own currencies control their money supply, which—should they choose to increase the supply faster or slower than the growth of the economy—will affect interest rates down or up. The Modern Monetary

Theory posits that a country with its own currency, such as the United Kingdom or the United States, can print as much as it needs. As such, it need not worry about national debt because it can always print more money to pay interest. (Note: This is a theory that can work for many situations but not all; if payments on debt must be made in a foreign currency and exchange rates are unfavorable, printing your own uncertain currency can only go so far in reducing sovereign debt.)

Of 41 central banks studied by the Bank of International Settlement (discussed later in this chapter), 50 percent or more design and print and/or mint currency, and are involved in managing its circulation.[93]

For example, in the United States, the Fed—which, as mentioned, constitutes the nation's central banking system, and is a network of regional banks with specific duties—places an order for bills and coins from the U.S. Treasury Department's Bureau of Engraving and Printing every year. The Fed decides how much of each denomination to order based on how much currency will need to be replaced due to being in unfit condition, and how much is needed to meet increased demand. In a recent estimate, the Fed said that 85 percent of new bills printed replaced old ones, while 15 percent were printed to "meet increased public demand."[94] As of January 2019 there were approximately $1.70 trillion in circulation, mostly in the form of dollar bills in $1, $2, $5, $10, $50, and $100 denominations—larger bills having been discontinued.[95]

Clearly, money in its most tangible form (dollar bills and coins) still plays a major role in the money economy, and these are typically created by central authorities overseen by the government. As noted in our opening chapter, the technology of money involves both hardware (physical currency) and software (credit money). Even though the world is trending away from hardware to become more virtual, physical money will still have a role for the foreseeable future.

### Currency and Banknote Design

National and regional currencies use images and symbols to express collective pride. In a typical currency system, there are multiple denominations of coins and bills, and each pictures a face and/or symbol (typically front and back) that is selected by the country's department of treasury.

Here are some commonly recognized images and symbols on today's currency (see Figure 3.2, licensed under Creative Commons attribution):

- All euro notes feature design elements with symbolic meaning. "The 12 stars of the EU represent the dynamism and harmony of contemporary Europe,

**Figure 3.2:** Currency images (Fig. Note 3.2).

while the bridges on the back symbolize communication between the people of Europe and between Europe and the rest of the world."[96]

- In the United Kingdom and in territories linked to it, a popular face is Queen Elizabeth. It is even possible to see her face from age 8 to the present day through a variety of themed currency.[97] Since 1963, her face has appeared on British banknotes from 5 pounds and above.[98] Newer additions are Jane Austen, JMW Turner, and Winston Churchill. Keeping up the pace of social innovation, currently there is a call to feature a man of color or a woman of color, probably on the 50 pound note.[99]
- On the U.S. $1 bill, we see the country's first president, George Washington, on the front and the Great Seal on the back, with its mysterious eye and pyramid first introduced in 1935. According to the U.S. Treasury, the pyramid "symbolizes strength and durability," and the unfinished pyramid means that the nation "will always grow, improve, and build." In addition, the eye above the pyramid symbolizes "divine guidance." The inscription *annuit coeptis* translates to "He [God] has favored our undertakings," while the inscription

*novus ordo seclorum* means "a new order of the ages," signifying "a new American era."[100]

## Monetary Policy

In addition to ordering bills and coins to put into circulation through the banking system, central banks also play a major role in the setting of monetary policy— defined succinctly by the Oxford Dictionary as "Those instruments, such as inter- est rates, reserve requients, and term controls, at the disposal of government for influencing the timing, availability, and cost of money and credit in an economy." How governments do this varies widely. In fact, the authority of central banks varies widely from country to country both by source (how they get their authority) and by domain (where they intervene).

As for *source*, the authority of a central bank may be set by law (national constitution, national statute, or international treaty) or by custom (published statement or accepted practice).

As for *domain*, a central bank may attempt to control one or more eco- nomic factors in the belief that these in turn will affect others—which may be at odds at times. For example, in the United States, the Federal Reserve's stated goal under the Federal Reserve Act is to achieve "long-run growth of the monetary and credit aggregates"—meaning growth in the amount of money in circulation and money loaned. This is done based on productivity, and in the belief that it will "promote effectively the goals of maximum em- ployment, stable prices, and moderate long-term interest rates."[101] In some countries, the central bank is tasked even more ambitiously with general eco- nomic welfare.[102] The price law in China aims to standardize prices "giving play to the role of price in the rational allocation of resources, stabilizing the overall price level of the market, protecting the lawful rights and interests of the consumers and operators and promoting the sound development of the so- cialist market economy."[103]

With respect to the domain of foreign trade, a central bank may need to de- cide among the competing goals of independent monetary policy, free capital movement, and fixed exchange rates—said to pose a "trilemma" in which only two of the three can be chosen.[104] In the Bretton Woods Agreement immediately following the end of World War II, the 44-member nations chose to peg currencies to the U.S. dollar and allowed countries to set their own interest rates; cross-bor- der financial flows would be minimal in those years.[105] In subsequent years, how- ever, a rise in cross-border flows and a decline in the use of fixed interest rates reduced the trilemma to a mere dilemma.[106]

But whatever their source or domain, central banks have one common feature that they have had since their origins: a connection to governments. The earliest central banks were formed to provide banking services and bank-notes (money) to governments.[107] In some cases, the banks were formed to restore monetary stability and the credibility of money after overissuance and collapse of convertibility (worthless paper money). Examples of this bank *deus ex machina* role include several of the banks mentioned above, namely the Austrian National Bank, the National Bank of Denmark, the Bank of France, and the Bank of Spain. (The Bank of Italy and the Bank of Portugal had similar origins.)

Eventually, central banks began serving the private banking system as a bank supervisor and as *lender of last resort*—that is, a lender that will extend credit to a financially important entity that has no other means of borrowing. In time, these roles became linked to public policy objectives. As the Bank of International Settlements recounts, "A sense of purpose had been identified. Their role was to discharge their functions in a manner consistent with the public interest."

One of the most important roles that central banks play is to *affect the supply of money*[108] by changing the volume of assets held in banks. When it comes to money supply, bear in mind that there are different classes of money. As the Financial Times Lexicon wisely notes, there are different measures of money supply—not all of them are widely used and classifications vary from country to country. In general, M0 and M1, called "narrow money," includes coins and notes or bills in circulation. M2 includes M1 plus short-term time deposits in banks and 24-hour money market funds and cash deposits.[109] M4 includes M3 plus other deposits. "Broad money" can describe any of the levels past M1, depending on the market.

However money supply may be defined, central banks clearly affect it. They do this using several different strategies.

- *Open-market transactions.* Central banks can influence interest rates through open-market operations, purchases, and sale of securities (such as U.S. Treasury bonds) in the open market by a central bank. The seller is the central bank; buyers are banks within the system, as well as other financial institutions. When banks in the system buy securities, they forfeit cash, so they have less to lend; conversely, when they sell them, they increase the cash they can lend.[110] These transactions can occur continually, changing the size or the composition of a central bank's portfolio over time.[111]
- *Loans to the government.* In some cases, central banks supplement other sources of government income (such as taxes and sales of treasury bonds)

by loaning money to the government. Many countries restrict the ability of central banks to loan to the government, considering this to be fiscally irresponsible.

- *Loans to banks.* A central bank can make short-term advances to the banks in their systems or to intermediaries. A key mechanism here is the *discount window* at which central banks lend money to banks and control the interest rate (discount rate). These "discounts" or "rediscounts," typically made on a short-term basis, carry a lower rate than what banks could normally get, so it is referred to as a discount or rediscount rate. By raising or lowering the rate, a central bank can affect the interest rate that banks charge on the loans they make to customers.
- *Credit curbs.* In some cases, central banks have set limits on how much banks can lend in certain circumstances—either by identifying companies that have too much debt[112] or through such formulas as maximum loan-value to purchase-price ratios and maximum maturities that lenders must prescribe.
- *Currency swaps.* Banks can lend one another their own currency through the foreign exchange market.
- *Prudential standards.* Many central banks have the authority to determine (often following Basel standards) the minimum cash reserves that banks must hold against their deposit liabilities.

A well-known standard setter in the realm of central bank policy is the Bank of International Settlements (BIS), a global organization that facilitates the settlement of payments across national and regional borders, an increasingly important aspect of the global economy.[113] Its stated mission is to "serve central banks in their pursuit of monetary and financial stability, to foster international cooperation in those areas, and to act as a bank for central banks."[114] BIS is owned by 60 central banks representing 95 percent of the world's GDP. It may be most well-known for the capital standards it sets at a forum in Basel, Switzerland, currently in the 3.0 version, "Basel III," being the third set of standards promulgated by the group. Many countries, including the United States, base their standards at least in part on these.

But monetary policy is not limited to money supply. Such policy can be used to support national objectives related to not only financial stability but also employment, growth, and welfare objectives. In some cases, central banks provide preferential treatments to state-owned enterprises or to enterprises designated by the government as in need of help.[115]

## Policy Shifts

Sometimes, national authorities such as legislatures can shift the goals of their central banks. For example, a central bank may move from monetary goals to social goals. As an economy that relies on market forces and the private sector to accomplish many social goals, the United States has traditionally not tasked its central bank with general economic welfare, but this could change. A bill introduced in October 2018 toward the end of the 115th Congress by Rep. Ro Khanna (D-CA) aspired to expand the mission of the U.S. Federal Reserve Banking System to include not only general goals "maximum sustainable employment, stable prices, and moderate long-term interest rates," the three primary mandates of the Federal Reserve, but also specific targets for employment. The bill defines maximum employment as meaning a labor market in which "job seekers can find work; involuntary part-time work is at a minimum; median wages are rising with worker productivity; and disparities in rates of unemployment and pay between and among racial, gender, urban, rural, and other demographic groups have reached their lowest practicable level."[116]

### Interest Rates Issues

There is some empirical evidence that de facto interest rates are also influenced by market forces beyond the control of a central banking authority.[117] Taken together, these forces—including policy and economic activity of the government, households, and firms—support what some call a "natural rate of interest."[118] However, it is clear that central bank policies have a direct and powerful impact on interest rates, and the banks themselves acknowledge this connection. In turn, interest rates have an effect on the economy. It was widely believed that the recession of the early 1980s was caused by the high interest rates triggered by the policies of Former Fed Chair Paul Volcker, and a mild recession in the early 1990s was blamed on his successor, Alan Greenspan.

It has been observed that an "economy can be seen as one long chain of interest rates," and that "at the start of that chain is the U.S.'s central bank, the Federal Reserve."[119] The chain begins, for example, with the bank's federal funds rate of, say, 2.25 percent. A bank may then charge 3.0 percent and a mortgage lender 4.0 percent. In countries other than the U.S., interest rates are often referenced to the "prime lending rate," such as prime + 1%, or prime + 2%, where prime is the lending rate that the bank charges to its best customers, and is tightly connected to the central bank lending rate. (See Figure 3.3.)

| Federal Funds Rate | Primary Credit Rate | Primary Loan Rate | Average Credit Card Rate |
|---|---|---|---|
| 2.0 – 2.25% ⟶ | 2.75% ⟶ | 5.5% ⟶ | 15.13% |

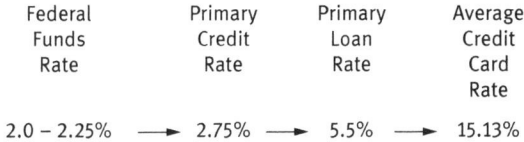

**Figure 3.3:** The chain of credit (illustrative) (Fig. Note 3.3).
Source: Federal Reserve.gov (various categories), as of 8/6/2019

In the business lending market, interest rates have traditionally been linked to LIBOR, the London InterBank Offered Rate or, secondarily, other *interbank rates.* The "IBORs" (LIBOR, EURIBOR, TIBOR) are the most actively used interest rate benchmarks in financial contracts today. IBORs are typically published for multiple forward-looking terms that measure expected wholesale, unsecured bank borrowing costs over specified periods (e.g., one, three, six, and twelve months. Now with the lead metric, LIBOR, about to expire in 2021, financial leaders are looking at reforms and alternatives.[120] A leader in this effort is the Benchmark Administration of the Intercontinental Exchange (ICE), owner of the New York Stock Exchange, which has created a benchmark called ICE Libor.[121]

In the aftermath of the financial crisis of 2008 to 2009, the federal funds rate (FFR) set by central banks had a strong impact on general interest rates. But when the central banks in the U.S. and UK added more money to the money supply through so-called quantitative easing, this diluted the ability of the FFR to affect interest rates, and the Fed began using new tools.

As the Federal Reserve Bank of St. Louis notes in a May 2019 report, "With such a large quantity of reserves in the banking system, the Federal Reserve can no longer effectively influence the FFR by small changes in the supply of reserves . . . . Instead, the Fed uses its newer tools—IOER and the ON RRP facility—to influence the FRR and short-term interest rates more generally." The report explains the workings of IOER (interest on excess reserves), and ON RRP (overnight reverse purchase agreement) as monetary policy tools.[122]

**Note 3.6 Quantitative Easing**
Central banks can work separately or together to affect money supply through various mechanisms. In the early 2000s, the Bank of Japan tried a new strategy dubbed *quantitative easing*, which entailed printing more money to buy government bonds and drive down interest rates. This spread to the U.S. and the UK in subsequent years, with mixed effects.[123] The current verdict on this experiment is that while quantitative easing lowers interest rates, it also increases the total level of consumer debt (because more people use credit cards and take out loans) and increases inflation and asset prices (too much money chasing too few goods).[124]

## The Future of Central Banks and Treasuries

Central banks and treasuries clearly play an important role in society, yet they are held in contempt by some corners of the influential blogosphere. While scholars spend years researching and debating over the nuances of central banking roles, online critics are posting comments, uploading blogs, and even creating entire websites accusing central banks of serving the private interests of their leaders. A second school of thought respects central banks but expresses fears that their independence could be co-opted by national governments.[125] This is a more reasonable concern, given the history we have seen from the Bank of England on.

Central bank agendas vary greatly in their form and function, and most of them have official goals to serve the public good in their own countries. Furthermore, the existence of overall global standards like Basel III and regional authorities in various continents ensure a level playing field, preventing national interests from trumping global good.

Indeed, if anything, the risk to economic well-being may come not from central banks—with their policy-oriented, highly regulated, transparent operations—but rather from the vast domain of the unregulated and underregulated institutions—a "shadow banking" sector that is continually emerging.[126] This $52 billion sector includes nonbanks, mentioned earlier, but also includes a wide variety of entities from simple pawnshops to sophisticated cryptocoin offerings[127] (discussed in Chapter 6).

In the words of Sir Howard Davies, the founding chairman of the United Kingdom's Financial Services Authority, anticipating global risks, "We may be about to discover whether the new credit creators, some of whom do not have to live under a rigorous regime of capital regulation, have priced risk correctly."[128] Mature markets anticipate risk and invest in preventing it, and in that sense they "price" risk.

Even the sacrosanct domain of deposits is fair game for nontraditional entities. A 2019 study found that in the U.S., 2 of 3 deposits and loan accounts opened online were with direct banks operating online rather than with traditional banks that still have physical branches.[129]

In Chapter 5, which covers fintech, we shall go further into the financial innovations in the areas of deposit and lending.

Yet another challenge to banks and their customers is the emergence of cryptocoins (discussed in Chapter 6) as an alternative to fiat currency. As one writer has opined in the British newspaper *The Guardian*, "You might be living in a time in which you will experience the end of central banking and perhaps even fiat currency, and their replacement by a completely new system."[130]

Banks have responded to this competitive threat by starting experiments with digital currency. Here's that "rebel currency" we mentioned earlier as an example of how innovation works. Already, several central banks are reportedly experimenting with this, including some in Canada, Denmark, Sweden, and the United Kingdom.

In the United Kingdom, Bank of England Governor Mark Carney gave a speech on June 20, 2019, in which he commented on Facebook's new currency by saying that "The Bank of England approaches Libra with an open mind but not an open door. Unlike social media, for which standards and regulations are being debated well after they have been adopted by billions of users, the terms of engagement for innovations such as Libra must be adopted in advance of any launch."[131]

In the United States, a blockchain start up called "WingCash Faster Payment Network" has suggested that its software platform could be "owned and operated by the Federal Reserve" as well as another governing organization. "The Federal Reserve would issue digital currency (digital Fed notes) . . . tied to the Internet domain (Fednotes.com)." Given such invitations, it is not surprising that another *Guardian* headline takes it upon itself to explain "Why Central Bank Digital Currencies Will Destroy Bitcoin."[132] In the battle between central banks (thesis) and cryptos (synthesis), a third reality is bound to emerge. This synthesis of trends will be explored in Chapter 6.

Meanwhile the most existential challenge for central banks is the obvious question: Can any institution control a monetary system, or is control an illusion? Already it is clear that the hegemony once enjoyed by the United States and the dollar is in decline, as the global marketplace welcomes an increasing number of players.[133] This is the theme of the following chapter, which asks how global markets help or hinder the societies they are intended to serve.

# Chapter 4
# Global Finance: Markets, Movers, and Motives

*Money makes the world go 'round.*
—Cabaret, 1968

No discussion of money would be complete without a close look at our global financial markets. Ever moving, ever changing, they impact our daily lives in many ways—some evident, some invisible. They may enrich us or impoverish us in ways that we do not always understand. In this chapter, we will define these markets and the motivations that drive them.

Arising from ancient street commerce and evolving over time into modern institutions of credit and exchange, global finance enables the flow of trade and investment through various activities, including governments issuing bonds, banks making loans, and various entities buying and selling commodities, currencies, and/or securities—including stocks, bonds, and derivative securities (that is, securities based on an underlying asset). These markets for credit and exchange emerge whenever and wherever large numbers of people and/or institutions agree to make economic trades involving the consideration of value in any form.

Financial systems exist along a spectrum from highly regulated, such as commercial banking, to relatively unregulated, such as nonbank lending (also called "shadow banking," to the dismay of its pioneers), to outright illegal activity well outside the scope of this book. As such, some financial systems are formal, regulated institutions such as stock exchanges or commodities exchanges, with fixed identities and brick and mortar locations—while others have a more informal, fluid identity.[1] New markets are most often started as informal, unregulated activities—as they expand, the need for society to formalize and regulate them arises. All affect our daily financial lives.

Taken together, both formal and informal markets are arguably indispensable for the functioning of our modern society, bringing together willing buyers and sellers to exchange money in return for a variety of goods and services.

Just like the money and assets that pass through them, the financial markets are constantly innovating and evolving to meet the changing needs of the society they serve.

And in specific economic sectors, new markets are being created all the time. Often, this is aided by the availability of new technologies to better link buyers and sellers, which reduces transaction costs. Think of Uber bringing together drivers and passengers, or Airbnb bringing together landlords and

https://doi.org/10.1515/9781547401116-004

renters. Global financial markets, in addition to serving individuals and institutions, also support these niche markets by giving companies like these the capital they need to pursue their missions. (Also see Chapter 5: Fintech.)

In this section, we will survey the four main established markets—stock, bond, currency, and commodity—and present some of the institutions moving them as well as the motives driving them—ending with new consideration of the *invisible hand*. In the second half we will move a little closer to the micro end, focusing on a series of problems facing markets—such as scams, speculation, and automation—with a focus on equity markets because of their continuing importance to the average person.

## Markets: Stock, Bond, Currency, and Commodities

Financial markets operate with relative freedom to buy and sell at prices the markets themselves set, but there are boundaries on that freedom. The exchanges that are used to effect trading have their own rules (hence the term *self-regulatory organizations* or SROs). Also, governments may exercise greater or lesser control through a central bank and/or treasury function, as explained in Chapter 3.[2]

When companies need capital, they can obtain it by issuing securities, in the form of either equity (i.e., shares of stock) or debt (i.e., corporate bonds, also called notes or paper). A security, generally speaking, is an instrument of investment, which may be classified as either an equity security (stocks) or a debt security (bonds). In the United States, the test used currently is based on a U.S. Supreme Court decision from over 70 years ago: *EC v. W.J. Howey Co.*, 328 U.S. 293 (1946).[3]

In this case, the court defined a security as "any note, stock, treasury stock, bond, debenture, evidence of indebtedness, certificate of interest or participation in any profit-sharing agreement, collateral-trust certificate, preorganization certificate or subscription, transferable share, investment contract, voting-trust certificate, certificate of deposit for a security, fractional undivided interest in oil, gas, or other mineral rights, or, in general, any interest or instrument commonly known as a 'security,' or any certificate of interest or participation in, temporary or interim certificate for, receipt for, guarantee of, or warrant or right to subscribe to or purchase, any of the foregoing."

Equity and debt securities have given rise to vast markets—namely, stock markets and bond markets. People buy stocks and/or bonds at one price in the hope that they can later sell them for a higher price, making a capital gain—or

receive ongoing payments from them in terms of dividends (for stock) or interest payments (in the form of bond dividends).

In addition, money flows to currency markets in which you may buy or sell
particular currencies or speculate on their future value. And finally, there is a
broad market for commodities futures. (See Figure 4.1.)

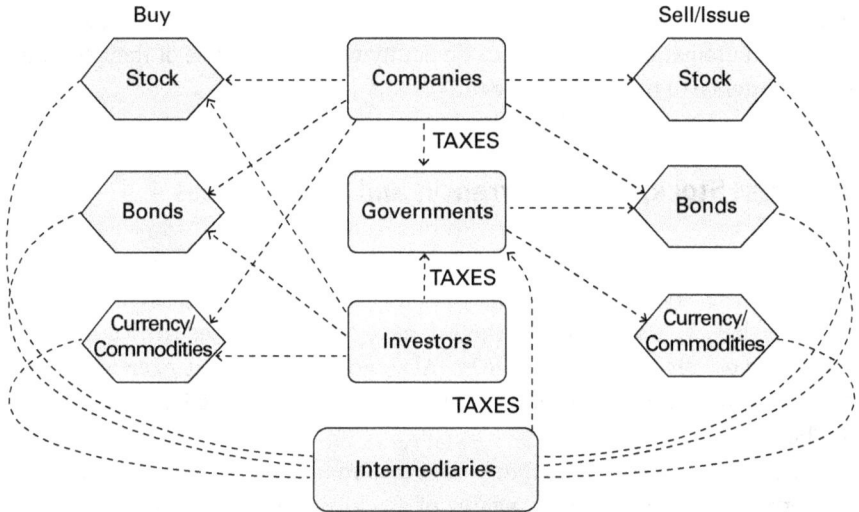

**Figure 4.1:** Key players of global finance. (Fig. Note 4.1).

The following four sections will explain these four key markets at a high level,
with market problems discussed toward the end of this chapter.

### Stock Markets

There are some 43 million companies listing stock in the world, according to the
World Bank Group,[4] and they have issued some $78 trillion worth of stock.[5]
Stockholders may consider themselves company owners, and many wise elders
such as shareholder activist and author Robert A. G. Monks[6] have encouraged
them to act as such, with prudent consideration for the long term. However,
many stockholders act more like renters—or in some cases, like guests in a hotel
or even a no-tell motel. Whatever the case may be, stock is considered to be a
security. (For more on securities, see the section "Securities Commissions.") Of
the approximately 200 sovereign nations on the planet, most have a stock market

to facilitate trading of equity securities during market hours—for example, in the case of the New York Stock Exchange, 9:30 AM to 4:00 PM Eastern Standard Time (EST). But high noon in New York is 5 PM in London (vagaries of daylight savings aside). Bearing in mind that it is "always 5 o'clock somewhere," a particular market may be open or closed at any given moment. Also, many markets have extended hours to settle trades—there is off-hour trading in market futures.

In many cases, these are trading floors housed in brick and mortar locations like the London Stock Exchange or the New York Stock Exchange. Other equity markets occur through a unified electronic system, overseen by brick-and-mortar headquarters, as is the case of the Nasdaq Stock Market with its famous Times Square billboard in New York. In addition, there are some brand new players in the stock exchange industry, such as MEMX.[7] (For more on stock markets, see the last section of this chapter, on market problems.)

The NYSE alone contains eight markets, including NYSE itself (by far the largest of the eight, with $22.9 trillion in market cap), NYSE American (for small caps), NYSE Arca Equities (for all-electronic exchange), NYSE National (for high-frequency trades), Chicago Stock Exchange (for hedge funds and day traders), NYSE American Options (for open outcry trading of options), NYSE Arca Options (for anonymous trading), and NYSE Bonds (for bond trading).[8]

## Bond Markets

A bond is a loan (from the bondholder to the bond issuer) that can be traded as a security. (A bond, in fact, is considered to be a security.) One could think of it as a fancy IOU that may be transferred from one holder to the other. Such a loan is typically structured with a specific face value (for example, $1,000). The bond comes with a guarantee that the issuer will pay interest periodically at a certain rate (known as the bond *coupon*), and a guarantee to repay the principal at a stated time (known as *maturity*). The price of a bond in the bond market and its *yield* (what it ultimately pays) have an inverse relationship. That is, if the price of a bond has risen, its yield has decreased. And if the price of a bond has declined, its yield has increased. Morningstar's explanation of this inverse relationship of price and yield is particularly clear.[9] When interest rates rise, bond prices fall—that is, they are sold at a discount from their face value. At that point, their yields must rise to match current market conditions. The buyer's yield will be higher than the seller's yield under these conditions, because the buyer paid less for the bond, yet is now receiving the same coupon payments, even while the redemption price is now higher than the purchase price.[10]

The global bond market currently has some 1 million bonds outstanding[11] worth approximately $41 trillion, with some $700 billion worth of bonds trading daily.[12]

The bond market, unlike stock markets, has no physical or electronic home—although some stock markets such as the New York Stock Exchange dedicate a market for bond exchange as well.[13] Rather, it is a vast series of transactions in an "over the counter" (OTC) market. OTC trading is trading that happens through a broker-dealer network operating without a formal stock exchange.

Bonds come in myriad forms, but there are generally three types: bonds issued by national governments (treasury bonds), bonds issued by states, cities, or counties (such as municipal bonds, including "green" bonds supporting environmental causes[14]), and bonds issued by corporations (commercial paper, which can sometimes be "convertible" into stock, or a plain bond that is "nonconvertible").

Currently there are more than 1 million bonds out there waiting to either be *paid* at maturity, *called* or redeemed before maturity date, or *retired* following purchase by a new investor or converted into stock. Some but not all of these are available to the ordinary investor, typically through a brokerage house licensed to buy and sell securities.[15] One exception to this rule is U.S. Savings Bonds, which are available directly to the public, though they are no longer sold over the counter via brokers, but must be purchased directly by registering with the U.S. Treasury's website, treasurydirect.gov.[16] Treasury bonds are the most common purchases for ordinary investors; corporate bonds are not as accessible.[17] This is partly because the U.S. government backs treasury bonds and is for all practical purposes in no risk of default (although it is notable that sovereign defaults have occurred in recent times in other countries, such as Argentina). By contrast, a corporation can go bankrupt and default on its obligations. Credit rating agencies like Moody's and Standard & Poor's publish bond ratings that affect what interest rates the bonds need to pay to succeed in the marketplace; the higher the credit rating, the lower the interest rate.

There are two basic markets for bonds: the primary market, where new bond offerings are sold for the first time (when the issuers borrow money from the market), and the secondary market, where these initial offerings can be sold again. Bond issuers must issue a prospectus following the rules of the government agency or department that oversees securities exchange. A prospectus describes basic terms of the bonds (also called notes) and details risks. A prospectus may run more than 100 pages with such details. For example, consider Bank of America's Medium Term Notes, Series N.[18]

In the secondary market, bond prices and the rate of interest they pay (coupons) are set through an auction process.[19] The price of the bond in the secondary market may be the same, higher, or lower than the bond's original face or par value based on the relationship between interest rate (*coupon*) and *yield-to-maturity* (the internal rate of return to the investor who buys at today's rate and holds until maturity).[20]

Calculating yield-to-maturity does not require any special analysis if one is buying the bond at its original par value. However, if one buys a bond at a premium or a discount, the yield will not be the same as its coupon rate and will require analysis

For example, a $100 one-year bond with a 10-percent coupon and semi-annual payments selling for a price of $106.50 still has a coupon yield of 10 percent but its current yield is only 9.0 percent. But conversely, if it is selling for $94.02 its current yield is 11.0 percent.[21]

Dropping bond prices imply that interest rates are going up as investors demand higher yields on their investments. Since the payout of the bond is fixed in dollars, the lower price of the bond has to provide the higher yield desired. The opposite applies to rising bond prices.

Whether the yield-to-maturity will be higher or lower than the coupon yield depends on the price of a bond in the market, which in turn depends on prevailing interest rate landscape and creditworthiness of the company. That is, if a company has a low credit rating, then the price set on its bonds will be lower, which then increases their anticipated yield-to-maturity. That is what "junk bonds" are all about: Generally, bonds with a rating of BBB- (on the Standard & Poor's and Fitch scale) or Baa3 (on Moody's) or better are considered "investment-grade." Bonds with lower ratings are considered "speculative" and often referred to as "high-yield" or "junk" bonds. The latter bonds are not for the faint of heart and best left to the professionals to trade.

Under normal circumstances, the yields of bonds tend to rise over time, with longer-term bonds delivering higher yields than shorter-term bonds. This leads to a *yield curve* that slopes upward over time. But occasionally, shorter-term bonds deliver higher yields, which leads to an *inverted yield curve*. For example, the yield on the 10-year U.S. Treasury note recently dipped below the yield on three-month paper.[22] Some experts say that the inverted yield curve can be a harbinger of near-term recession. Because when a yield curve inverts, it shows that investors lack confidence in the near-term economy. "They demand more yield for a short-term investment than for a long-term one because they perceive the near-term as riskier than the distant future," notes analyst Kimberly Amadeo of The Balance.[23] However, causes and effects of inverted yield curves vary.[24] The prevailing interest rate has many causes, and one of them is central banks. Any country's central bank is able to influence interest rates through open market transactions. When the central bank buys bonds, the prices of bonds will rise and interest rates will be pushed down. When it sells bonds, the prices of bonds will drop and interest rates will rise. This power has given rise in the United States to the adage, "Don't fight the Fed."

## Currency Markets (Foreign Exchange or FX)

The foreign currency or foreign exchange (Forex or FX) market is a decentralized worldwide market for trading currencies, both physically and, increasingly, virtually, via market "electronification."[25] The market involves some $5.1 trillion in in currencies on any given day, making it the world's largest market.[26] The U.S. dollar and the euro are the most commonly traded currencies, with the British pound, the yen, and other currencies trailing behind. The market grew out of the need for individuals, banks, companies, and governments engaged in international trade to buy and sell currency—both to accomplish fundamental transactions, and to hedge against risks of change in currency values. Major centers of FX trading include Bahrain, Chicago, Frankfurt, Hong Kong, London, New York, Tokyo, Toronto, and Zurich.

Currency markets can be extremely sensitive to external events. A recent article on the exchange value of the dollar mentioned eight different factors that were influencing this rate, including effects from economic strength, trade policy, fiscal deficits, current account deficits, tariffs, trade deficits, possible government shutdowns, and a possible infrastructure program. (See Note 4.1.)

### Note 4.1 Forex Sensitivity to External Events

"Following a year of broad dollar strength—due to *widening interest rate differentials*, a *booming US economy*, and investors seeking the reserve currency's safety amid *global trade tensions*—the risks surrounding the greenback in 2019 appear to be subsiding . . .

Separately, although markets have turned a blind eye lately, investor concerns about the twin *fiscal and current account deficits* could return, especially if the economy slows more sharply than anticipated and the *higher tariffs* have no impact in narrowing the huge *trade deficit* with China. Political gridlock in Washington and the constant threat of *government shutdowns* could also haunt the US currency.

However, there are also upside risks. Any further deterioration in US-China trade relations may in fact see the dollar attract fresh safe-haven bids. Likewise, if Congress agrees on a *massive infrastructure program* that has the potential to boost growth and inflation, it would be a game-changer."

Excerpted from *World Finance*, April 15, 2019. https://www.worldfinance.com/markets/the-dollars-stability-seems-illusory-as-tumult-abounds-in-currency-markets

## Commodities Markets

While stocks, bonds, and currencies can be considered key factors in global finance (per Figure 4.1), there is a fourth market that also has considerable influence—namely, commodities. There are three main classes of commodity markets, as well as some additional discreet commodity markets of various types. The main classes of commodity markets are for *energy* (e.g., oil, gas, electricity, and renewables), *metals* (both precious metals like gold and industrial metals like aluminum), and *agricultural products* (e.g., grains, cotton, and livestock). Annual trading can be counted in trillions of dollars for the major commodities like crude oil and industrial metals. In addition, although one normally associates commodity markets with tangible (physical) commodities such as the aforementioned, a growing number of intangible (non-physical) commodities like freight forwarding and emissions credits are also traded on commodities markets.

Commodity markets are themselves innovations in how we exchange money for particular types of goods, and they typically evolve through three stages of maturity. The first stage is physical trading of the goods, with participants who are mainly producers and consumers of the goods. Initially there is little standardization. The second stage sees new entrants like brokers and banks come to the market, a higher degree of standardization, and the formation of indices. The focus here is on over-the-counter (OTC) trading of both physical and financial products like commodities derivatives or commodities futures.

The most mature stage is when there is heavy trading in standardized products on exchanges, in addition to OTC trading. There is now significant participation of financial traders, and prices are highly transparent due to reference data and indices. Commodity markets typically start (stage 1) due to some event like the breakup of the traditional supply chain and are enabled by a decline in transport costs relative to the value of the commodity.

As the market matures, the need for financial management and the opening of the market to new participants leads to stage 2. Pressure for more transparency from regulators and participants is usually what leads to stage 3. For example, the market for crude oil was based on long-term supply contracts prior to the 1973 OPEC oil embargo, but afterward became more of a spot trading market. In the early eighties, it moved on to OTC trading, and then in the late eighties made the transition to regulated trading with more liquidity and derivatives like Brent futures attracting Wall Street firms. Crude oil futures are now a major benchmark in the United States.

The global commodities market is a vast and loose trading system for commodities, commodities derivatives, and commodities futures, with numerous price-drivers, including supply disruptions, interest rates, currency trends, trade relations, and the financial state of the countries supplying the commodities—often in emerging markets.[27]

The Futures Industry Association (FIA), the leading global trade organization for the futures, options, and centrally cleared derivatives markets, keeps statistics on commodities futures based on 79 exchanges operated by 54 companies in 34 countries. Volume is based on number of contracts, not money value involved. Currently, volume is at 25 billion contracts.

The World Bank keeps a pink sheet of global commodities prices.[28] It shows some 80 commodities organized into groups: energy (coal, crude oil, and natural gas) and non-energy (agriculture, types of beverages and food, raw materials, fertilizers, metals and minerals, and precious minerals). Each of these can become an important sub-market, per Note 4.2. Investors in commodities, like all investors, want to buy low and sell high. The Nasdaq Stock Market in the United States maintains a heat map of commodities trends as rising or falling.[29]

**Note 4.2 The Ag Futures Market**
Within every market there are sub-markets with value chains. Let's take a look at one of them—agriculture, a dominant commodities market. The largest agricultural commodity exchanges are the New York Mercantile Exchange (NYMEX), the Chicago Mercantile Exchange (CME), the New York Mercantile Exchange (NYMEX), the Zhengzhou Commodity Exchange (ZCE), and the Dalian Commodity Exchange (DCE). Global agricultural production exceeds $3 trillion per year.[30] The top two agricultural exporters—the European Union and the United States—exceed 50 percent of global output.[31] Pricing tends to be more regional than global, with cost differences driven by tariffs, transportation, and storage costs. Major agricultural commodities are typically traded on futures exchanges. Long-term futures markets for agricultural commodities are typically shorter-term and less liquid than for other major commodities such as crude oil.

The lion's share of value taken in the agricultural value chain is added during retail and distribution. The second largest share goes to the suppliers of crop inputs like seeds and machinery like tractors. The lowest share goes to agricultural production. Put bluntly, the farmers who grow our food get by far the smallest share of the money we pay for the food we buy in stores.

## Intermarket Financial Analysis

The movements of various global financial markets—for stocks, bonds, commodities, and currencies—can be compared with one another, as shown in

**KEY**

■ Positive correlation
☐ Negative correlation

**During inflation**

Bonds     ■ Stocks

U.S. Dollars ☐ Commodities

**During Deflation**

Stocks     ■ Interest rates

Stocks     ☐ Commodities

Bonds     ☐ Stocks

U.S. Dollars ☐ Commodities

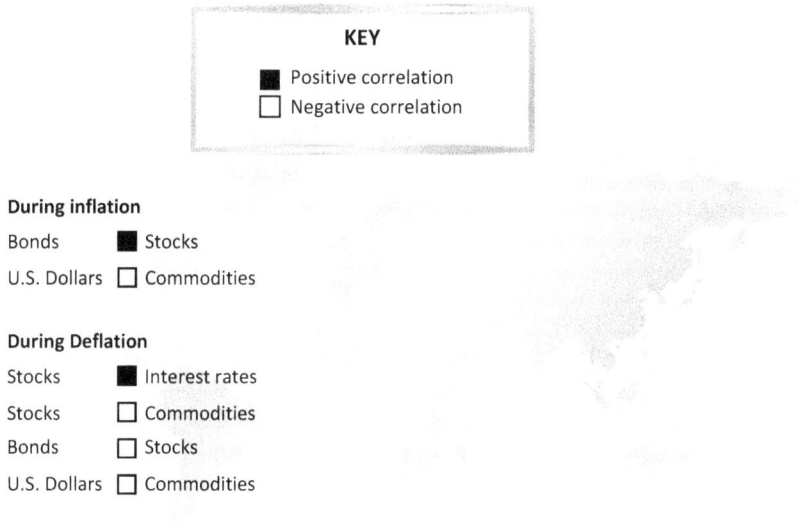

**Disclaimer:** *"Correlations revealed through intermarket analysis are not guaranteed to remain stable. Changing economic conditions may lead to changing correlations. Positive correlations between asset classes may become negative correlations, or a correlation may cease to exist altogether." CFI*

**Figure 4.2:** One view of market interdependencies (Fig. Note 4.2).

Figure 4.2. This *intermarket analysis* can be studied either in pairs or with more than one comparison occurring.

If market movements are identical (which would be rare), there is a positive correlation of 1. As noted by the Corporate Finance Institute, any correlation between 0.7 and 1.0 sustained for a long period of time indicates that the two variables are statistically significant to each other. Although correlation is not causation, it can be, and this is where it gets interesting for investors. Because if an investor knows that a particular movement in one asset class will cause another movement in another asset class, this can suggest a buy/sell/hold decision. For example, if it is believed that low interest rates and high stock values are correlated, then an announcement of higher interest rates would trigger a sell signal for equities. Of course, determining causality is rife with challenges, including the well-known statistical problem of endogeneity.[32] Nonetheless, according to the Corporate Finance Institute, the markets have certain predictable relationships to each other.

For example, during inflation, stocks have a positive correlation to bonds, but during deflation, the two have a negative correction, according to the Corporate Finance Institute (see Figure 4.2).

The interrelationship of stocks, bonds, commodities, and currencies impact investment decisions by individuals and institutions. There are times to "get out of stocks and into bonds" and vice versa, but most investment portfolios keep a prudent balance.

## Market Movers

The four markets described above don't operate by themselves. They rely on the work of many "movers"—generally, global institutions in the private sector. Here are just a few of the most important ones.

### Bank of International Settlements and SWIFT

The Bank of International Settlements (BIS) based in Basel, Switzerland, introduced earlier in Chapter 3 as a network of 60 central banks, facilitates payment settlements around the globe.[33] The Society for World Interbank Financial Telecommunication (SWIFT), the main service for payment transfer, is merely an enabler, not a driver. Based in La Hulpe, Belgium, it is a cooperative enterprise to which banks around the world belong. Its messaging services, using a hardware-based Public Key Infrastructure (PKI) technology, are used and trusted by more than 11,000 financial institutions in more than 200 countries and territories around the world, sending more than 7 billion messages in a year's span.[34] SWIFT helps clear transactions by enabling international funds transfer. This includes the kind of fund transfer needed to make any global payment, as when countless people around the globe made contributions for the reconstruction of Notre Dame Cathedral in Paris, France, following a devastating fire in April 2019.

SWIFT technology can get slowed down by legacy systems within banks, but its standards are evolving to help. For example, SWIFT will soon be rolling out SWIFT Standards MT Release in 2020 to "prepare the community for a more systematic approach to compliance."[35]

Dan Tapscott, blockchain evangelist and expert of The Tapscott Group, has suggested that blockchain's distributed ledger technology could revolutionize or replace global payments.[36] As we will see in our chapter on blockchain (Chapter 7), this prediction may prove optimistic, as transmission via current blockchain technology can be slow and cumbersome.

## National Securities Commissions

Most nations that have stock markets also have securities commissions to regulate the issuance and exchange of securities. Examples include the Financial Conduct Authority in the United Kingdom[37] and the U.S. Securities and Exchange Commission in the United States. Most of these commissions have voluntarily joined a self-regulatory association of International Organization of Securities Commissions.[38] IOSCO has three categories of members: ordinary, associate, and affiliate. The ordinary members (128) are national securities commissions. Associate members (27) are usually agencies or branches of government (other than the principal national securities regulator) that have some regulatory competence over securities markets. Affiliate members (64) are "self-regulatory organizations, stock exchanges, financial market infrastructures, investor protection funds and compensation funds, and other bodies with an appropriate interest in securities regulation."[39]

U.S. securities laws can apply not only to offerings of traditional stocks and bonds but also to any offering that is based on a commodity, including a digital one. For example, in the United States, cryptocurrency is considered to be a "digital asset" and, like a tangible asset such as gold, it is considered to be a "commodity." However, as noted by Securities and Exchange Commission chair Jay Clayton, products linked to the value of such assets "may be structured as securities products subject to registration under the Securities Act of 1933 or the Investment Company Act of 1940."

## The "Great" G's

In modern times, nations have banded together to cooperate on economic issues. They are all called "G" because they are groups.

*G7.* The G7 (formerly G8 until Russia was pushed out in 2014) is a group of highly industrialized countries that meet to further global economic prosperity.[40] Members are the heads of government of Canada, France, Germany, Italy, Japan, the United Kingdom, and the United States.

*G20.* Every year, the heads of government for the world's most prosperous countries participate at an annual Summit on Financial Markets and the World Economy.[41] Known as the G20, the group describes itself as "the premier forum for international economic cooperation." Although only 20 of the nearly 200 nations participate, they represent some 80 percent of world gross domestic product (GDP). The presidency of the group rotates, with the president in any year hosting the summit, as well as related ministerial meetings. In June 2019, for example, Japan's Prime Minister Shinzō Abe hosted the summit in Japan, which also included meetings of ministers of agriculture, energy, finance, foreign affairs, health, labor, tourism, and trade. The impact of the meetings on financial markets has generally been minimal.[42] (This is likely because these meetings are rarely used to announce new policies; most of the policy work is done in advance and priced into the markets by the time the meetings happen.)

### Global "NGOs" (Nongovernmental Organizations)

*Financial Stability Board (FSB).* The (FSB) is a global body that monitors and makes recommendations about the global financial system. It promotes international financial stability by coordinating national financial authorities and international standard-setting bodies engaged in development of strong regulatory, supervisory, and other financial sector policies.[43]

*International Finance Corporation (IFC).* A member of the World Bank Group, IFC is the world's largest global development institution. It was established following the Bretton Woods Agreement forged after World War II. The IFC supports the private sector in developing countries using funds from the bonds it issues in a variety of markets and formats, including U.S. dollar benchmarks bonds, "themed" bonds that support a specific program such as green bonds; uridashi notes (secondary offering of bonds outside Japan using yen or another currency); private placements; and discount notes. In addition, IFC issues local-currency bonds to develop domestic capital markets and facilitate local-currency lending. IFC takes equity positions in companies in developing countries and places directors there to ensure good governance.[44]

*International Monetary Fund (IMF).* The IMF, another Bretton Woods creation launched in 1944, is a cooperative association of 189 country members, formed for the purpose of monetary cooperation among members.[45] One of its most important activities is the provision of special drawing rights (SDRs), an international reserve asset created by the IMF in 1969 to supplement the official reserves of its member countries. SDRs are based on a basket of major currencies—the U.S. dollar, the British pound sterling, the euro, the Japanese yen, and the Chinese yuan. Additional goals include financial stability, international trade, increase of employment and decrease in poverty, and sustainable economic growth. IMF sponsors research in emerging monetary issues, including fintech.[46]

*World Bank.* A sister organization to the International Finance Corporation and a member of the World Bank Group also founded after Bretton Woods, the bank provides low-interest loans, zero- to low-interest credits, and grants to developing countries. Some projects are cofinanced with governments, other multilateral institutions, commercial banks, export credit agencies, and private sector investors. The World Bank also provides or facilitates financing through trust fund partnerships with bilateral and multilateral donors.[47]

*World Economic Forum.* The World Economic Forum is hosted by the International Organization for Public-Private Cooperation, headquartered in Geneva, Switzerland under the supervision of the Swiss Federal Government.[48] The forum engages political, business, and other leaders to "shape global, regional, and industry agendas."[49] Founded by Klaus Schwab, a prominent engineer and economist known for his contribution to stakeholder theory[50] and his insights into the Fourth Industrial Revolution, the WEF hosts an annual summit in Davos, Switzerland.

## Motivations: Market Forces

So much for the markets and their movers. Now comes the more interesting question: What motivates the movers to act? What are the forces that connect and drive them?

Global financial markets have a dynamic of their own, comprising multiple players and, even more deeply, multiple *drivers*—some human (behavioral), some beyond human control.[51] How, then, could one nation, institution, or group control markets?

Yet, beyond the complexity, there do seem to be some principles organizing markets. To determine them, let us first look at the players, and then the driving forces and the dynamics that link these forces together.

Global finance has many drivers. The list of drivers defies full enumeration, as each driver is connected to another. The following discussion is offered as a selection of some key drivers related to self-interest.

### Drivers

*Individual human self-interest.* One human driver of global markets is *individual self-interest*, the desire of each participant to make exchanges that increase his or her wealth. This basic selfishness can be exacerbated by the carelessness with which one can spend other people's money (nicknamed

"OPM.[52] The theory of human selfishness (with or without the Voltairean twist) is consistent with classical economics and continues to have support in modern research. The social impact of self-interest can be positive, paradoxically enough. Adam Smith described this paradox in *Wealth of Nations* when he explained that in producing items of value (e.g., in our present case, trading in global financial markets), the merchant "intends only his own gain; and he is in this, as in many other cases, led by an invisible hand to promote an end which was no part of his intention." Smith notes that the force that guides human commercial behavior is providential, because "By pursuing his own interest, he frequently promotes that of the society more effectually than when he really intends to promote it." Many economic thinkers in the free enterprise or libertarian school of thought have cited this wise observation in arguing against government controls over business. But even while accepting self-interest as a driver, it is important to acknowledge that we have certain built-in inhibitors to our self-seeking. Our experience, as well as research, reveals additional motives such as cooperation, fairness, and enforcement of norms.[53] In addition, human self-interest is often foiled by human folly, as noted later in this chapter. A good example of this is the "irrational exuberance" identified by past U.S. Federal Reserve Chair Alan Greenspan.[54]

Finally, transcending self-interest, altruism, and folly in a kind of supreme act of individuation, there may be the life-sustaining impulse of "animal spirits" identified by John Maynard Keynes. In his book on *The General Theory of Employment, Interest, and Money* (1936), Keynes observed that "a large proportion of our positive activities depend on spontaneous optimism rather than mathematical expectations, whether moral or hedonistic or economic. Most, probably, of our decisions to do something positive, the full consequences of which will be drawn out over many days to come, can only be taken as the result of animal spirits—a spontaneous urge to action rather than inaction, and not as the outcome of a weighted average of quantitative benefits multiplied by quantitative probabilities."

The notion of animal spirits gives us a window into human choices that defy logic, setting the theoretical groundwork for an entire system of economics deemed behavioral. In the last section of this chapter, on problems plaguing markets, we will address the issue of "Robot Roulette," in which financial decisions are automated based on algorithms, with no human choice involved once the formula is set.

*Corporate self-interest.* Another arguably human actor in the field of global finance is the corporation, which shares many traits with the humans that form them. Corporations are formally recognized as legal "persons" in many jurisdictions—for example, in the United States and various nations in Europe. Courts have cited this personhood as a justification for certain corporate actions, such as political expenditures.[55] As shown earlier in Figure 4.1, corporations have a major role in both trade (exchange of good and/or services for money) and finance (exchange of one kind of money for another kind of money (e.g., cash for stock). Corporations participate in global trade by being part of global value chains of mining, design, production, and distribution that are increasingly intricate.[56] They also participate in global finance by issuing debt (aka corporate paper) and securities (aka stock), and through their pension or retirement plans. (This aspect of corporate behavior dovetails with both individual self-interest and investor self-interest because these plans may be directed by employees or agents they authorize; they invest employee contributions in securities and defer taxation on gains until the employees withdraw the funds.)

*Investor self-interest.* Individuals and institutions that invest in corporations also operate largely out of self-interest, seeking to maximize returns on their investment. There is a wealth of empirical research on the behavior of investors (also known as "behavioral finance") showing that investors can be irrational. These economists have identified types of irrational choices (explored further below, but generally, at least from the point of view of conscious decision making (as opposed to unconscious bias), choices generally fall on the side of maximizing return. This influences corporate behavior as well, as shareholders and securities regulators alike apply pressure to corporations to link executive compensation to shareholder returns, creating a strong incentive for corporations to maximize the latter, at least in the short term.

*National self-interest.* Along these same lines is *national self-interest*—the policies of sovereign nations to maximize their productivity and wealth, measured by level of exports, strength of currency, and other indicators. Within global finance, nations participate as issuers of debt, selling treasury bonds with interest rates set at auction,[57] and they also participate as buyers of equity, through sovereign wealth funds. Certain areas of global finance, such as infrastructure investment, are dominated by government debt (government bonds), not private debt (bank loans).[58] Balance of trade is one metric that nations watch in their own self-interest, desiring to export more goods and services than they import. In addition, there is *foreign direct investment(FDI)*, which along with balance of trade (export-import), is an important part of a country's overall balance of payments, and can have a major impact on a particular currency's exchange rates.[59] In general, nations would prefer for their companies to acquire (through outbound acquisitions) than to be acquired (through inbound transactions), and in sensitive industries, there may be restrictions on the latter.

The counterweight to national self-interest here is the rise of global institutions and movements leading to "one world" in finance as well as in politics—for some, a valid and positive movement evident in the rise of numerous influential global organizations and initiatives;[60] for others, a form of tyranny to be resisted. In any event, it appears that with or without the "globalist" interference, national self-interest is both expressed and occasionally inhibited by national laws, rules, and regulations, set and enforced by governments and the exchanges and other institutions they authorize.[61]

Of course, the drivers of national self-interest may move in diverging directions when it comes to capital flows. For example, in a December 2018 study, scholars writing for the Bank of International Settlements found that the properties and drivers of capital flows vary considerably across sectors, instruments, and country groups.[62] Nonetheless, the movement of pure capital across borders has a homogenizing effect.

An earlier paper found that "the correlation between capital inflows and outflows has increased substantially over time in a sample of 128 advanced and developing countries. This is a result of an increase in financial globalization (stock of external assets and liabilities). This dominates the effect of an increase in trade globalization (exports plus imports), which reduces the correlation between capital inflows and outflows."[63] To put it another way, capital inflows and outflows are becoming more closely correlated, which points to an increase in financial globalization (cross-border financial holdings) rather than an increase in trade globalization (exports plus imports), which would have the opposite effect.

## Equilibrium and Feedback Loops

Human and non-human forces in global markets interact with each other in patterns best understood as systems that go in and out of equilibrium, with both major driving feedbacks that are both positive and negative all operating together. To understand global finance, we have to understand equilibrium and feedback.

Equilibrium characterizes a system that is stable and well balanced. Over time, equilibrium can be disturbed. Not every change needs to result in a feedback effect, but in complex systems, many changes will. What happens then will depend on whether a positive or negative "feedback loop" is operative. Feedback loops can occur in a number of domains studied by scientists, including electronics, biology, and economics.

Positive feedback loops amplify changes, moving a system away from its equilibrium state and making it unstable. Negative feedback loops counter changes; they attempt to hold a system to its equilibrium state, making it more stable. Putting it mathematically, in a positive feedback loop, a change (increase or decrease) in some variable results in the same type of change in a second variable. With the one change feeding into the other, there is an amplification effect. Think of what happens when you hold a microphone too close to a speaker. In a negative loop, a change in some variable results in the opposite change in a second variable.[64] Think about riding a bicycle: when it leans over too much to one side, a negative feedback would correct that effect and bring it back to the vertical. But positive feedback would amplify the tipping of the bicycle and eventually make it fall over.

Each of these feedback scenarios can occur in a complex, dynamic system like the global finance system. The point is that each can create a self-reinforcing cycle of change. Tracing feedback loops is not easy because real-world systems are complex, non-linear, and will change over time. As geologist Steve Hurst has observed, "In many complex systems, delays are intrinsically related to feedback and so it is important to look at models that contain both explicit and implicit delays. Implicit delays are not obvious from how the models look or the underlying equations but are found in the characteristic time that it takes for a process to run. Such delays are often indicated in terms such as half-life, residence time, equilibrium time, mixing time, compounding and others."[65]

Negative feedback loops are familiar to students of economics. One such loop is the relationship between supply and demand. Demand for a resource decreases due to the higher prices that get charged when the resource becomes scarce.

Systems can also oscillate. The classic (theoretical) example that can be modeled by a couple of differential equations is that of fox and rabbit populations. Starting with a low fox population, the rabbits multiply quickly. That increases the food available for the foxes, who can now increase their population. At some point, the fox population becomes large enough that the rabbit population is overhunted. With less rabbits, some of the foxes starve and the fox population is reduced. Then the cycle starts all over again.

An economic system either self-regulates (classic supply and demand theory) or one force regulates another (public regulators versus private interests).

Negative feedback naturally occurs in both economic and political systems; where it is natural and desirable.

Positive feedback loops are another matter. They can be good ("success begets success"), but they can happen not only for positive things like wealth but also for negative things like poverty, as discussed in Chapter 2. Also, the process is not sustainable in a positive feedback loop. Eventually, extremes are reached and a negative loop sets in.

In today's economy, it would seem that positive feedbacks occur more often than people realize, and can cause crises due to their amplifying effects.

When currency markets began to float—no longer based on a commodity or on money supply, and no longer subject to limits on exchange rates, then once exchange rates began to float—positive feedback loops became more common. As one study noted, the world has seen "a remarkable increase in trading volume and volatility and many major currencies have seen major swings in the floating market since 1990."[66] Both rises and falls were steeper. In equity markets, index trading and algorithmic trading are self-reinforcing rather than self-correcting.

## The Invisible Hand

Patterns in markets are well known, and quickly discounted as just so much white noise. Profit-seeking market quants with PhDs in rocket science are looking for large and small patterns all the time, with the intent on trading on that knowledge. Any pattern may be elusive because people will trade on it as soon as they find it. If too many catch on, that pattern will be traded away and a new pattern will emerge, as noted by billionaire investor George Soros in his 1987 book *The Alchemy of Finance* on the theory of reflexivity.[67] (We cited this book in Chapter 2 for an equally important point—the importance of perceptions when assigning value, and we will return to Soros later in Chapter 6 on cryptocoins.)

More importantly, the patterns reinforce themselves. For example, in equity markets, traders may be programmed to buy when they see a large upward jump in a closing price after three consecutive days of decline—because they think prices will soon rise.[68] If they all buy this stock, then this indeed will happen. These events become a standard for buy and sell behavior. The pack believes that they exist and that makes it so. They can now generally be relied on to come true as enough traders act on the trend. This situation can be abused, as a little manipulation (up or down) can create such a pattern.

But sooner or later, participants in economic markets may ask a more profound question: Is there an order to financial markets that is akin to the order of the physical universe? Adam Smith, father of classical economics, believed this. As mentioned earlier, he called it the "invisible hand," implying a divine ordering from God.[69] Although Smith only uses the term once in *Wealth of Nations*, it is considered to be a central idea in that work—one based in the Deist beliefs of his generation.[70] Support for an "invisible hand" design can also be found in Philip Mirowski's book *More Heat Than Light*, which reveals a strong connection between early economics theory and early physics theory.[71]

Meanwhile, the best we can do may be to understand finance one market at a time. The next section discusses six problems in equity that can be solved by a return to true investment.

## Six Problems Plaguing Markets

Moving now from the what and why of global finance, we now look at certain problem areas that are now plaguing it, and what people can do to counteract these issues. We shall start this section with a few thought-provoking quotations.

> In the long run, stock returns depend almost entirely on the reality of the investment returns earned by our corporations. The perception of investors, reflected by the speculative returns, counts for little. It is economics that controls long-term equity returns; emotions, so dominant in the short-term, dissolve.
> —John C. "Jack" Bogle (May 8, 1929–January 16, 2019) in *The Little Book of Common Sense Investing: The Only Way to Guarantee Your Fair Share of Stock Market Returns* (New York: Wiley, 2007)

On January 16, 2019, at the height of earnings season on a strong trading day, John C. "Jack" Bogle passed away at age 89. As soon as his death was announced by Vanguard, the company he founded as an "experiment" in May 1975, tributes poured in from every corner of the world. This was a man who had seen it all. Born in the speculative Hoover Bull Market of May 1929 and raised in the post-crash depression, Bogle was known as a long-term value investor who opposed speculation and short-termism. In *The Little Book of Common Sense Investing*, he said, "Owning the stock market over the long term is a winner's game, but attempting to beat the market is a loser's game."

More than anything else, Bogle was known as the inventor of the mutual fund—the use of the open-ended investment fund, owned by many investors to purchase a variety of stocks and/or bonds selected according to the fund's stated purpose.[72] This has become the vehicle of choice for retirement accounts (401ks) of average workers and, for many, their only financial investment. As such, this innovative financier, perhaps more so than anyone since Adam Smith, had a profound impact on the wealth of nations. Today there are more than 10,000 funds in existence, including mutual funds and the exchange-traded-fund innovation they inspired.[73] So the legacy lives on.

But as with the passing of any larger-than-life figure, we sense that the loss of John Bogle may have marked the end of a golden era of value investing. "The true investor ... will do better if he forgets about the stock market and pays attention to his dividend returns and to the operating results of his companies," said Bogle. This strategy has been possible during our lifetimes. But as we approach 2020, conspiracy theories persist, along with scams, short-termism, speculation, human folly, and trading automation.

### Problem 1: Possible or Perceived Conspiracies

A number of conspiracy theories have arisen to explain the workings of global finance. From the times of the earliest central banks in the seventeenth century, observers expressed distrust of banking institutions, as noted in Chapter 3 on central banks and treasuries.

In our modern times, mistrust continues. There are people today who believe that there is a "new world order" that is run by a small and powerful group with key players such as some wealthy family (e.g., the Rothschilds) or some religious or spiritual order (e.g., Jesuits or Masonic Illuminati). These crackpot notions coexist with more serious attempts to understand global finance in a holistic framework—generally, a negative one. Consider recent books on "global financial collusion,"[74] the "global power elite,"[75] a "secret plan for the next financial crisis,"[76] and one on "what they do with your money."[77]

### Problem 2: Scams and Other Scandals

Unfortunately, in the four markets we have presented, there are enough global market scandals to fuel such negative views, whether populist or academic in platform. In short, market scandals "have happened," as some laughable late-night pharma commercials state when talking about drug side effects.[78] This includes the mother of all financial scandals, manipulation of the London Interbank Rate (LIBOR) affecting global interest rates from 2005 to 2010.

Bad behavior in financial markets led to a total of $26.5 billion in fines levied worldwide in 2017 alone, according to a leading bond rating agency, Duff & Phelps (itself a subject of regulatory scrutiny, along with other commercial rating agencies in the aftermath of the financial crisis a decade ago).[79] These fines were levied for variety of violations, including not only failures in corporate governance, market conduct, and business obligations, but also downright "financial crimes," accounting for 24 percent of the incidents and 16 percent of the fines from 2013 to 2017. Of all countries, the United States was by far the most punitive during that period, accounting for 96 percent for the five-year period.[80]

Here are a few more examples of when markets veered from their social purpose to enrich a few at the expense of many. We are using "scam" as a shorthand to include any economic behavior meant to manipulate or game a market. As for "scandal," lengthen the list to include any type of fraud or money laundering perpetrated on a global scale.

*Stock scams.* Throughout the history of equity markets there have been companies large and small that make false statements to investors or keep them in the dark in order to inflate their stock prices—this occurs despite often stringent requirements for prompt and accurate disclosure of all material information. This is a common theme in many stock scams. The largest such scandals occurred in the United States at the turn of the century, with the well-known failures of Enron and WorldCom, together blamed for a total of nearly $200 billion in investor losses.

But such giant-sized stock market swindles are relatively rare, occurring only once or twice in a typical decade. But every single year, hundreds of *small* frauds are perpetrated. In 2018, the SEC's Office of the Whistleblower, created by the Dodd-Frank Act of 2010, and growing annually ever since then, received 5,200 whistleblower tips. While not all were deemed credible, it does go to show how widespread securities fraud—or the perception of fraud—can be, considering that only about 5,000 companies trade on the major exchanges.

Some critics consider stock buybacks by companies to be against the public interest A bill proposed by Rep. Jesus G. Garcia (D-IL) would "prohibit public companies from repurchasing their shares on the open market, and for other purposes." Populists criticize buybacks because they use company funds not to increase jobs or wages but rather to boost stock price. The left-of-center magazine *New Republic* has even referred to the practice as a "scam."[81]

*Bond scams.* Bond market scandals also occur. For example, recently a group of leading global banks—including Bank of America, Credit Suisse Group AG, Crédit Agricole SA, and Deutsche Bank AG—were accused of attempting to rig the prices of dollar-denominated supra-sovereign, sovereign, and agency sovereign bonds between 2009 and 2015.[82]

*Commodities scams.* Like other markets, the commodities market can be manipulated. The biggest example of this is the time that the Hunt brothers hoarded $4.5 billion in silver in Switzerland, creating a false scarcity, which pushed the price of silver so high that the government stepped in and stopped silver trading. Like most scams, this one met a bitter end, as the price plummet caused the younger Hunt to remark that "a billion dollars isn't what it used to be."[83] There are also small-time scams, through a "pool" (small group of investors). In a "commodity pool fraud"[84] investors may be asked to put their money in a pool that does not really exist (it is a scam), or if it exists, it may operate for the sole profit of its founders, who "cherry-pick" opportunities.[85]

*Currency scams.* Currency market frauds are fairly common, and for good reason. As Bloomberg bloggers Joel Weber and Jason Kelly have observed, "Unlike in equities, where large trades leave little left unknown, friction and arbitrage are everywhere in foreign exchange," which has left the market open to "scandal."[86] At least seven global banks have been accused of improper FX behavior, including charges of a "cartel" allegedly involving Barclays, Citigroup, JPMorgan Chase, and Royal Bank of Scotland.[87] There is also a credible claim that the billionaire George Soros singlehandedly succeeded in attacking the British pound sterling, forcing its retreat from the original European Exchange Rate Mechanism (ERM) that preceded the launch of the euro currency.[88]

*Other scandals.* Beyond these market-centric ruses, global markets are affected by various types of fraud and money laundering. Fortunately, there is a new cop on the global beat to fight such crime. The Financial Action Task Force (FATF), founded in 1989 after the global financial crisis, is an inter-governmental body founded by the ministers of finance in many leading economies. Today the crime-fighter has 70 members—37 countries, 2 regional bodies (the European Commission and the Gulf Cooperation Council), and 31 non-governmental organizations. FATF sets standards for "legal, regulatory, and operational measures for combating money laundering, terrorist financing and other related threats to the integrity of the international financial system."[89] Among other activities, the FATF monitors the threat of money laundering and terrorist financing techniques and determines or reviews counter-measures. Its ultimate goal is to protect the international financial system from misuse.

### Problem 3: Speculation

But even more problematic at the systemic level than scams is speculation. Every century sees them. Ever inventive, human beings can make a market bubble out of everything—even Beanie Babies.[90]

The long list of previous market bubbles caused by speculation is well known.[91] We will review some examples here, and add the latest bubble—namely, the cryptocoin bubble of 2018—just a short while ago.

*Tulipomania (1634–1637).* The Tulip craze of the Netherlands in the 1630s rocketed to fame with the publication of Charles Mackay's Extraordinary *Popular Delusions and the Madness of Crowds* (1841)—a compelling collection of market panics. As it turns out, the situation was a little more banal. A relatively small number of investors was affected and losses were not dramatic. That is the conclusion of *Tulipmania: Money, Honor and Knowledge in the Dutch Golden Age* (2007), in which historian Anne Goldgar shows that the mania was not as extreme as commonly portrayed. However, she does acknowledge that the market did fall prone to speculation. In 1637, prices rose 1,100 in a single month. Switser bulbs went from 125 florins a pound on Dec. 31, 1636, to 1,500 florins on Feb. 3, 1637.

*The South Sea Bubble* (1716–1720). The popular imagination was all too ready to buy in when executives of this British trading company talked up the value of the firm's trading rights. When inventor Isaac Newton lost his fortune in that crash, he lamented, "I can calculate the movement of the stars, but not the madness of men."[92]

*The Mississippi Bubble* (1718–1720). This dream crashed and burned in the New World but it began in the Old Country when an inventive Scotsman named John Law convinced the French government to start a new bank, which in turn financed economic operations overseas in a 3,000 mile territory bordered by the Mississippi River. This economic empire, considered by some historians to be a fundamentally sound prototype of legitimate big business financing in future generations, eventually crashed due to overleverage.[93]

The *Global "Railway Mania" Bubble* (1840s–1894). Railroads were a paradigm-changing innovation in their time, and optimism about their prospects was high. Rail companies overbuilt their way into bankruptcy, both in the United Kingdom and the United States, where one quarter of all railroad companies went bankrupt, leaving their owners with investment losses.

*The Dot-com Bubble* (1995–1999). When the internet first opened up the possibility of electronic commerce through websites, the costs of creating these was high and expectations of returns were higher. Website businesses with negative cash flow went public for fantastic sums. Investors were left with losses when the stock prices plummeted. There was even a belief that this "New Economy" would be immune to business cycles of boom and bust. In early 2000, when investors realized that the dotcom emperor had no clothes, the Nasdaq hurtled down from 5,000 to less than 1,000 within two mournful years, ushering in a recession.

*The Bitcoin Bubble* (January 2017–January 2018). During 2017, bitcoin values rose from less than $1,000 to almost $20,000. Then, in February 2018, they plummeted to below $7,000, and were barely half that by year's end. In retrospect, it was a bubble.[94] Note, however, that in 2019, there were signs of recovery, with price levels at around $9,000 by mid-year.[95] Even so, as we will explore further in Chapter 6 on bitcoin, the volatility that bitcoin has detracted from its status as a store of value; its ups and downs have a huge impact on its chances in the long run. Volatility is simply not a good trait for any type of money.

## Problem 4: Short-termism

Some investors hold their purchases for a very short time, buying and selling securities in rapid succession. An extreme example of such short-termism is the individual day trader, who executes trades to capitalize on intraday market price action—in contrast to the institutional investment manager, who makes selections for a portfolio based on research into long-term value prospects. Increasingly, however, institutional investors also have a short-term mentality. The portfolio turnover ratio of mutual funds (percent of holdings that are new at the start of any given year) has risen to 79 percent at last calculation (in 2015), up from 45 percent in 1975 and 26 percent in 1945. Some predict that it will go to 100 percent, with entirely new stock picks every year, while others believe that the hot-potato trend has plateaued.[96]

While there is nothing necessarily illegal or unethical about a short-term investment, it is not desirable to have an entire economy built on it. When long-term consequences are ignored, their impact is more severe.

For example, if a company wants to boost its earnings in a particular quarter, it might postpone plans to invest in research and development (R&D). This is because earnings are calculated as revenues minus expenses, and R&D costs are accounted for as an expense, so in the short term they depress earnings. The reason a company might want to boost earnings in a particular quarter is that it may know that many of its investors are oriented to the short term. If these investors are using an automated trading algorithm that is set to "sell" when earnings drop, then a choice to invest in R&D could trigger selling by investors. To be sure, there are still value investors as described by John Bogle, but these are becoming rare, as described in the section "Automation: Robot Roulette."

## Problem 5: Human Folly

Behind speculation and short-termism is human folly—in particular, *irrational exuberance*, a term famously coined by former Federal Reserve Chair Alan Greenspan in a December 5, 1996 speech during the dot-com bubble. Economist Robert Schiller, writing a book of this title in 2009 (after the contagious meltdown of the mortgage market) defined this as "a situation in which news of price increases spurs investor enthusiasm, which spreads by psychological contagion from person to person, in the process amplifying stories that might justify the price increases, and bringing in a larger and larger class of investors who, despite doubts about the real value of an investment, are drawn to it partly by envy of others' successes and partly through a gamblers' excitement."[97] This is similar to a theory advanced by financial columnist Anne Kate Smith of Kiplinger's Personal Finance. She notes that follies vary throughout a market cycle. The same person who has an anchoring bias in a bear market may catch a contagious fear of missing out in a bull market, then become biased via representativeness and familiarity, and move back to anchoring.[98]

Investment follies may also vary by temperament. One typology says that humans may be bargain hunters, risk avoiders, price accepters, loyal buyers, or indifferent buyers, and their susceptibility to economic foibles various accordingly.[99] For example, a risk avoider may be more prone to anchoring than to the fear of missing out.

If markets at times resemble a "ship of fools"—to join the many who have appropriated this title from the prescient Dutch Renaissance writer Sebastian Brandt—this is in part because of twists and turns of the human mind. (For a catalog of such human folly, see Note 4.3.)

### Note 4.3  A Catalog of Behaviors Driving Human Folly

**Anchoring**

A single event or trend can bias the mind into thinking that this situation is permanent; the mind "anchors" in the past rather than observing what is present or possible.

**Attribution bias**

Past successes tend to generate overconfidence. People take too much credit for successes and too little blame for failures; they attribute successes to their own prowessbut failures to forces beyond their control.

**Cognitive dissonance**

This is a state of mind in which contradictory ideas and/or actions coexist.

**Confirmatory bias**

People have a tendency to overweigh data confirming prior beliefs while dismissing data-contradicting prior beliefs.

**Conformity**

People change their behavior as a result of pressure from others—similar to the bandwagon mentioned earlier.

**Control illusion**

Many suffer from the false belief that they have control over something uncontrollable. Conformists are likely to rationalize.

**Disposition effect**

When an investor overvalues a company and refuses to sell its stock even though itspricing is steadily declining, this irrational behavior is called the disposition effect.

**Emotional attachment**

Sometimes, emotional attachment to an investment position masquerades as the exercise of discretionary judgment. One study showed that investors who fared best during a recent market downturn had restrictive rules that prevented them from holding on to stocks (for emotional or other motives) that did not meet the criteria.

**Familiarity bias**

This bias occurs when an investor prefers an investment in his or her own country or industry.

**Fear of missing out (FOMO)**

When markets are rising or falling, an investor may buy or sell hastily in order to avoid "missing out" on an opportunity.

**Group thinking**

Different answers given by individuals converge to a single answer when the individuals are in a group. Also, individuals sometimes give wrong answers in order to conform to group norms.

**Optimism**

People are generally optimistic. In one study, undergraduates were asked to relate how likely various life events were to happen to them. The result: students systematically thought that good events were likely to happen to them while bad events were more likely to happen to other students.

**Rationalization**

Cognitive dissonance causes people to rationalize actions that differ from their own preferences. Conformists are more likely to rationalize.

**Self-serving biases**

People reach conclusions about reality (including their own skills) that favor them.

**Status quo bias**

People may prefer the present state over an unknown future state, leading to inaction even when action is called for.

*Excerpted and expanded from Robert A.G. Monks and Alexandra R. Lajoux,* Corporate Valuation for Portfolio Investment *(Wiley, 2010).*[100]

Any person can fall into one or more of these traps at any time—even the most logical among us.[101]

## Problem 6: Automation—Robot Roulette

Last but not least, markets today suffer from a lack of real-time, discretionary intelligence. They have evolved into a system that is very different from the origins of corporate finance, and into a kind of casino.

Once upon a time, corporate finance worked like this: Companies needed debt and equity capital. To get capital, they made disclosures about what they do and aspire to do, issued shares, and offered them to investors. Investors then decided to buy or sell those shares based on company and other information. They also voted their annual proxy cards based on what they knew. Companies, seeing buy/sell/hold trading patterns and proxy voting patterns, continually improved what they were doing in the world. That was how it was supposed to work, and the system prospered. The buy-sell signals of the market as a whole were "efficient," as descried in the classic efficient market theory.

But this time-honored paradigm is changing. The number of public companies available for stock investment (trading on exchanges) is down from more than 8,000 in 1996[102] to fewer than 4,000 today. Public companies play a special role in investment because they must follow disclosure rules that help stockholders know what they are buying. In the United States., with some exceptions, any company with more than $10 million in total assets and more than 500 shareholders must register as a public company.[103] Exceptions are made for individuals who are "accredited" (having high income or net worth) or funds directed by an individual who is "sophisticated" (having knowledge and experience in business). In these cases, the triggering threshold is not reached until 2000 investors.[104] Today, however, only a few thousand companies in the U.S. are registered to sell securities to the public; many are closely held (with a small number of owners). Ownership has shifted from individual (retail) to institutional stock ownership. Investment has moved from active to passive (via index funds). The few remaining "active" stock investments (not linked to an index) use algorithmic trading. Proxy votes are largely delegated to proxy voting advisors who vote according to a formula.

In the United States, investor identities are not known to the companies due to rules that distinguish between objecting beneficial owner (OBO) and the non-objecting beneficial owner (NOBO). These rules allow companies to know the identifies only of NOBOs, not OBOs. Since many brokers treat the "OBO" status as a default, and don't actually ask their clients whether or not they object, companies can be in the dark needlessly about their owner base and unable to communicate with it directly.[105]

There are also "dark pools." National market systems in the U.S. now have alternative trading systems (ATSs), which meet the definition of a national securities exchange, but are not required to register as one. These include trading centers are called "dark pools" due to anonymity. Many alternative trading systems are operated by multi-service broker dealers, which have a potential conflict of interest between their role as a broker for the issuer of the stock to be listed, and as an operator of the exchange. (For example, as a broker, the dealer would want listing fees to be low; as an operator, a dealer might want them to be high.) As of March 31, 2018, there were 21 national securities exchanges in the U.S. and 87 alternative trading systems, with some 11.4 percent of the trading volume, and slightly more (11.5 percent) of the dollar volume.[106]

In recent years, there has been a shift from active "value" investing based on analysis of specific company fundamentals to passive investing tied to an index, along with a rise of algorithmic trading—automated trading based on algorithms that force buy-sell-hold decisions based on market patterns.[107] J.P. Morgan has estimated that the prevalence of sentient investors (not automated trades) may be as low as 10 percent.[108] A J.P. Morgan research report released November 30, 2018, stated, "Today most micro-level trading decisions in equities and electronic future contracts are made by algorithms: they define where to trade, at what price, and what quantity."[109] Such automated trading poses some potential risks, including the following:

*Limited decision-making framework for the trades.* Client orders take days in some cases (as noted in Chapter 7 on blockchain[110]), while trading agents need to make decisions every few seconds or faster. This built-in lag limits the agent's sampling frequency, which will be lower than what is necessary to fully integrate all available information about market dynamics.[111]

*Volatility caused by positive feedback.* When many mutual funds are tied to a particular index, this means that if the index moves in a particular direction, it will drag all the fund trades with it. This can cause deeper swings in the marketplace, often triggering buy sell decisions based on exuberance or panic, rather than an eye for value.

*Creation of a market in perceptions.* Brett Scott said it well in *The Heretic's Guide to Global Finance* (2013): "They don't try to trade 'reality,' they try to trade other people's perceptions of reality. If a market is dominated by enough technical traders, it could lapse into a 'postmodern' state, with traders trading perceptions of perceptions of reality."[112]

In addition to these trends, we also see the emergence of day traders using zero-commission trading apps such as Robinhood, Webull, and MI Finance, which allow millions of individuals to buy and sell stocks all day without paying for an intermediary.[113]

The above problems may seem troublesome but even worse is the risk of the robot company. Earlier we mentioned corporate self-interest as a driver of global finance. Consider what would happen if some corporations were controlled entirely by autonomous systems. Thomas Burri, Assistant Professor of International Law and European Law at the University of St. Gallen in Switzerland, notes "some existing national laws are sufficiently flexible so as to enable attribution of personhood to artificial intelligence."[114] In support of this alarming prospect, he cites Shawn Bayern,[115] a U.S. scholar at Florida State University, who has shown how current company law in the US can be used to establish a company that is controlled by artificial intelligence, and he has joined a group of European scholars to describe a similar application of European law.[116] If an autonomous system ever did get control of a corporation under the plausible scenarios described by Bayern and his coauthors, a non-human corporation could become an "investor."

## Reforming Markets from Within

The cumulative lesson to be learned so far from this chapter is that money and markets can take on a life of their own with their own goals and dynamics, but we as participants need to be proactive. Raffaele Savi, co-chief investment officer of BlackRock Active Equity, put it well. As a counterculturalist in this world's-largest investment company, which is a major index investor, he had just the right words,[117] "As an investor, you have to work extra hard to reinvent yourself constantly and change practices you've established over decades to succeed in a new world."

To balance out the robots, investors can reclaim their heritage. Individuals and institutions alike can return to the origins of corporate finance described earlier in this chapter as "once upon a time." By becoming more active in voting their shares and proxies, investors will add brainpower to global markets—for the good of all participants.

Part III: **Money and Technology**

# Chapter 5
# Fintech: When Money Meets Technology

*Any intelligent fool can make things bigger and more complex ...*
*It takes a touch of genius—and a lot of courage to move in the opposite direction.*
—E.F. Schumacher, *Small Is Beautiful: Economics as If People Mattered* (1973)

At the start of this book, we explained why money should be thought of as an important technology that was invented to serve society. How, then, does this old technology evolve further when it is combined with the latest information technologies? The answer to that question is fintech.

Fintech, short for financial technology, is a term that has been popularized in the recent digital age. *Fintech* is the marriage of finance and information technology. It is typically associated with the financial applications of mobile data, digitization, big data analytics, the Internet of Things (IoT), chip cards, and, more recently, with cryptocurrencies and artificial intelligence (AI). Some writers only associate the term *fintech* with financial services provided by technology companies, particularly startups, but the established financial sector uses the term to apply as well to technology-based innovations introduced or adopted by financial incumbents.

Fintech is a fast-changing terrain, so references to some companies and offerings (especially in the world of startups) may be dated by the time you read this. For that reason, we have endeavored to provide readers with a good introduction to the topic and insights into the most important trends we see. We hope this will allow you to interpret new events and innovations armed with this understanding.

## Financial Innovations We Use Every Day

The concept of fintech has evolved over time. We have seen many innovations introduced over the last few decades that would be called fintech today, but were not at the time. Think of credit cards, automated teller machines (ATMs), and online banking in retail banking. Think of electronic trading. And then there are the unheralded back office applications of computer technology, of which the most consequential was the change-over from paper-based bookkeeping to electronic financial records that enabled all the other applications. These were all huge fintech innovations that changed the way we handled money, executed transactions, and kept records. But most importantly, these

https://doi.org/10.1515/9781547401116-005

earlier innovations changed our relationship to money—how the financial sector did business with us, and how we chose to spend our money.

These are all important innovations, but we do not think about them enough because we have been using them for a while now. (One could argue that metal coins, paper money, and so on were the fintech of their time. But we shall confine ourselves to the modern era.) When we take innovations for granted, we become desensitized to their opportunities and risks, and we miss recurring patterns as they manifest themselves in the next generation of innovations. But if we look in the right places, we will see, for example, the win-win that happens when an innovation (e.g., online banking) increases consumer convenience while lowering institutional cost, or the synergy that occurs when two separate fintech inventions (e.g., online auctions and online payment) leverage each other.

Let us now look at some well-established fintech innovations with fresh eyes—they may help us see the way future financial innovations could go. We will also see how far we have come just in the last few decades.

### Automatic Teller Machines (ATMs)

Today, there are ATMs everywhere—even in Antarctica! But like every new technology, ATMs had a beginning, followed by an adoption curve.

Enabling technologies that preceded ATMs were the magnetic strip card, first used in electronic ticketing gates, and vending machines. The first ATMs were indeed little more than cash vending machines. The technology began in 1969, when several banks in Britain, Japan, and the United States rolled them out for this purpose.[1] As is typical for a new technology in its early stages of evolution, the designs were all over the place. Some machines dispensed cash directly, others in plastic cartridges. Some used magnetic cards, others tokens. Some used PINs, others did not. The first machines were mechanically unreliable, and security was very poor.

Yet, banks persisted installing ATMs because it extended their very limited hours at a time that labor unions, especially in Britain, were resisting working longer hours and on Saturdays. The shining new technology and the aura of automation and modernity that they carried were attractive to customers. In addition, ATMs helped the banks to shift the loyalty of customers to the bank and its brand, away from their local branch and the individuals who served them there. Banking deregulation also helped. A 1984 U.S. Supreme Court decision essentially lifted the limit on the number of ATMs that banks could have, ruling that ATMs were not bank branches and therefore exempt from geographic concentration laws that applied to banking at the time.

Today there are close to half a million ATMs in the United States.[2] ATMs still dispense cash, but modern optical scanning technology also enables them to take deposits of stacks of cash and checks.

## Credit Cards

Merchants have extended credit to their customers for thousands of years. More than a few old movies feature the line, "Put it on my tab." But all these credit arrangements were always based on one-to-one relationships: a merchant would extend credit to a good customer, allowing that customer to "buy on account." Cash was the only means of payment that would be accepted by all merchants. To effectively buy on credit at many merchants, you would need to go get a loan at the bank and then put the borrowed cash in your wallet. The credit card did away with this constraint. What was novel about the credit card was that it could be used at a large number of merchants.

In the early 1900s, department stores and oil companies started to issue their own charge cards to customers.[3] This was an evolution of the old buy-on-account facility. In the 1940s, a bank-based charge card appeared, with Franklin Bank issuing the first one. By mid-century, this idea evolved further. Businessman Frank McNamara was caught short without his wallet and, after paying with the help of his wife, returned to the restaurant the next day with a cardboard card convincing the restaurant to accept it. He had the dream that one card would one day be accepted by all restaurants in New York instead of just one restaurant. That was what led him to starting Diners Club in 1950.[4]

Note how this innovation did not come from the banks of the day, but from a start-up. Diners Club subsequently gained wide acceptance, even though merchants were charged 7 percent fees on each transaction. They were willing to do so because they were assured by the card company that card users would spend more than other patrons. By 1958, bigger companies caught on to the idea, particularly American Express (which was an express mail company by origin) and Bank of America in California. The latter's card operation became BankAmericard, and from 1966 its cards were licensed out to banks in other states in order to grow faster. Eventually BankAmericard was spun off and became Visa. A separate group of California banks had started ICA, which eventually became Master Charge and finally MasterCard.

At first, cards were captives of their sponsors. In the seventies and even into the eighties, it made sense to choose your credit card based on the network logo on it to make sure it was accepted at the merchants you used most. So, if you liked to dine out in New York City and more restaurants there accepted Diners Club than Visa, you would choose Diners Club. It was all about not being told, "Sorry sir/ma'am, we don't accept your card here." But as acceptance of the all the main cards became ubiquitous, that was no longer a differentiator and card companies had to compete on other grounds, such as financing terms, sign-up bonuses, and other perks.[5] And compete they did.

Today, the total outstanding credit card debt in the United States exceeds $800 billion.[6] This is near a historic high but, as we saw in Chapter 3, credit card debt is still dwarfed by mortgage debt and is still less than auto loan or student loan debt in the United States. Yet credit cards have played an important role in making those liabilities possible. Probably the largest impact that the adoption of credit cards had was to forever change how and when people make decisions on spending money. (We cannot strictly say spending *their* money, since, by definition, all spending on credit cards is on credit, even if it is just for a month.) With a credit card, the decision of spending money on a purchase is effectively severed from the consideration of how to pay for it, or whether the purchase is affordable in the first place. That is why credit card companies have always been able to confidently claim that consumers would spend more on cards than with cash. They are counting on the fact that you will spend more freely if you don't have to dig in your pocket for the cash and notice that you don't have much left.

### Debit Cards

Once ATM designers had settled on plastic cards modeled on a credit card as the preferred way for people to identify themselves to ATMs, it did not take long for them to realize that these cards could also be connected to the big credit card networks such as Visa and MasterCard. Thus, the ATM card became a dual-purpose magnetic card, and could be used as if it were a credit card when making purchases facilitated by those payment networks. The only difference, of course, being that no credit was being extended but that the purchase amount would be debited immediately from the holder's account. Debit cards offer the convenience of credit cards without the credit facility.

### Credit Scoring

We may not think of credit scoring as a consumer product but, as explained in Chapter 3, it affects our access as consumers to almost all financial products.

Credit scoring has almost totally automated the evaluation of loan or other credit applications from individuals. That is why you can get an instant decision on a new credit card application online, and can get a very quick decision on your mortgage application. (This assumes that you already have a credit history. If you don't, you are out of luck.) Taking human judgment out of the evaluation process has also reshaped the financial services industry because it has moved us away from local markets for financial services and toward national markets. There is no longer a need for a local loan officer to look an applicant in the eye to assess how likely that person will be to pay or to default. This has led to a substantial reduction in underwriting and compliance costs for lenders, and the transparency of credit scores has facilitated secondary markets for retail loans through securitization.[7] This move from local to global is changing the very nature of the average person's relationship to money and, ultimately, his or her access to wealth.

### Online Banking

Today, it is hard to imagine a world without the convenience of online banking. But online banking only started in the late 1990s. Though today there are online-only banks, online banking is most frequently a complementary channel to brick-and-mortar bank branches. The online-only banks typically offer better interest rates and lower (or even zero) fees to make up for their lack of a physical presence.

The first financial institution to provide online (internet) banking was Stanford Federal Credit Union in 1994. As online banking caught on quickly, the first internet-only bank, NetBank, was founded in 1996. By 2001, Bank of America reached three million online banking customers, representing about 20 percent of its customer base at the time.[8] (Today the online customer percentage at BoA is 79 percent.[9]) By 2006, a full 80 percent of U.S. banks offered online banking.[10]

Online banking was preceded by telephone banking, which was the first conduit to allow customers 24/7 access to their account information without leaving the house. It was thus also the first virtual conduit, which made us comfortable with not doing our banking face-to-face, and with not seeing our money being counted and physically changing hands. The heyday of telephone banking was in the 1980s and early 1990s, after which the online channel largely took over from it, though telephone banking is still available at almost all financial institutions. Telephone banking first demonstrated the cost-saving benefits of customers switching to automated channels, which meant they were not coming into branches and using the time of bank employees to obtain balance information, pay bills, or transfer money between accounts. Customers enjoyed a new freedom, no longer limited by banking hours or branch locations. Instead of having to take the time to drive to a branch, they could pay their utility or other bills late at night from the comfort of their homes, a major new convenience.

This fundamental quid pro quo—the customer gaining convenience or another thing of value, while the financial institution reduces costs or extracts additional customer value—is at the heart of every successful fintech innovation.

### Mobile Banking

In the United States and Canada, mobile banking was first introduced in the early mobile phone era at the turn of this century. (The BlackBerry was the reigning "smartphone" of the day and the leading mobile phone to offer email and internet access.) Initial mobile banking adoption was slow, patchy, and limited to tech-savvy early adopters, as network incompatibility and digital versus analog contrast plagued early smartphone technology.[11] Everything changed with the smartphone era that started with the introduction of the Apple iPhone in 2007. Today, the high-resolution cameras on smartphones, together with sophisticated optical character recognition (OCR), enable customers to not only check their balances, transfer money, and get text alerts, but also to deposit checks for up to a few thousand dollars by taking photographs of the checks.

In the developed world, mobile banking was introduced as an additional convenience to customers who were already banking online and had access to physical bank branches. But in the developing world, it was revolutionary because it enabled millions of people who were previously unbanked to bank for the very first time. In Kenya, M-Pesa, a Vodaphone financial solution that facilitates B2B (business-to-business) and P2P (peer-to-peer) payments over a mobile phone platform via a local service provider, just turned ten years old. The service is now offered in ten African countries and used by around 30 million customers. In 2016, it processed around 6 billion transactions.[12] M-Pesa has been life-changing for people in cash-based economies, where only a small percentage of the population typically has access to conventional financial services. Mobile banking allows such customers to avoid the risks of having their money taken in street robberies, burglaries, or even by corrupt officials. According to McKinsey & Company,[13] more than half of all active mobile accounts are in sub-Saharan Africa (followed by South Asia, the Middle East and North Africa, and Latin America), showing the power that fintech has to rapidly bring millions of previously unbanked people into the global financial system.

### Electronic Funds Transfer (EFT) Networks

The term *EFT* is not the name of a particular product but broadly refers to payment vehicles that use electronic networks to make or process payments. There are two main types of EFT networks: wholesale and consumer. Wholesale networks are used by financial institutions for large-dollar electronic transfers, while consumer EFT networks handle small-dollar amounts. The origins of the EFT industry go back to the introduction of the ATM and its associated cards. The first ATM networks were all proprietary systems owned by particular banks or payment processors, typically limited in the geographical areas that they served. This soon created the need for communication and payment processing between banking networks.[14] Financial institutions quickly recognized the benefits of sharing IT and network costs. Economies of scale could be achieved through greater transaction value. But most important, the sharing of ATMs on a network would enable the classic *network externality*, now called the *network effect*, where the value of the network to each user increases exponentially as more users join.

### Online Payments

When you think about online payments, the first company that comes to mind is PayPal. Though it is by no means the only player in this space, which has become quite competitive, the rise of PayPal coincided with the rise of the internet and of ecommerce. Its story is therefore instructive.

PayPal was founded in 1998 as a money transfer service. At the time it was called Confinity. The company's origins were in cryptographic security, but they were not making money from it and needed a commercial application for it. This was during the time of the first mobile devices, then called personal digital assistants (PDA), and the Palm PDA was the dominant device. The Palm did not have wireless capability like today's smartphones, but one could send data from one Palm to another close by (about an arm's length away) using its built-in infrared port. Business users of the Palm often used this functionality at the time to exchange electronic business cards, calendar invites, and contact details. Confinity was founded to offer a secure way of sending IOUs (money) between Palms by using cryptography. The founders soon realized that their process could be modified to exchange obligations via email or web. This new product was called PayPal.[15]

In order to rapidly build the PayPal user network, the company offered $10 cash incentives for opening a new account and also for referring a new user.

The timing was perfect as eBay, an online auction site founded three years earlier, needed a better way to complete transactions online. Sellers on eBay embedded PayPal's advertisement for online payment, which took users to the PayPal homepage where they could enroll. This was the start of a long-running symbiotic relationship between the payments provider and the ecommerce site. Each has enjoyed a level of success that may not have been possible without the other—a sign of the interconnectedness of fintech innovation.

In 2000, PayPal merged with its major competitor, X.com, headed by free-spirited technologist Elon Musk, who subsequently headed the combined organization for a while but was eventually pushed out as a consequence of board-level intrigue. (Musk famously went on to found SpaceX and Tesla Motors.) The original PayPal founders, led by venture capitalist Peter Thiel, took back control of the combined company and proceeded with a successful IPO that valued the company at $1.2 billion. Shortly after the IPO in 2002, PayPal agreed to be bought by eBay for $1.5 billion. The original founders Thiel, Levchin, and Hoffman cashed in, and went off to play significant roles in other ventures like Facebook and LinkedIn. In 2015, eBay spun off PayPal and it became an independent company again. Today, PayPal has over 200 million active users and 17 million merchant accounts. It processed $7.6 billion payments in 2017, about one third of which were mobile payments.[16]

The digital payments business has now grown to handle $4 trillion in digital payments annually.[17] PayPal is still a big player, but it is facing stiff competition. For example, PayPal was recently displaced as the main eBay payments processor by the Dutch fintech Ayden, which also processes Uber's payments.[18] Another big player in online payment processing is the payment platform company Stripe, which counts Amazon and Lyft among its customers.

## The Current Fintech Landscape

Perhaps the most helpful topology of the fintech landscape comes from the World Economic Forum,[19] which has divided the landscape into six major sectors by function:
- Payments
- Insurance
- Deposits and Lending
- Equity Crowdfunding
- Investment Management
- Market Infrastructure

Each major sector is further subdivided into one or two thematic clusters, as seen in Figure 5.1, adapted from the WEF.

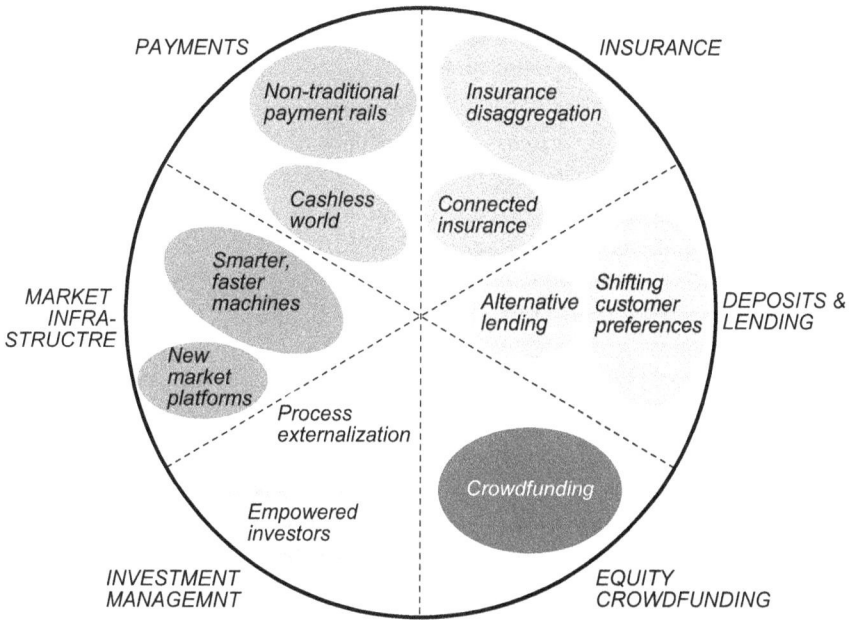

**Figure 5.1:** WEF's functions of financial services, simplified (Fig. Note 5.1).

Let us look now at each of these major sectors, using the World Economic Forum's six functional sectors and the clusters within them as our guide.

### Payments

The modern evolution of payments and remittances is moving away from cash and toward digital channels. That is why futurists and visionaries have been promising us a cashless world for a while now. Though this world has not yet arrived, we are getting ever closer to it. Within the cashless cluster of fintech, we mainly see new consumer functionalities built on existing payment infrastructure. This includes mobile payments, which have caught on and have even become dominant in some geographies.

The other cluster within payments is non-traditional or emerging payment rails. A *payment rail* is a payment platform or network that moves money from a payer to a payee. This is where we find the more disruptive technologies that promise direct or peer-to-peer transfers between parties that cut out financial intermediaries. For example, cryptographic protocols can obviate the need for a trusted third party like a financial intermediary or, in the case of cryptocurrencies, even the issuer of money. The world has not yet experienced, much less understood, the full impact of this disintermediation.

Enabling this trend has been *near-field communication* (NFC) technology, a set of very short-range wireless technologies embedded in smartphones to facilitate the exchange of small packets of data at very short range, around 4 centimeters or 1.5 inches.[20] It is this technology that facilitates mobile payments to be made between the smartphone in your hand and a merchant's point-of-sale (POS) terminal with embedded NFC abilities. The payment app on your smartphone needs to be preloaded with funds or your credit card information.

Recently, U.S. credit- and debit-card issuers have been building NFC technology into the cards themselves. Banking customers receiving new cards may have noticed that their cards now have the contactless-payment capability. By the spring of 2019, 78 out of the top 100 U.S. merchants (ranked by transactions) that accept Visa payments were able to handle contactless transactions. The contactless cards actually offer improved security by transferring encrypted data when you pay. This transfer obviates the skimming devices that fraudsters use to intercept payment data from conventional cards and create counterfeit cards.[21]

NFC has been available since the approval of the standard by ISO in 2003. Barclay Card introduced its first NFC-based payment card in the UK in 2007. In 2011, Google launched the first NFC-based mobile app, Google Wallet. Apple Pay was launched in 2014, adding its iPhone fingerprint scanner as a validation measure.[22] Google Pay (the new name for Google Wallet) and Apple became the first major mobile payment rails within the developed world, and they are seeing some use. However, developed-world consumers are still more comfortable with already well-established non-cash payment methods such as credit cards, which continue to work well for them. This means initial optimism for Apple Pay and Google Pay has tapered off. However, in China an offshoot of Alibaba, the Alipay app of Ant Financial, owned by Alibaba founder Jack Ma, has over 500 million users and handles $2.4 trillion in mobile payments every three months.[23] Alipay is similar to Apple Pay and Google Pay in that it is an e-wallet or digital wallet with payment cards or funds stored inside. Customers contract directly from their mobile devices.

A big difference between western mobile payment products and those found in China, is that the former piggyback off of credit-card forms' networks, while the latter access bank accounts directly, cutting out the credit card middlemen.[24]

In the mobile payment realm, as in others, fintech innovators have the greatest early-mover advantage in less developed economies. Complex regulation and ingrained consumer habits still protect established financial institutions against the full onslaught of fintech in developed economies like the United States. But in Asia we can see a glimpse of the future to come as traditional banks there find themselves on the frontline against giant fintech encroaching on their territory. For example, Singapore-based DBS Group Holdings Ltd. is Southeast Asia's largest bank, but it is investing billions in new technology, including its own mobile payments app, DBS PayLah!, in the face of competitive pressure from the Alipay app described earlier. DBS Group's concern about Ant Financial's ambitions is well-founded: Ant has been expanding in other countries' local subsidiaries and affiliates, already owning half of Paytm, an Indian digital-payments star, and it has bought stakes in fintech firms in Thailand, Singapore, Indonesia, the Philippines, and South Korea.[25] Ant Financial's main rival in China is Tencent, a social media and gaming behemoth that also owns WeChat. In 2013 it started offering a payment app called WeChat Pay over the WeChat platform. WeChat Pay has the advantage that it is part of an app that most Chinese citizens use many times a day. According to an analysis done by *The Economist*, Alipay has 54 percent and WeChat Pay 39 percent of the Chinese mobile payment market by value.[26]

The meaning for the average consumer is clear: As fintech evolves worldwide, consumers everywhere will need to keep up with financial technology. Increasingly, the option to use cash will become more limited.

Not all new payment methods are that visible to the customer. The wildly successful and patented Amazon "one-click" is actually a new payment method, even though it piggybacks on your credit card registered with Amazon. Amazon accounted for 53 percent of overall U.S. ecommerce growth in 2016, largely as a result of the success of Amazon Prime. After initially defending once-click as proprietary, Amazon is now rolling out one-click to other merchants and turning it into more of an ecosystem. In China, the shift to online purchases is exemplified by Taobao, the Alibaba-owned website, which is the world's biggest ecommerce site, with over 600 million users.[27]

## Deposits and Lending

For many people, having a bank account at a local bank is the first step in managing their money. Technology has enabled significant developments in the traditionally staid banking business of deposits and lending.

As far as deposits go, Bank of America has been experimenting with fully automated mini-branches to lower costs. This is only the latest development in a rationalization of brick-and-mortar branch networks by traditional banks, which may have the undesirable consequence of driving frustrated customers to online competitors.

Another trend is that some nonbanks that are fintech innovations are trying to become banks. One pending application for a bank charter is from payment processor Square; Social Finance (SoFi), a U.S. online provider of student and mortgage loans, withdrew its application following turmoil at the online student and mortgage lender.[28]

These recent attempts by nonbanks to become banks show the continuing value of becoming a true depository institution not only for the convenience and safety they offer the consumer, but also because of the money that these banks can collect, which can be loaned to businesses.

Will this new interest in bank charters for nonbanks, however modest, be enough to reverse the trend of the disappearing bank branch? One would hope so, because some small businesses need local banks to thrive, particularly in lower-income areas where entrepreneurs are already at a disadvantage when looking for business loans. Such loan applicants often need higher-touch services, and they have a better chance of getting loans from local bankers who may give preference to building their own communities.[29]

Unfortunately, however, the face of lending is changing from the friendly local banker to the anonymous computer interface.

Data and analytics have enabled new techniques to adjudicate credit applications. This includes using new data sources such as social media and mobile data to assess the credit worthiness of individual borrowers who may lack a credit bureau history. It also includes better analysis of existing data, and new credit risk models that provide better ways of assessing the risk of such borrowers. An example of the latter is LendUp, a direct online lender that serves subprime borrowers at lower rates than payday lenders, using its proprietary underwriting model. ZestFinance sells machine-learning underwriting technology to banks to improve pricing, and is developing a credit-scoring platform for Chinese customers after an investment by Chinese search giant Baidu, which is making its search data available to improve credit-pricing decisions.

These fintech lending innovations are not limited to consumer lending. Amazon now offers credit to its merchants using sales data to measure risks, and has the ability to suspend sales on its platform should a merchant default on its loan.

These innovations have conditioned customers of all kinds to expect a good digital experience and rapid decisions from their potential lenders. Quicken

Loans, the largest originator of mortgages and home loans in the United States, offers Rocket Mortgage, a digital home-loan service that verifies credit, property, and income information online and uses sophisticated algorithms to provide approvals within minutes.

Does this mean that anyone with the right technology and some start-up capital can start a bank? Hardly. As mentioned, there are regulatory barriers to starting a bank anew. While startups in the lending business can beat traditional financial institutions with lower costs and credit pricing sophistication, they still have to pull in the funds to lend out. It is here where they are at the biggest disadvantage against incumbent deposit-taking institutions. Customer acquisition costs are high because it is expensive to find and attract new depositors. The advantage of having no costly branch networks can be wiped out by higher funding costs—for example, by being forced to pay investors a premium due to perceived or actual higher credit risks. This is a common flaw in the business model of fintech startups that makes them prone to stumbles. It may also lure fintech players into earlier than planned exits as they allow themselves to be acquired by incumbent financial institutions who have access to cheap funds.

Marketplace lending is another new technology-supported form of lending that is changing the financial landscape for the average consumer. A marketplace lender uses an online platform to offer consumer and small business loans, which it then will bundle and sell to wholesale lenders or institutional investors. Prospective borrowers fill out a standard application form on the website, including standard criteria like credit scores. The marketplace lender then uses a (typically proprietary) risk rating that yields an automated lending decision. It bundles the resulting loans and sells them in bulk to institutional investors, with bundles priced based on the risk rating. The online marketplace lenders themselves do not assume any credit risk of the loans done through their platforms because they do not hold the loans. They make their money mainly from origination and service fees.[30] For the average consumer, the risk lies in being seen as just a number rather than a person. Individuals with a low credit rating who are determined to dig out may not get a chance in an automated world.

On the other hand, the emergence of new lenders on the scene could spell opportunity for neglected borrowers, as long as they have an internet connection (or maybe only a mobile connection). Even century-old banking behemoths are inspired by the low-cost service models of their online competitors, as well as the potential of reaching currently unserved segments in the hopes that they will be lucrative. In 2016, Goldman Sachs—better known for advising clients on corporate mergers, trading, and wealth management for multimillionaires—started an online-lending business called Marcus that markets directly to consumers and has a significant share of subprime borrowers.[31]

### Insurance

Insurance is one area where fintech innovations have been largely good news for the average consumer. Insurance value chains are becoming more modular, thus enabling players to combine with one another in different ways. This value-chain disaggregation threatens large incumbents in the property and casualty (P&C) and life businesses as well as the renter's insurance sought by many millennials, creating new opportunities for so-called "insurtechs." At the same time, the measurement and underwriting of risks are being changed by usage and consumption-based methods, often enabled by new technology. The Israeli insurer Lemonade is a good example of this trend; its proprietary algorithm for insurance decisions reportedly includes many soft measures, including cell phone charging patterns.[32] These constitute new ways of looking at borrowers, always good news for the average person, since they can be judged by more than one or two aspects of their economic behavior, reducing the chance of being typecast as deadbeats.

In emerging markets, insurers are evolving a variety of new products, often making use of fast-growing mobile payments platforms. In Africa, BIMA provides mobile health coverage for low-income, emer ging market customers that pay prepaid mobile credit. To pull in a new type of customer, Ladder, a U.S.-based insurtech start-up, offers term-life without medical check. Its competitor, Haven, is owned by MassMutual.

The electric carmaker Tesla offers lifetime auto insurance provided by third-party insurers for most of its cars sold in Asia. The insurance premium is included in the cost of the vehicle at point of sale. While the insurance premium is not quantified, it is probably fairly low, reflecting Tesla's calculation that its self-driving and related safety features will greatly improve the risk profile of its cars. Tesla may also be able to track the driving habits of its owners, although that is not publicly known.

The Internet of Things (IoT) has enabled additional insurtech innovations. For home insurance, Liberty Mutual offers a free (internet-connected) Nest Protect smoke detector together with discounted insurance premiums. For life insurance, John Hancock Vitality Program rewards customers with premium savings and retail discounts for healthy lifestyles. Customers may choose to opt-in to tracking of their daily activities. While connected devices are proliferating, making it feasible to monitor almost anything, insurers are having only limited success so far in convincing privacy-concerned or tech-shy customers that using these devices will be in their interest. Time will tell.

## Investment Management

The field of investment management—another sector identified by the World Economic Forum—has embraced fintech fully. It starts with empowering investors to perform increasingly sophisticated investment management functions formerly reserved for Wall Street firms. (Investment management and wealth management services for retail investors are essentially equivalent terms, with the distinction that wealth management is often branded to cater to more affluent investor segments.) By employing robo-advisors and other algorithmic tools, retail investors no longer need to rely on professionals to make investment decisions and even to effect trades; increasingly, these functions are being offered in a "do-it-yourself" platform. New entrants providing these tools to investors squeeze the profit margins of traditional players as the competition between them heats up. For the sophisticated consumer, the result of robo-investing is greater choice and lower cost; for the less tech-savvy, who must rely on full-service institutions, costs may rise.

Most people invest in the market not directly but, rather, through retirement plans. The shift away from defined-benefit retirement plans (pension plans) that employers used to offer their workers, toward defined-contribution plans such as 401(k)s in the United States or RRSPs in Canada is increasing the demand for investment allocation tools, typically offered by mutual fund managers as a customer-centric service to their end users. A leader here is Vanguard, founded by John Bogle, mentioned in Chapter 4 as the inventor of index funds. A long-time leader in such low-cost, passive financial product investing, Vanguard has benefited greatly from the defined-contribution trend. Charles Schwab's Intelligent Portfolio[33] is an online robo-advisory product for mass-affluent customers that compete against fintechs like Wealthfront.[34] Robinhood is a purely digital discount brokerage that allows users to trade securities with zero commissions from their computers or mobile devices.[35] At the meta-level, the giant investment firm, BlackRock, is consolidating a large number of mutual funds that rely on algorithms and rules-based models to pick stocks.[36]

Another cluster of fintech innovations entail the outsourcing of non-core functions in the investment management value chain, typically in the middle and back office. Declining margins are causing investment management firms—themselves in a sense an "outsourced" function for the funds they manage, which have no staff[37]—to look to process externalization (a fancy term for outsourcing a process) in order to reduce costs. For example, BlackRock's Aladdin platform provides risk analysis, portfolio construction, and compliance tools for institutional investors and retail wealth managers. Using external service providers can allow asset managers to focus on the more strategic side of investment.[38]

## Equity Crowdfunding

This sector contains only one major cluster: crowdfunding. The big new development in capital raising in the last decade has been the democratization of capital raising through crowdfunding. Crowdfunding entails raising money from large numbers of people who each contribute a small amount. It is typically done via the internet to quickly reach a large audience, and contributions are made and received online.

Crowdfunding has already changed how many startups have raised capital, and holds the potential of even larger changes in how ventures are financed. Kickstarter is probably the most well-known crowdfunding site for startups, and it claims to be the world's largest crowdfunding platform for creative businesses on which it is focused.[39] For individuals, including those in distress, there is GoFundMe, a crowdfunding platform that allows people to raise money from strangers on the internet for personal or community causes ranging from birthday celebrations, legal representation. treatments for illnesses, to local causes such as architectural, cultural, or environmental conservation.

The raising of any significant funds from individuals obviously creates the possibility that financially unsophisticated people may lose money, whether due to poor choices or to outright fraud. In the case of new charities, or those hybrid entities known as B Corporations (serving both a social and financial purpose), governments impose extensive rules and regulations on such entities to prevent them from becoming false advertisements covering individual enrichment. In the case of new for-profit companies, government regulations typically prevent startups from soliciting substantial investments from unsophisticated so-called *non-accredited investors* who do not meet certain minimum income or net worth requirements set by the Securities and Exchange Commission (SEC) in the United States, or its counterparts in other countries.

Under the SEC's Regulation D, the term *accredited investor* is used to signify individuals who are considered financially knowledgeable enough to look after their own investing activities without SEC protection, currently requiring an income of more than $200,000 annually and a net worth of more than $1 million, excluding the value of their primary home.[40]

In the past several years, a number of new SEC regulations have eased such restrictions, including Regulation Crowdfunding[41] and a revised version of Regulation A[42] that permits offerings up to $50 million without going through the full registration process for a public offering.

Similarly, in the United Kingdom, restrictions have eased. In the United Kingdom, the crowdfunding platform SEEDRS is open to unaccredited investors who may invest as little as £10 in a startup, and it has funded over 700 deals now with tens of thousands of individual investments.[43]

But despite strong demand and some deregulation, the old order continues. Frequently, startups that raised early capital through crowdfunding revert to the established providers of capital as they scale up. For example, Pebbl, a Smartwatch start-up, raised over $10m on Kickstarter but then got its next round of $15m from traditional investors due to burdensome disclosure requirements.

There is a need for more investor education and for better connections between crowdfunding platforms and the larger financial system to make them more scalable. One example of how such connections are being established is iCapital Network, which connects accredited investors and their advisors to private equity and VC funds through a digital-first process. It received a BlackRock investment in 2016. An example of crowdfunding being scaled up is the creation of secondary markets that allow the trading of crowdfunded securities launched by Crowdcube.

## Market Infrastructure

Market infrastructure is another important sector, since well-functioning markets require platforms and technological support. Smarter, fast machines are an important element enabling market infrastructure. Market infrastructure development is now being driven by disruptive technologies like machine-accessible data, big data, and machine learning or artificial intelligence. This is actually just the latest phase in the ongoing development of algorithmic trading, which takes the human mind out of the immediate loop to achieve faster, and maybe smarter, responses to events as they happen. (For more on algorithmic trading, see Chapter 4.)

In contrast to corporate equity (shares of stock), which has been moving from a live bidding "pit" to an electronic board, corporate debt (bonds) has up until now been mostly traded over the phone. Trumid is a new electronic bond trading platform, in which Deutsche Börse has taken a 10 percent stake. This is a sign that even holdout parts of the financial trading industry are going electronic.

Other parts of the trading technological infrastructure are getting retooled to make use of blockchain technology. (We shall devote Chapter 7 to a discussion of blockchain after introducing cryptocurrencies in our next chapter.) For example, Depository Trust and Clearing Corporation (DTCC) is using blockchain to rebuild its platform for processing $11 trillion of credit default swaps. And Thomson Reuters has launched BlockOneIQ, a "smart oracle" that provides users with cryptographic proof of the source of external securities pricing data. This is an essential building block for many future smart-contract use cases of blockchain in financial services. While the impact of these innovations—providing more efficient, secure, self-automating tools to reduce cost and improve or guarantee the accuracy and speed of transactions—may not be obvious to the general population, their overall effect is and will be positive. These innovations will help ordinary consumers who are doing their daily business, by providing more efficient, secure, and self-automating tools to reduce cost and improve the accuracy and speed of transactions.

The second cluster in the market infrastructure sector is for new market platforms, which serve to create new ways for market participants to connect with one another. This makes markets more liquid, efficient, and accessible to more people.

Algomi, another fintech company, provides software solutions to bond market participants to improve their workflow and liquidity by enabling data aggregation, pre-trade information analysis, and execution facilitation.[44] This addresses the problem of a highly fragmented fixed-income trading world, and creates new trading opportunities between counterparties within the current client-to-dealer market.

## The State of Play in Fintech

While new fintech entrants generate a lot of buzz, they are mostly not considered a major threat to established financial institutions in developed countries. (As mentioned earlier, dreams of empire-building can prematurely cede to exit plans when faced with the hard reality of raising funds.) Needing scale and regulatory blessings, new fintech firms often have to partner with (or even sell themselves to) large incumbent financial institutions. In the United Kingdom, newcomers have taken 14 percent of total payment and banking revenues, in the United States only 3.5 percent, and across Europe 7 percent. A good example of a high level of activity with low market penetration is Canada, where

47 percent of banking and payment institutions by number are classified as new, yet they have captured less than 2 percent of banking.[45] However, in developing countries fintechs have been able to gain traction and scale much faster as they fill the unmet needs of a largely unbanked population.

## What to Look for Next

### Biometric Identification

Biometric identification leads the parade when it comes to futuristic financial innovations. This unique new technology authenticates a person's identity by using technology that checks his or her unique biological traits such as voice, fingerprint, iris, or face against stored data. The need for bio-ID arose from the fear of cybercrime. Many well-publicized security breaches have decreased confidence in the reliability of traditional passwords. Too often, customers leave themselves open to password breaches by choosing predictable passwords, repeating passwords between institutions, or succumbing to scams like phishing where they are tricked into revealing their passwords.

Biometrics are considered to be inherently more reliable and user-friendly than passwords—whether the technology is by voice, fingerprints, iris, or facial recognition.

Voice recognition, a $1 billion + market projected to growth to some $7 billion by 2025, is now used by many banks and other financial institutions—in some cases, using Amazon's Alexa.[46]

Several financial institutions have introduced biometric identification, with fingerprints being the dominant biometric method currently. Iris identification is also predicted to become more widespread across the next few years. Facial identification systems are being boosted by incorporation in the latest Apple and Android smartphones. The technology of facial recognition is maturing fast and is already in use by government agencies like U.S. Customs and Border Protection, which uses it at airports to identify departing passengers.

Generally, the increased use of biometrics has been identified as a major trend in banking.[47] In fact, biometrically-enabled transactions are here already and customers are quickly getting used to them. For example, if your smartphone is set to unlock by scanning your fingerprint or your face, and it contains an ewallet application like Apple Pay or Google Pay which is activated by its mere proximity to a payment terminal, you are already using biometrics to secure your financial transactions.

### Fintech Applications of Artificial Intelligence

Despite the widespread publicity given to it, there is no universally accepted, standardized definition of artificial intelligence (AI). Some experts even prefer to avoid the term altogether because of its imprecision. (The IEEE prefers the term, "autonomous and intelligent systems," which encompasses both robotics and what others call AI.[48]) However, a pragmatic way to define it is to say that AI is when computers (machines) behave in ways that we previously thought (until recently, at least) required human intelligence.[49] It does not take much thought to realize that this definition is inherently a moving goal-post definition. What we thought was AI in the not too distant past, like spell checking in our word processor programs or ABS braking assistance in our automobiles, we would not consider to be AI today. By this definition, we constantly need to be surprised and impressed by AI. In that sense, AI is always aspirational.

There are multiple ways of implementing AI, and each of these techniques has created a new kind of AI. Indeed, we can classify different subsets of AI based on the techniques used.

One new kind of AI machine learning which is commonly conflated with AI today is only one subset of AI. In machine learning, we let the machine (i.e., computer) figure out or implement the decision-making rules because they are too hard for us to figure out, too complicated to explain, or too complicated to process. Machine learning is closely associated with neural networks, modeled loosely on the neural pathway architecture of the human brain. Machine learning allows us to sidestep the problem of not knowing the rules ourselves and therefore being unable to teach the machines what to do. We can train multilayer neural networks by making them understand what outputs are expected from certain sets of input data, and then allow the neural networks to reconfigure themselves to achieve the desired outcome. For example, looking at animal pictures and identifying whether the animal is a dog or a cat is the type of problem that lends itself well to such machine learning. Machine learning is based on a neural network architecture modeled on how we think the brain works[50] and, in this application, requires the availability of large amounts of data to train the machine.

On the other hand, if the rules are known to us—even though they may be highly complicated, such as the U.S. tax law—we can program such rules directly, frequently making use of decision trees that use if-then logic. We may not think of our tax preparation software as AI these days, but twenty years ago we would have for sure. Tax preparation software is an example of an expert-system type of AI, although the term *expert system* is most often used in other contexts, like medical decision-making systems, which contain extensive databases. Yet, the principle is the same.

Algorithms and sophisticated mathematics, aka quant techniques, have been used in investment decisions for quite a while, especially by Wall Street professionals. As noted in Chapter 4 on global markets, algorithmic trading is responsible for a large portion of the trades made in the wholesale market these days. As a result, the traders who embraced algorithmic trading are always looking for the next tool that might give them even the tiniest bit of an edge. Their hope is that AI can learn to make smart, automated decisions by studying and emulating the successful strategies of human experts facing ever-shifting conditions.

In the widely used and taught capital asset pricing model (CAPM), alpha is the rate of return on an instrument that exceeds what the market expects for that class of asset. Increasing alpha is thus the aspiration of any active investor. Some believe that artificial intelligence holds the promise to increase alpha.[51] But unfortunately the alpha goes only to the pros; in the new AI-powered marketplace, individual retail investors cannot win against the pros who have all the heavy guns in this battle.

AI is also useful in interacting with consumers. In June 2019, Manulife Bank in Canada launched a digital-only banking bundle called All-in Banking, which includes an AI-based digital assistant called MAI. MAI is intended to help banking customers, particularly millennials, get a better handle on their finances. It is trained to provide expert advice on Manulife's range of products.[52] The aim for banks using such AI technologies is to handle as many as possible customer interactions digitally, thus saving call center and branch costs.

## Blockchain/Distributed Ledgers

No discussion of fintech would be complete without a discussion of blockchain as well as bitcoin and other cryptocurrencies. While mainstream financial institutions and government agencies remain highly skeptical of cryptocurrencies, they are considerably more enthusiastic about the potential of blockchains when applied to other areas. As we conclude this chapter on fintech, we would like to offer a preview of such applications. This section is also effectively a preview of the next two chapters: We shall dedicate Chapter 6 to cryptocurrencies, so we will not cover them here in detail. In Chapter 7 we continue to explain and discuss blockchain, which is the technology behind bitcoin and other cryptocurrencies.

As explained in more detail in Chapter 6, blockchain started as an insurgent technology behind bitcoin, the first and most well known cryptocurrency. The rebel pioneers who created it wanted to create a new space outside the global monetary order. Blockchain can facilitate trust in a distributed system between users and agents who do not have to know or trust one another, which means that it has application far beyond cryptocurrencies. Bob Greifeld, CEO of Nasdaq, has called blockchain "the biggest opportunity set we can think of over the next decade."[53] It is ironic that a technology so closely associated with people who wanted to stay outside the global monetary order has all of the establishment organizations so excited!

So what exactly is a blockchain? In short, it is a distributed ledger system that can be thought as a chain of blocks, each representing a transaction that, once completed, is immutable and added to the chain. The chain is then secure, and the transactions cannot be changed after the fact. A *distributed ledger* is a recordkeeping system that may be updated independently by each participant in a large network.[54] But blockchain has an iron-clad mechanism that validates additions to the record—changes are generally not allowed, hence the chain concept. Blockchain uses two technologies to make it work. The first technology that makes this system work is *public key cryptography*, which serves to validate the identity of actors through the exchange of public and private keys. This technology preceded the invention of blockchain. The second technology, which is novel to blockchain, is a *cryptographic hash function* that validates transactions and the resulting ledger. The resulting ledger of transactions can be secure in a totally decentralized architecture without a third party (like a banker) acting as an intermediary and a source of trust.

This is a major paradigm shift for finance, and its implications for us are still unfolding. We are so used to using trusted third parties in any monetary transactions that this radical concept deserves additional appreciation. When your employer pays you a salary, that money does not go directly to you but into an account you hold at your bank. When you pay a merchant by credit card, that transaction is facilitated by one of the major credit card networks, such as Visa, MasterCard, American Express, or Discovery. The merchant trusts the credit card company to deliver the funds, and you trust the credit card company to deliver only the agreed amount. Now, with a blockchain and its immutable ledger, one does not need such a trusted third party anymore.

What can blockchains be used for aside from cryptocurrencies? These secure, distributed ledgers systems have broad applications—from electronic land registries that accurately reflect all transactions of land to *smart contracts* that execute themselves. In the current manifestation of this technology, money and software become intertwined in a contract that executes itself like a computer program based on predetermined inputs and progress milestones. Is this the next evolution of money; could we be seeing the birth of a new kind of money that has a mind of its own: smart money?

Since we are concerned here with the topic of financial technology, smart contracts are perhaps the most interesting blockchain application, and potentially one of the largest. Imagine a supply chain where the movement of goods are tracked by IoT devices. Each contractual step is automatically recorded through an entry in a blockchain-based ledger. Fulfillments of, or deviations from, contractual terms are automatically credited as payments or debited as penalties are transacted via the blockchain. (For example, a deviation may be late delivery.) The supply-chain application of blockchain is a particularly poignant one since trillions of dollars flow through global supply chains, changing economic lives and the way business is done at every level. Reshaping these supply chains will transform the global marketplace and the money flow associated with it.[55] This is but one example of the kind of blockchain applications that will be discussed in more depth and breadth in Chapter 7.

## The Battle for Fintech Supremacy

Fintech is a fascinating landscape not just because of its novel applications and its possibilities for changing how we interact with our money, but also because of all the players who are active in it.

We can discern at least four types of players: fintech startups; banks (more broadly, all traditional financial institutions); the tech giants (like Amazon, Alibaba, Apple, Facebook, and Google, who own the platforms and billions of active customer relationships); and the large technology providers (like IBM and Microsoft, who have the technology know-how and thousands of developers).

We see how these players are constantly trying to get the ascendancy over one another, but also that they often form alliances in order to do so. It's an ever-shifting landscape of alliances and partnerships, punctuated by the demise or acquisition of startups by larger players, the breakup of old alliances, and the formation of sometimes surprising new alliances. (It is akin to the plotline of HBO's recently concluded *Game of Thrones* series, complete with the untimely demise of your favorite characters, and the unexpected transformation of heroes into villains.)

Each type of player in the fintech universe brings something unique to the party: The fintech startups have the new ideas and the zeal to change the world. The banks have the licenses and the networks. The tech giants have established customer relationships and big data. The technology providers have the know-how and the armies of developers.

In one recent example of an alliance between different types of players, Apple and Goldman Sachs announced in March 2019 that they were teaming up to launch a new credit card. Forbes commented somewhat skeptically that it was an "attempt to bolster waning sales in their core products which are iPhone sales and securities-trading, respectively."[56] The new card will replace Apple's credit card partnership with Barclays. The card will be known as the Apple Card and will fully integrate with Apple's iPhone, to the extent that a customer will be able to directly apply for the card on the iPhone and, if approved, start using it within minutes. The Apple Card will live electronically inside the Apple Wallet, but holders will also be issued a physical credit card which they can use elsewhere. The credit card should be seen as a further step by Apple to dominate the digital payment space, where it already has established a good foothold, expecting to surpass 10 billion transactions in 2019.[57] For Goldman Sachs, one of the biggest names in the world of finance but much less well-known as a consumer brand, the Apple Card is an opportunity to expand the business of its new consumer unit, Marcus.[58]

The tech giants all seem keen on expanding into the banking business. Amazon has already provided billions in loans to the small businesses operating on its Marketplace platform. The ecommerce giant is also using the brick-and-mortar presence it obtained when it bought the Whole Foods organic grocery chain to allow customers to deposit cash directly into their Amazon accounts.[59] In the next chapter, we'll discuss Facebook's push into the online remittance market by means of its soon-to-be-launched cryptocoin, Libra—already under attack by wary regulators.[60]

In a recent survey, 82 percent of U.S. financial services businesses said they are concerned about losing revenue to fintech innovators.[61] Banks are right to worry that the tech giants are moving onto their turf. Banks have generally been slower than the tech industry to adopt new technologies to serve latent, unexpressed, or evolving customer needs, or to reach new types of customers. (However, they have generally been good at improving technologies which they expect their existing customers to use. You may have noticed the constant upgrades in your bank's ATMs.) In a 2017 Bain survey, more than half of U.S. respondents said they would be willing to buy financial products from a tech company, with that percentage being 73 percent in the 18 to 34 age group. In the same survey, the most trusted tech companies were PayPal and Amazon.[62]

However, the banking business is conservative and staid for a reason (even mergers, while disruptive, are often pursued for survival reasons rather than for growth). Banking has to be a serious business. It's one thing if a company like

Blockbuster (rental videos) or Toys "R" Us (toys) closes down because it has been overtaken by innovation. Innovation may well be creative destruction. But is another thing altogether when a large bank fails. The shock to the economy due to mega-bank failures was only too apparent during the financial crisis that caused the Great Recession in 2008. In addition, regulatory compliance is complex, and fintechs often do not have the experience or culture necessary for it. In a recent example of a regulatory stumble that could harm consumers, *USA Today* reported in December 2018 that the fintech investment platform Robinhood (mentioned earlier) had inaccurately claimed on its website that its saving and checking accounts were insured by the Securities Investor Protection Corporation (SIPC), when they were not according to the SIPC.[63]

Fintechs' biggest challenge is *scaling* their operations and business models. Though the number of tech IPOs were up in early 2019, there were few fintech IPOs. While fintechs have no problem getting financing pre-IPO—the first quarter of 2019 saw 170 such financing in the United States—they seem to be in no hurry to go public for capital. An analysis by SeekingAlpha[64] suggests that part of the reluctance are the disappointing track records of the most recent fintech IPOs. For example, LendingClub went public at about $25 per share a few years ago, but its stock price was languishing at $3 in July 2019 after suffering a series of losses. As we write this, even prominent fintech startups like Stripe, Robinhood, and Credit Karma have no current plans to list themselves on a stock exchange.[65]

According to *Forbes*, recent disappointing performance is not the only reason fintech IPOs are currently rare. The fintechs seems to have no trouble attracting large amounts of investment in private rounds, so are not pressed to go public for funds. But the biggest thing holding them back is scale. And the reason they don't scale is most likely because they lack a viable, scalable business model. For example, too many B2C startups think digital distribution and services are sufficient. They suffer from the misconception that bank customers want to replace their branches with digital offerings. But the reason these customers have been attracted to digital offerings is because of better interest rates and lower fees, not a fundamental desire to go branchless. The biggest opportunity is to change the cost structure of banks.[66]

Still, the hopes for technology-driven progress in the money world remain high. In a recent leader on the world of banking, *The Economist* emphasizes the need for a change in the cost structure of banks. It predicted that the benefits of technological change could be large, and pointed out that savings from shutting bank branches, retiring legacy IT systems, and trimming bureaucracies in banks could save a third of banking costs, worth $80 a year for every person on the planet.[67] But it also acknowledged the risks. Power could become even more concentrated in a few mega banks who learn to exploit data the way social media companies like Facebook do. Or the industry could become totally fragmented, which could undermine the necessary work that banks do to intermediate between savers and loaners. Still, a widespread fintech-driven revolution in banking could have big benefits for the global economy.

While greater banking efficiency may benefit the economy and the average consumer, there are increasing concerns that, as is so often the case (see Chapter 2), the gains will not be evenly divided. A particular concern is the effect of disappearing bank branches as banks rationalize their brick-and-mortar networks. U.S. Banks shut almost two thousand more branches than they opened between 2015 and 2018. However, banks have been cutting branches much faster in lower-income neighborhoods than in more affluent ones. Consumer advocates fear that the thinning of branch networks is leaving lower-income neighborhoods with less competition. This makes it hard for local businesses to get loans.[68] And holding back these small businesses holds back the development of the areas they serve.

The fintech innovations we have reviewed in this chapter offer a net plus to society, for the most part, for all the reasons enumerated so far. However, fintech innovations can also have drawbacks. It is up to consumers and citizens to be aware of both aspects of our new financial world. As consumers, we have to choose wisely which technologies are in our long-term benefit to adopt, and as citizens we should care about the effects these technological changes have on society as whole, and particularly on those who are less well-off to start.

# Chapter 6
# What's New about Cryptocurrencies and What's Not

> *Implicitly, the story my friend told to these people was not that, as a model for censorship-resistant, disintermediated money, bitcoin has the potential to enable peer-to-peer exchange without rent-seeking financial institutions dictating the terms.... No, his story was quite simply that if you hang onto this thing—never mind understanding it—you too can get rich like me.*
> —Michael J. Casey, "Crypto Winter Is Here and We Only Have Ourselves to Blame," Coindesk.com, Dec. 3, 2018

So-called cryptocurrencies have now been with us for a decade and there still is much hype surrounding them. You can buy books entirely dedicated to cryptocurrencies, and there are many blogs, websites (e.g., coindesk.com and cointelegraph.com), and online newsletters devoted to the latest cryptocurrency news, most of them run by unabashed cryptocurrency enthusiasts. Established financial media players like CNBC and Forbes have also dedicated resources to covering the cryptocurrency space. In a single chapter, we cannot match the depth and breadth of all these media, and no doubt some of our references may be outdated by the time you read this—the crypto industry is evolving so rapidly—but we do want to offer you a helpful introduction to the topic. In the next chapter, we will cover the non-currency applications of blockchain, which is likely a more important long-term advancement with broader applications than the cryptocurrencies it powers today.

None of our opinions should be construed as investment advice. For full disclosure, neither of this book's authors now hold or have held cryptocurrencies. This does not necessarily identify us as cryptocurrency skeptics, and we will make every attempt to offer you a balanced view of the industry. The insights we provide come from both a study of mainstream business and specialized cryptocurrency information sources, as well as interviews with actual cryptocurrency participants, like coin miners.

A brief note about nomenclature: We prefer the term *cryptocoin* over *cryptocurrency*, for the simple reason that the word *currency* implies something that is universally accepted as payment (i.e., money). Since even the well-known cryptocoins like bitcoin or ethereum cannot meet that test, we will favor the term *cryptocoin* over *cryptocurrency* in this chapter.[1] Cryptocoins are trying to become money, but they cannot be considered money yet in the full sense of the word. They are currently more like casino tokens, which are worth a lot of money and are exchangeable for real money in the proper

https://doi.org/10.1515/9781547401116-006

setting, but not universally. We cannot buy groceries with casino tokens. And that can be a good practical test of any alternative to money: Can you buy groceries with it at the store? Can you buy street food with it from an informal vendor? Can you pay your utility and medical bills with it? Can you buy gasoline and pay your taxes with it? As we shall see, despite the hype, cryptocoins have not completed that journey yet. They are a means of account (maybe) and a store of value (hopefully), but they are certainly not yet a full-fledged medium of exchange.

## A Brief Introduction to Cryptocoins

Despite the physical energy required to "mine" them (as explained below), cryptocoins such as bitcoin exist only in the digital realm. Unlike government-issued fiat money, which is mostly created electronically but still exists in bill and coin formats too, cryptocoins have no tangible equivalent. Even more importantly, they are not backed by any government. (At least not yet— as mentioned in an earlier chapter, some centrals banks say they are looking at potentially issuing government cryptocoins one day.) Cryptocoins are private money, created out of nothing by loosely formed consortia of private individuals.

Pause for a moment to appreciate this important point: Cryptocoins like bitcoin are fiat money too, but they are privately-created fiat money as opposed to the government-created fiat money that we are used to. Unlike conventional fiat money, the typical cryptocurrency has no central authority that can back it up, trace counterfeit bills, or police fraudulent transactions. The integrity of cryptocurrency transactions is wholly dependent on the concerted efforts of thousands of freelancers and the complex software that runs their cryptocurrency transactions across hundreds of thousands of computers distributed around the world. These computers are owned by volunteers who record and verify transactions for a small commission, paid in cryptocoin. This system can be compared to the original "invisible hand," used by Adam Smith to describe the forces of the market at work—a theme we explored in our earlier chapter on global finance. But unlike the invisible hand that Smith envisioned, this one has no special intelligence. Rather, the cryptocoin invisible hand is comprised of a rigid rulebook and the players who follow it: It comprises a set of software algorithms that represent clearly-stipulated rules only changeable by consensus, and the efforts of thousands of self-interested individuals employing computer technology to execute these rules for each transaction, each in the hope of earning a small share of the transaction.

Blockchain, a technology invented barely a decade ago, makes all crypto-coins possible. At a high level, you can think of it as a collective digital ledger, almost like a communal spreadsheet such as a Google Sheets document that is saved across many computers and is very, very hard (but not entirely impossible) to tamper with. As people do transactions, the volunteers, who are called *miners*, run computationally heavy software to check and record these transactions in an *immutable record*. No previous records are ever overwritten but the record grows with every validated transaction. Every addition to the record is called a *block*, which is being added to the chain of pre-existing blocks, hence the name *block-chain*. The miner who successfully adds a particular block gets a payment in the form of a small fraction of that transaction. (We shall explain the technicalities of blockchain in more detail later in this chapter and in the following.)

As we write this chapter on cryptocoin it feels like the concept has gone from new and shiny to old and a bit tarnished in a very short period of time. This is not only because more people have heard of it and many have dabbled in it, but also because a significant degree of disillusionment or even cynicism has set in after the wild ride of the first decade. If, for instance, you bought bit-coin in the early days for less than a hundred dollars and held on to it, you would be pleased with your investment now. But if you were late to the party and bought bitcoin near its peak price of $19,000 dollars, you would be under-water at this time. If you have never owned cryptocoin, you may wonder if you missed out on its best days, and whether it is already too late to get into them. To be sure, if you have an appetite for risk, you still have options. Today there are more than a thousand cryptocoins, with new ones being created all the time. However, bitcoin, the most well known cryptocoin and the one that started it all, is still the biggest by far and its history of price volatility casts a long shadow.

What started as a populist currency rebellion intended to fight both govern-ment power and banking greed has developed a split good/evil personality like the main character in Robert Louis Stevenson's classic book *The Strange Case of Dr. Jekyll and Mr. Hyde.* Cryptocoin has become an attractive, albeit highly volatile, asset class for some of the already-moneyed classes. It is still viewed with childlike enthusiasm by its early adopters, like tech enthusiasts and stu-dents, and by the true believers, the money revolutionaries. But cryptocoin is also the preferred financial asset for money launderers, fraudsters, black-mailers, international terrorists, and other unsavory characters lurking in the darkest corners of the financial and online worlds.

It may also be that we now realize how much of what we thought was new and wonderful about cryptocoins is maybe not that novel after all. It is starting to feel like we have seen at least some parts of this movie before.

## The Invention of Bitcoin and Why It Is Like Napster

### The Genesis of Bitcoin

Bitcoin originated in the 2007 to 2008 financial crisis and the Great Recession that followed. Everyone's confidence in the global financial system was shaken. But different institutions and individuals reacted differently to the crises. National governments, central banks, and regulators took drastic steps to stabilize the global financial system. New laws and new standards were passed that would force banks to set aside more cash that they could not risk via lending or investing—the equivalent of putting it under a mattress. But even before that, the first and most urgent course of action was to recapitalize large cash-strapped and essentially bankrupt financial institutions so that they wouldn't close and to avoid a run on the banks—in some cases, this meant governments literally bailing out banks by recapitalizing them. The second course of action was to inject fresh liquidity into the global financial system by creating money at an unprecedented scale. While the techniques had new names, like "quantitative easing," most people recognized it as an old-fashioned money-printing operation when they saw it. Central banks have traditionally had this power, as explained earlier in Chapter 3, and in the post-crisis environment, they used it to the hilt. The expression "running the printing presses day and night to print money" comes to mind, but of course central bankers only had to enter numbers on a computer screen. The third major course of action in response to the last financial crisis was large government deficit spending (fiscal stimulus) to stabilize the economy as a whole by making up for a rapid drop in private and corporate spending.

While all of these measures arguably helped to stave off an even bigger calamity—namely, a possible second global depression like the one in the 1930s—they all had vehement opponents. In the first case, there was resentment that many of the big banks that had contributed to creating the financial crises got bailed out and their executives walked away scot-free while private individuals with underwater mortgages lost their homes and had to declare bankruptcy. Meanwhile, hundreds of smaller local banks were declared insolvent and their officers and directors became subject to lawsuits and even clawbacks of compensation, but that just seemed like more suffering by the "little guy."[2] As for money printing, there was the age-old concern that the currency was being debased by the treasury for the sake of government convenience. And when it came to government spending, fiscal conservatives were outraged by the scale of anti-recession government spending which created large deficits that had to be funded by borrowed money. In the latter case, this anger led to the emergence of the right-wing Tea Party political movement in the United States.

While in the United States the Tea Party was founded as a political move-ment to oppose loose government *fiscal policy*, another movement arose world-wide among people who were disgusted by the accompanying loose government *monetary policy* and bank malfeasance.[3] (This latter movement also included the usual advocates for a return to the gold standard.)

But it was a subgroup within this anti-establishment monetary move-ment—a band of private, tech-savvy individuals with a strong libertarian world view called the *Cypherpunk*[4] movement—who took matters into their own hands and created a private currency that would never again suffer from the weaknesses of government-issued and bank-created money.[5] At least, that was their fervent hope. The desire for a private, digital currency pre-ceded the financial collapse of 2007 to 2008, but proponents needed a trig-ger. More importantly, they needed a technical solution to an existential challenge of digital currency: how to create a digital coin that could not be spent twice or more, and could only be held in a single person's account at any given point in time. Their desire was for a solution that would exclude the involvement of a financial intermediary like a bank. We now know that the trigger was the Great Recession of 2007 to 2008, which led to a crisis of confidence in the established financial order. The technical solution turned out to be *blockchain*.

While there had been previous attempts by the Cypherpunks and others to create a digital currency, the age of cryptocoin only started with the distribu-tion of a short white paper to the digital currency innovator community (i.e., an existing Cypherpunk mailing list) in August 2008. The paper titled, "Bitcoin: A Peer-to-Peer Electronic Cash System," was written under the nom de plume of Satoshi Nakamoto.[6] Satoshi's paper finally provided a practical design for how to use cryptography to prove the authenticity of transactions without a central authority, something the Cypherpunks had been working on for a number of years but had failed to completely solve. Here is the abstract of that now-famous paper:

A purely peer-to-peer version of electronic cash would allow online payments to be sent directly from one party to another without going through a financial institution. Digital sig-natures provide part of the solution, but the main benefits are lost if a trusted third party is still required to prevent double-spending. We propose a solution to the double-spending problem using a peer-to-peer network. The network timestamps transactions by hashing them into an ongoing chain of hash-based proof-of-work, forming a record that cannot be changed without redoing the proof-of-work. The longest chain not only serves as proof of the sequence of events witnessed, but proof that it came from the largest pool of CPU power. As long as a majority of CPU power is controlled by nodes that are not cooperating to attack the network, they'll generate the longest chain and outpace attackers. The network itself requires minimal structure. Messages are broadcast on a best effort basis, and nodes can leave and rejoin the network at will, accepting the longest proof-of-work chain as proof of what happened while they were gone.

Satoshi laid out the concept of a blockchain in succinct mathematical terms in the second half of the paper.[7] This was a novel concept and an invention that solved the aforementioned problem of potential double-spending of virtual money: Since any data on a computer or other digital device can easily be copied multiple times, any form of digital money (that is solely to exist in such a medium) has to be impossible to duplicate. If Sandra sends John a bitcoin, there needs to be an iron-clad mechanism to prevent Sandra from spending that bitcoin again elsewhere. Only John can now be allowed to spend that particular bitcoin (and only once). The person receiving the coin from John needs to be assured that it is indeed his or hers to spend. Put in more abstract terms, a very strong mechanism of ensuring *digital scarcity* is needed when anything digital can otherwise be easily copied. (Remember from Chapter 1 that money has to be believed to be scarce to be valuable.) In the technical terms often used in this context, a cryptocurrency has to be *finite* and *immutable*.

After seeing Satoshi's white paper, excited volunteers in the Cypherpunk movement helped write the software that would make the concept of bitcoin come alive. A bitcoin forum was established and a logo was designed. The first bitcoin exchange that allowed people to buy bitcoin with their PayPal accounts was set up. (It was called Mt. Gox, an acronym for "Magic: The Gathering Online Exchange.") It took a long time to get anyone to accept bitcoin as payment, but it eventually gained traction and started appreciating as demand for bitcoin grew.

The rest is now history. The contributions of the different pioneers, the play-by-play intrigue of the early cryptocurrency industry, and the evolution of the technology all make for interesting reading and can be found in sources such as *Digital Gold*, a book by Nathaniel Popper.[8]

The mysterious Satoshi has since become the world's most elusive billionaire based on his or her personal bitcoin holdings. There continues to be much speculation as to the identity of Satoshi, which includes rumors that the identity of Satoshi has become known to the U.S. National Security Agency (NSA).[9]

## The Bitcoin Bubble

Bitcoin was launched early in 2010, and one bitcoin initially sold for cents on the dollar. In April 2011, bitcoin crossed the U.S. $1 threshold for the first time. In July 2012 it was worth $10, and merely a year later in July 2013, it reached $100. By January 2017 it was worth $1,000. After that, bitcoin's rise continued at a dizzying pace until the $20,000 mark seemed within reach, but it peaked at $19,065.71 in December 2017 (see Figure 6.1). After that, bitcoin suffered a number of sharp declines, followed by only partial recoveries. The year 2018 was the worst, as bitcoin fell from $15,000 at the beginning of the year to less than $4,000 at the end, an 80 percent drop in the price of the asset. So while 2017 was the year of the big bitcoin boom, 2018 was the year of the big bitcoin crash. In the view of many mainstream financial commentators, the rapid decline in 2018 represented the burst of the crypto bubble.[10]

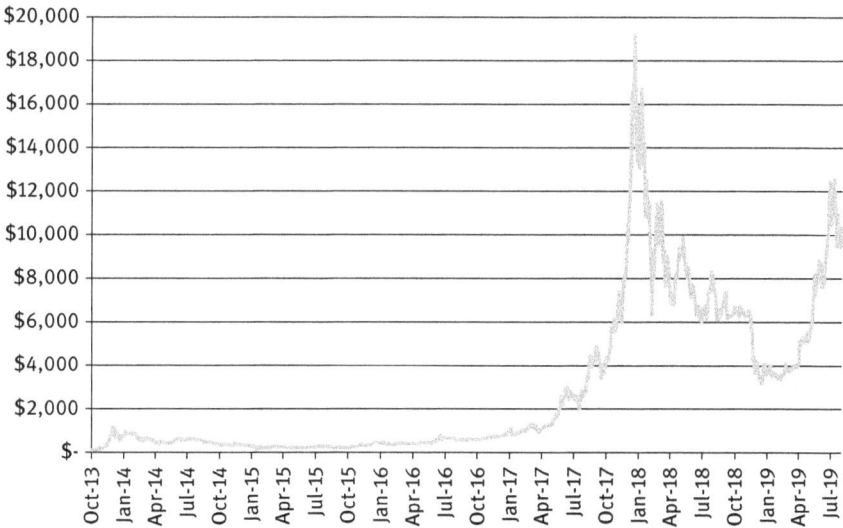

**Figure 6.1:** Bitcoin closing price in U.S. dollars, Coindesk (Fig. Note 6.1).

Some cryptocurrency industry insiders agreed: In December 2018, the official arrival of "Crypto Winter" was announced by Michael J. Casey, the chairman of CoinDesk's advisory board and a senior advisor for blockchain research at MIT's Digital Currency Initiative. Casey lamented the fact that so many people got on the bandwagon and caused an "insane market bubble" purely for speculative gains without seeing the real benefits of cryptocoins that a true believer like him sees. He described the actions of a generous friend who handed out bitcoin as gifts so they could also share in the tremendous gains like he did, and Casey objected to what he saw as a false message (almost a betrayal) that too many people believed:

> Implicitly, the story my friend told to these people was not that, as a model for censorship-resistant, disintermediated money, bitcoin has the potential to enable peer-to-peer exchange without rent-seeking financial institutions dictating the terms. Nor was it that we now have the makings of digital cash, a means of transferring value from anyone anywhere to anyone anywhere that doesn't require a bank account or the approval of some authority.
>
> The underlying message was not that bitcoin is the first digital asset, a representation of value that can live on the Internet without risk of replication or counterfeiting. Neither was it that we now have an ostensibly immutable, consensus-based record-keeping system, the first in history that cannot be changed by someone in power.
>
> No, his story was quite simply that if you hang onto this thing—never mind understanding it—you too can get rich like me.[11]

But could a crypto spring and crypto summer follow a cold crypto winter? After bitcoin languished below $4,000 during the first quarter of 2019, it started to make what looks like a remarkable recovery in the second quarter of 2019 from about $4,000 at the start of April to $12,000 at the end of June. It then softened to trade in the $10,000 range at the start of August. At the time of this writing, the bitcoin bears had disappeared with the first signs of spring weather in the northern hemisphere, and the bulls were stampeding through the summer months of 2019. But who knows what the fall will hold?

Even after the supposed burst of the bubble, many people still enter the cryptocoin market every day. What could motivate them? Recall the "FOMO" folly outlined in our chapter on global markets. The fear of missing out, powered by primal emotions such as greed and envy, for them still seem to trump any concerns about cryptocoin volatility or underlying value. These emotions are stoked by news reports about people who got fabulously rich by investing in cryptocoins. For example, it was reported early in 2018 that Peter Saddington, an unassuming 35-year old computer programmer, bought a Lamborghini Huracan with 45 bitcoins, which he bought when bitcoins cost about $3 each.[12] This type of news triggers the same emotional response as the noise and the flashing lights coming from a one-armed bandit announcing that some other lucky gambler in a casino has received a huge payout. The next time it could be you! Provided you keep on playing, of course.

Facebook's announcement in early June 2019 that it would launch its own cryptocoin, Libra, lifted the confidence of the cryptocoin market in general. (We shall discuss Libra in our section on the Bitcoin Bubble.) Though Libra is supposedly a rival to bitcoin, the fact that Facebook is entering the cryptocoin business did wonders to boost confidence in the industry. The sentiment is that if a massive digital company like Facebook is getting into cryptocoin, there must be something to it and other types of crypto-assets. Particularly, the move by Facebook was seen as a breakthrough because it would get millions of mainstream users, not just cryptocoin enthusiasts, to start transacting with cryptocoin. Those holding bitcoin and other cryptocoins felt vindicated in their earlier confidence, and others feared being left out. Bitcoin took off on this surge of positive segment as buyers stampeded back to the cryptocoin market.[13] Was 2018 just a temporary correction and are the cryptocoin happy days here again to stay this time? Only time will tell.

This wild rollercoaster ride of the last few years begs a fundamental question: For a financial asset that was supposed to be more stable than government-issued fiat money, aren't the huge price fluctuations of bitcoin a glaring contradiction in terms? Of course, most cryptocoin enthusiasts do not care about this as long as the asset they hold is wildly appreciating. As with monetary follies past, greed pushes logic and sober reflection aside. Wouldn't we all have liked to buy a financial asset that appreciated from less than $1 to almost $20,000 in less than a decade? At the current valuation of $12,000, bitcoin represents an incredible appreciation over what bitcoin cost just a few years ago. Even at the recent low point of just below $4,000 it was a terrific investment if you bought it for $100 in 2013. Wouldn't owning such an investment make us feel smarter than all the naysayers? Wouldn't we keep rooting for our asset's success? Few people can answer with a decisive no—the activity known as investment seems to bring out the folly in humans, a theme explored in Chapter 4 on global markets.

### Why Is There Always Another Bubble?

We've had a tech bubble burst in 2000, a housing bubble burst in 2008, and, most recently, a cryptocoin bubble burst in late 2017. That's three big bubbles in less than twenty years. Why don't we see them coming?

A few years before the dotcom crash, U.S. Federal Reserve Chairman Alan Greenspan said that buyer demand isn't always rational. In a speech titled "The Challenge of Central Banking in a Democratic Society," Greenspan famously said that central banking is tough because nobody really knows exactly when "irrational exuberance has unduly escalated asset values."[14] Indeed, bubbles are much easier to see in retrospect than in real-time. To see bubbles for what they are right before they start to blow up, we need a theoretical model that recognizes how we tend to buy, sell, or hold assets based on biased perception or faulty logic—such as buying based on an unfounded hope that there will always be an unlimited demand for the asset, or selling based on unfounded despair that an asset has lost all value forever.

One such framework is the *Theory of Reflexivity* first expounded upon by the prominent financier George Soros in the wake of the 1987 market crash in his book *The Alchemy of Finance*[15] and revived in the wake of the 2008 financial crisis.[16] As noted briefly in earlier chapters, the theory attempts to explain bubbles in a way that mainstream economic theory cannot because it is based on the assumption that actors will behave rationally. However, in the real world, events often unfold due at least in part to the views held by the actors. And sometimes this means that situations can get out of hand, like a run on a bank, or when everyone piles into the same asset, believing that it can only go up. The theory applies to situations where the actors or participants are *thinking*, perceiving the situation in its present state and processing the information, and then *acting* or *reacting*, which changes the future state. The core idea is based on two propositions. The first, the *principle of fallibility*, is that participants' view of a situation is always partial and distorted. The second, the *principle of reflexivity*, is that these distorted views can influence the situation, as false views held by participants lead them to take inappropriate actions. While both of these principles sound like common sense, Soros points out that conventional economic theory does not allow for either of them. Economic theory is built on the concept of market equilibrium, which requires a degree of certainty that is unrealistic when applied to human affairs. Modern advances in understanding the functioning of the human brain also substantiate the principle of fallibility.

As Soros acknowledges, the theory of reflexivity is really about the existence of a feedback loop between perception, action, and outcome. Such a feedback loop can be either stabilizing, in the case of negative or self-correcting feedback, or destabilizing, in the case of positive or exaggerating feedback. (The feedback-loop is a well-understood element of control theory in engineering, which Soros may not have been as familiar with since his expertise is in business and investing and his interests are in philosophy.) An asset bubble is then a positive feedback loop where unrealistic expectations about future rises in value encourage buyers to overpay for a type of asset, leading new buyers to enter the booming market, which will fuel further rises in the price and so on, until there is an eventual moment where confidence drops and sell-off is precipitated. The trigger for the drop in confidence may be a random extraneous event, which makes it hard to predict when a bubble will burst. (For more on feedback loops in markets, see Chapter 4.)

A list of potential bubble-bursting triggers has been compiled by Harvard University lecturer Vikram Mansharamani, the author of *Boombustology:*

*Spotting Financial Bubbles Before They Burst.* In a LinkedIn blog early in 2017, Mansharamani listed his criteria for the existence of a bubble, and opined that bitcoin did not yet meet all of them at that time.[17] The one bubble criterion that was missing in the cryptocurrency situation until late in 2017 was widespread participation. The *Wall Street Journal* reports that media mentions and Google searches reached a crescendo that almost exactly mirrored bitcoin's peak.[18] But Mansharamani also relies on an old rule of thumb (which may need to be updated to reflect ridesharing innovations of Uber and Lyft): "When taxi cab drivers start asking about it, then you know it's a bubble." Another criterion is the use of leverage (i.e., debt) to buy the asset. When many people start using credit card debt or other loans to buy such an asset, a correction is near. When these criteria were met late in 2017, the bubble did burst. This validated Mansharamani, who also made a handsome profit acting on his own theory, as he bought bitcoin for about $1,000 when he posted his blog and sold it before it peaked.

It is interesting to note here that if bitcoins themselves (and not merely offerings of bitcoins) were treated as securities, then there would be more restrictions on what owners could write about them. Bitcoin is only one example of technological innovations that can totally change established business models and transform an industry, raising potential regulatory questions along the way. This has happened before. The comparatively recent story of Napster is therefore instructive.

### The Lesson from Napster

The original Napster[19] was a pioneering peer-to-peer internet file sharing service, in operation from June 1999 to July 2001. It was mostly used to share digital audio files saved in the MP3 format. (MP3 is an audio file format that sacrifices some sound quality in exchange for a smaller file size.) In its heyday, Napster was widely used particularly by the younger generation to access and download free digital music in a format that users could play on their mobile devices. The problem was that no one was paying royalties to the copyright holders of the music, and legal challenges to the unauthorized distribution of copyrighted material eventually closed down the original Napster. (Though it reappeared in subsequent incarnations with a legal distribution model under different ownership.)

Looking back, the main contribution Napster made was to change how people accessed and acquired music. It proved the existence of consumer demand for a massive searchable catalog of instantly downloadable music files. But maybe even more important, it showed the music industry that during the digital age, consumers did not want to be forced to buy whole albums anymore when they just wanted to listen to one song. There was just one big problem that needed to be solved: how to get users to pay for the copyrighted material they wanted to download. Many file-sharing applications were spawned by Napster's popularity, but none gained traction. It took a large, established company with both the technological expertise and the business clout to negotiate with the companies who held the music rights to bring the concept to its full potential. And so Apple decisively solved the copyright problem with the launch of the iTunes Store in April 2003 after Steve Jobs negotiated digital music rights with five major record companies.[20] Users had to pay to download music from the iTunes Store, which enabled the copyright holders to receive royalties and solved the big legal problem Napster had. In June 2019, Apple announced the end of iTunes, but the royalty-paying model continues in Apple Music, Apple Podcast, and Apple TV.[21] Meanwhile, Spotify,[22] a music streaming service with a business model that allows users to stream music for a monthly subscription (or a more limited service that is free with ads), presents the latest evolution of online music. Pandora, an older music streaming service, fulfills a similar consumer need.

All in all, the story of Napster is a cautionary tale for bitcoin. Though we are not predicting bitcoin's imminent demise, it is similar to Napster in the sense that it was started by rebels intent on disrupting their industry, but eventually ran into legal and practical limits that could not be overcome without the cooperation of established industry players and governments. Both introduced a powerful new technology to the world—*peer-to-peer file-sharing* in the case of Napster, and *blockchain* in the case of bitcoin. But eventually, innovations pioneered by rebels were embraced and adopted by the "establishments" they opposed.

Napster has forever changed how we think of accessing music. Bitcoin has forever changed how we think about keeping shared records of online financial transactions. While bitcoin may never conquer the money world in the way that its strongest evangelists have proposed, it has laid the groundwork for a new transaction model for digital money just as Napster laid the groundwork for a new transaction model for digital music. We may one day remember bitcoin more for the new technology it introduced to the world (blockchain) and for how this technology has enabled economic transactions between counterparties without the need for a third party, trusted or otherwise.

## Cryptocoins Today and Tomorrow

So where does this leave us now? The horizon is broad indeed. Today it is easy to start your own cryptocurrency because the technology is well-established and the code you need may be easily downloaded for free. You only need to find people who will want to own your new cryptocurrency. There are currently about five thousand cryptocoins by some counts, but the big two, bitcoin and ether (from Ethereum), still have by far the largest market cap and market share. Together, bitcoin and ether have more than half the total market share, but there is a long tail of alternative currencies. Cryptocoins are traded on around 200 cryptocurrency exchanges worldwide, with Bitfinex and Binance being the largest exchanges in terms of trade volume.[23]

## Exchanging Dollars for Cryptocoins

In order to own cryptocurrency, you need a service that will exchange your dollars for the cryptocurrency of your choice. Such a service is akin to a stockbroker, but is more often than not in app form. You can also exchange dollars for cryptocoin at machines similar to ATMs, where you deposit dollar bills and leave with the codes that verify your ownership of cryptocurrency.

Currently, the most popular exchange service is Coinbase.[24] This service can withdraw dollars from your bank account to pay for bitcoin, ether, litecoin, or bitcoin cash (a variant of bitcoin). The mobile apps have face recognition ID verification as a security feature.

Another exchange service, which only sells bitcoin and ether, is Gemeni.[25] Based in the United States with U.S. customer support, it was started by Cameron and Tyler Winklevoss, who became billionaires after their payout from Facebook as a result of their lawsuit with Mark Zuckerberg over who invented the concept of Facebook.

Binance[26] is an exchange service with a wide range of cryptocoins on offer. This service claims to be the world's largest exchange, and even offers an online "academy" to educate customers about blockchain and the cryptocurrency market. (The academy contains a helpful retelling of the Tulip Bubble story, with an explanation about why investing in cryptocurrency is not like buying tulip bulbs. Spoiler: Tulip bulbs have a limited life and could not be a good store of value, unlike cybercurrencies which have no natural lifespan restriction.) For professionals and serious amateurs, there is Bitfinex, which currently requires a minimum balance of $10,000 but offers many trading options.

## Cryptocoin Exchanges

For most newcomers, the first step to cryptocurrency starts at an exchange where you can trade government fiat currencies like the U.S. dollar or the euro for cryptocoins like bitcoin or ether. Such exchanges link the worlds of cryptocoins and the traditional financial system. Coinbase has become the most popular exchange in the United States, and has received several rounds of venture investments.

It is important to understand the business models of these exchanges and how they make money. Up until now, their revenues have come mostly from transaction fees, but as speculative trading slowed down following the crypto-crash of

2018, these fee revenues have been falling quarter over quarter. To remain competitive, exchanges are trying to increase trading volume by listing additional cryptocoins and launching new trading products catering mainly to institutional investors. CB Insights, a leading tech market intelligence platform, predicts that from 2019, the exchanges will have to deal with increasing competition from established traditional players. For example, the Chicago Board of Options and Exchange (CBOE) now offers bitcoin options, and the Intercontinental Exchange (ICE), owner of the New York Stock Exchange (NYSE) and one of 14 stock exchanges regulated in the United States, is planning to launch bitcoin futures next year.[27] A big question is whether the big financial firms will start to take over the trading of cryptocoins from now on.

As respected and established players enter the cryptocoin exchange business, we can also expect to see increased regulatory scrutiny of unregulated cryptocoin exchanges that sprang up like mushrooms earlier. The industry seems in need of regulation: A recent report filed with the SEC claimed that up to 95 percent of all trading in bitcoin is artificially created by unregulated exchanges. The accusation is that unregulated exchanges fake trading volumes to improve their rankings and attract higher listing fees.[28]

## Cryptocoin Transactions

It may surprise the older generation to know the high level of comfort that young tech workers (particularly those working in the industry) have with cryptocoins—so much so that they are even willing to be paid in it. The volatility of bitcoin or ether does not scare them off. On the contrary, they seem to be hoping that a rise in the value of these cryptocoins can help them pay their student debts off faster. The risk-taking nature of this proposition is revealed by the 21.2 percent of college students (more than one in five) who have used student-loan money to buy cryptocoins, according to a recent survey.[29]

College students are not alone: The main cryptocurrency exchanges all have facilities for margin trading. This is so that you can borrow old-fashioned fiat money issued by national governments, like U.S. dollars, to buy the new private fiat money that exists only in cyberspace. This all makes perfect sense for cryptocurrency believers and for gamblers who do not care about underlying value, only the possibility for a huge upside.

While cryptocoins are not nearly as widely accepted as cash in dollars or other government-issued currencies, or as bank credit or charge cards, they can be used for legal transactions in sometimes surprising places. For example, you can use cryptocoin to buy tech products like Xbox game consoles, as well as movies and apps from the Microsoft store. (But you cannot buy Microsoft software with cryptocoin.) However, during 2018, some businesses have pulled back on their previous acceptance of cryptocoins. For example, Expedia, the major travel-booking site, did accept bitcoin for a while as payment for hotels and flights but then stopped accepting bitcoin in June 2018.[30] Much of this pullback can be attributed to the high volatility—mainly seen as a massive recent drop in value, with some swings in between—over the 2017 to 2018 period.

Cryptocoins can also be used to overcome the slow and expensive process of sending money between countries and converting between different currencies. Ripple (XRP), formerly OpenCoin, is a cryptocoin used by over 100 financial institutions to rapidly transmit money between countries. The RippleNet network is being built on top of a distributed ledger database (XRP Ledger) with the main goal of connecting banks, payment providers, and digital asset exchanges to enable faster and more cost-efficient global payments.[31]

Regrettably, we also have to point out here that many criminals, particularly those of the online variety, have developed a strong preference for being paid in cryptocoin. Such modern criminals do not want to receive the classic briefcase with unmarked 100 dollar bills anymore. Instead, the hackers who hold your personal or corporate data hostage after penetrating your security systems now insist on their ransom being paid in bitcoin or another cryptocoin of their choosing. Around the globe, cities have been faced with such demands and, sadly, some felt that they had no option but to pay the ransom. This vulnerability to the dark side of the cryptocoin world may eventually encourage governments to explore this form of payment for legitimate purposes.

**Sovereign Cryptocoins**

So far, of the 200 sovereign nations in the world, Venezuela is the only one that has attempted to create a government-backed cryptocurrency. Perhaps because the country has been experiencing hyperinflation and a shortage of hard currency for years, it is more willing to experiment than others. President Nicolás Maduro has been heavily promoting the *petro* to Venezuela's trade partners, but no one has yet been willing to adopt it or accept it as payment for Venezuela's debts.[32] As always, the economic laws of gravity apply: If there is no confidence in the ability of a currency to maintain its value, people do not want to accept it as payment.

Despite the Venezuelan petro's false start, there is life in the idea of central-bank-issued cryptocoins. We mentioned in our discussion on central banking in Chapter 3 that central banks may view the idea of cryptocurrencies as both a threat and an opportunity. It seems that more and more central bankers want to embrace the opportunity and get ahead of the game. According to a November 2018 IMF discussion paper,[33] at least 15 central banks worldwide are already exploring the idea of a central bank digital currency (CBDC), a widely accessible digital form of fiat money that could be legal tender one day.[34] There are three main policy objectives driving this interest—although not all central banks share the same objectives. First is the *reduction in cash usage* as new digital money takes over the role of cash. Second is *financial inclusion*, where the new technology could reach the hundreds of millions of people who do not yet have a bank account or access to modern financial services. Third is *cost efficiency*, as central banks see the potential to reduce costs by replacing costly physical banknotes with digital ones.

In a speech accompanying the release of this IMF paper, Christine Lagarde, former head of the IMF (at press time, nominee to head the European Central Bank), raised some profound issues regarding the use and status of money in the future. In a speech provocatively titled, "Winds of Change: The Case for New Digital Currency"[35] Lagarde delivered an overview of the history of money in a way that emphasized the always-changing nature of money. She asserted that we are at another historical turning point in the history of money in that the winds of change driven by widespread digitalization have reached the central banking world as well. Lagarde also commented on some of the biggest problems with cryptocurrency and how they may be mitigated. For example, there is a tradeoff between the privacy of the holder and the financial integrity of the system. Users may not want their spending patterns to be tracked by companies or governments, but governments want to prevent money laundering and other illicit uses of money. A solution may be a central-bank-owned authentication system where identities are not disclosed to third parties or governments unless required by law. Lagarde concluded with this statement: "My message is that while the case for digital currency is not universal, we should investigate it further, seriously, carefully, and creatively."

### Cryptocoins as an Investment

The story of cryptocoins extends beyond their use as a medium of payment and a "get rich quick" asset buy. They can also be traded like a commodity. Today it is easier than ever to trade in cryptocoins. Cryptocoin exchanges like Coinbase show streaming up-to-the-minute buy-sell quotes for hundreds of cryptocoins, streaming charts with price history, and news articles. The cryptocoins have symbols just like stocks. For example, bitcoin is BTC, ethereum is EHT, and ripple is XRP. And the screen image representing these trades looks just like a stock exchange dashboard from Nasdaq or the NYSE. This all creates the impression of a widely traded financial asset class that has arrived. And indeed, it has arrived in at least one corner of the market—the arbitrageurs. Cryptocoins are held by established investment professionals, such as hedge fund managers, who like highly volatile financial assets that may appreciate tenfold or more in a short period of time. Speaking of Nasdaq, dx.exchange, launched in 2018, is the first cryptocurrency exchange powered by the Nasdaq's infrastructure, and obviously benefits from the Nasdaq brand.[36]

But the cryptocoin industry still craves broad acceptance as an investment class asset, and its fragile ego is easily bruised. When Goldman Sachs Group announced[37] in September 2018 that it was ditching plans for establishing a much-anticipated bitcoin trading desk, the news, coupled with delayed approvals for initial coin offerings (ICOs) by the SEC, triggered a selloff that brought the price down below $6,500—less than half the price it opened that year.[38] In a more positive development the previous month, NYSE owner Intercontinental Exchange (ICE) announced that it would form a new startup exchange called Bakkt that would provide a safe, regulated environment for investing in digital assets.[39] A month later, Fidelity Investments announced that it would store and trade bitcoin for hedge funds and other professionals, a move seen as a milestone toward achieving mainstream credibility.[40] The cryptocurrency industry was also cheered when researchers working for the banking giant Morgan Stanley seemed to acknowledge cryptocoins as a new institutional investment class in a report on the topic.[41] And we have already mentioned the substantial market boost that followed the mere announcement of Facebook's cryptocoin, Libra, in mid 2019.

Every bit of news indicating cryptocoin acceptance by the establishment is eagerly embraced, and every bit of bad news causes a market tantrum. If cryptocoin were a human, it would probably be somewhere in its preschool years. It is able to walk on its own and is starry-eyed about the wonderful possibilities the world holds for it. But it is still disappointed easily and prone to wild mood swings. It needs adult supervision. Those thinking of investing in cryptocoins would be wise not to base their decision on one or two favorable reports, or a few good months, unless they have a very high-risk appetite. And as new exchanges run by more reputable organizations become available, would-be investors should still consider the inherent riskiness of the digital assets they are contemplating purchasing. Just because an exchange is reputable does not mean buying a security listed on it is always a good idea, as many investors on the traditional stock exchanges have discovered over the years.

In 2018, there was much talk about the potential approval of a bitcoin investment fund that could be traded on a traditional stock exchange as an exchange-traded fund—in essence, the first bitcoin ETF. Having an ETF is seen as a catalyst for the next bull run in cryptocoins and a sign of maturity. While one member of the U.S. Securities and Exchange Commission (SEC), Hester Peirce, is seen as a pro-cryptocurrency regulator, she has indicated that the approval of a bitcoin ETF may be some way off. And it appears that other SEC commissioners need even more convincing.[42]

## Regulation and Taxes

One interesting perspective on cryptocurrency comes from taxing authorities—which often take unique views on transactions, generally geared toward increasing income to a national treasury. According to a 2014 notice, the U.S. Internal Revenue Service (IRS) currently treats cryptocoins as investment properties like stocks and bonds, and not as currency. This means that no tax is due when someone buys or holds the cryptocoin, but a tax is due if a profit is realized upon the sale of the cryptocoin. The IRS is cracking down on abuses, so if you have made a profit on the sale of cryptocoins, you need to declare it. In one case reported in the *Wall Street Journal*, the IRS has sent information on 11,000 digital currency accounts held at Coinbase Inc. (a major cryptocoin exchange) to revenue officers countrywide to look for matches with tax collection cases. Faced with a federal court order, Coinbase turned over information on 13,000 accounts worth more than $20,000 apiece between 2013 and 2015.[43] In what is likely the next chapter of the same story, the *Wall Street Journal* reported in July 2019 that the IRS had begun sending out letters to more than 10,000 cryptocoin owners, warning them that they may have broken federal tax laws.[44] It is becoming harder to hide cryptocoin holdings (and profits) from the government.

On the regulatory front, cryptocoin participants in the United States often complain that the SEC is applying an over 70-year old decision by the Supreme Court, *Securities and Exchange Commission v. W. J. Howey Co.*, 328 U.S. 293 (1946), to regulate digital currencies. According to that ruling, any transactions that qualify as "investment contracts" are considered securities. As a result, the SEC has been effectively regulating all initial coin offerings as securities. ICOs are bundles of cryptocoins issued to investors, usually in digital start-ups in return for real (government fiat) currency. The ICOs take the place of the

traditional initial public offering (IPO), which entails the issuance of stock certificates to founding investors. As stated by the SEC's Corporate Finance Director
William Hinman, "The digital asset itself is simply code. But the way it is sold—
as part of an investment; to non-users; by promoters to develop the enterprise—
can be, and, in that context, most often is, a security, because it evidences an
investment contract. And regulating these transactions as securities transactions
makes sense."[45]

Thus, ICOs are viewed by the SEC as securities because of the expectation of
a return by a third party. In contrast, the two major cryptocoins, bitcoin and
ether, are considered to be commodities because they are decentralized, and are
regulated by the Commodities Futures Trade Commission (CFTC). In April 2019,
Rep. Warren Davidson (R-OH) reintroduced the "Token Taxonomy Act,"[46] a bill
he first proposed in the lame-duck session of the previous l Congress to amend
the two main U.S. securities laws—namely, the Securities Act of 1933 and the
Securities Exchange Act of 1934—to define what a cryptocurrency (called a "digital token" in the bill) is and is not. If the bill passes, it would exclude digital currencies from the decades-old definition of a security, and cryptocoins would fall
under the purview of the Federal Trade Commission or the Commodity Futures
Trading Commission (CFTC) rather than under the SEC.[47]

### Fraud, Manipulation, and Other Risks

All this regulatory attention aside, and despite the promise of iron-clad digital
security, cryptocoins have not been immune to fraud, manipulation, and heists.
On the contrary, cryptocoin is the perfect space for the famous "fraud triangle":
pressure, opportunity, and rationalization.[48] In the case of the cryptocoin market, the pressure to commit fraud comes from price volatility. The opportunity
comes from the low level of regulatory scrutiny, and the rationalization is easy
to come by: Everybody does it!

In May 2018, Bloomberg reported that the U.S. Justice Department has
opened a criminal probe into whether traders were manipulating the price of
bitcoin and other digital currencies. According to the report, federal prosecu-
tors are working with the CFTC, the financial regulator in charge of policing
derivatives. Practices that attempt to manipulate prices, like flooding the market with fake orders to trick other traders into buying or selling, are under investigation. Practices under investigation include *spoofing*, in which a trader
submits a spate of orders and then cancels them once prices move in a desired
direction, and *wash trading*, which involves a cheater trading with himself to
give a false impression of market demand that lures other to dive in too.

Because of malpractices, China has banned cryptocoin exchanges.[49] Bloomberg also reported that the SEC has opened up many investigations into ICOs in which companies sell digital tokens that can be redeemed for goods and services, due to suspicions of scams related to them.

What makes it harder to police is that cryptocoin trading is spread over dozens of platforms across the globe, and many aren't registered anywhere, much less with the CFTC or SEC. Because it is primarily a derivatives regulator, the CFTC focuses on futures linked to cryptocoins and not on the spot market for digital tokens, where the buying and selling of the actual cryptocoins take place. But the *Wall Street Journal* reported that CFTC recently subpoenaed four cryptocoin exchanges for their trading data as part of an open investigation into whether traders colluded to manipulate bitcoin prices.[50]

*Forbes* contributor Peter Tchir points out that the industry is ripe for manipulation because of three conditions.[51] First, there is a concentration of holdings in bitcoin and other cryptocoins, which gives certain individuals a tremendous incentive to push prices higher. While highly concentrated holdings attract extra scrutiny in the traditional stock markets, that is not the case in the cryptocoin world. Second, miners, many of whom also hold high positions, have a similar incentive to manipulate prices upward, as they get a cut of the proceeds. The third and final reason is the desire of price arbitrageurs to get repaid. Tchir points out that we have seen actual manipulation of real markets like LIBOR interest rates and foreign exchange, which are much more heavily policed than the fragmented cryptocoin exchanges. It is hard to believe the same is not going on in this world, but with the much lower probability of getting detected.

Manipulation is one thing. Outright theft is another. In 2014, Mt. Gox, the pioneering bitcoin exchange mentioned earlier, lost the equivalent of $400 million of its users' coins and had to cease operations. News of cryptocoin thefts is now becoming a regular feature of the landscape. For example, CNN[52] reported the two recent thefts in mid 2018: A security breach at South Korea's Coinrail exchange in which 30 percent of its virtual currencies, representing nearly $30 billion, was stolen. At Japan's Coincheck, hackers stole $530 million of currency from users of the exchange.

Chainanalysis, a cryptocoin analyst organization, claims to have identified patterns in seemingly random hacks. In January 2019, the *Wall Street Journal* reported that two groups of sophisticated hackers have likely stolen $1 billion in cryptocoins. This sum accounts for the majority of the estimated $1.7 billion lost in bitcoin hacks so far.[53]

It is important to point out that the theft of your coin from a cryptocoin exchange means that you suffer a direct, unrecoverable personal loss, unlike when money is stolen by robbers at your local bank branch. In the latter case, several institutional bank and government mechanisms kick in to ensure the integrity of customers' deposits and to make you whole. The irony is too obvious: Cryptocoins were supposed to be safer and more secure than traditional deposits, yet keeping money in cryptocoin holdings is in many ways riskier than conventional currency holdings in the traditional banking system.

*The Wall Street Journal* estimates that in less than a decade since their inception, cryptocoins worth more than $15 billion at peak prices have been stolen, much of it in hacks like those that precipitated Mt. Gox's collapse.[54] This counts only publicized thefts, not the many other illicit uses to which cryptocoins may have been used, like buying stolen credit cards or paying ransom to hackers.

Other risks related to the cryptocoin exchanges are related to operations and governance, which are too often informal and key-person dependent. This was illustrated by the recent collapse of QuadrigaCX, the largest Canadian cryptocoin exchange. After the founder, Gerald Cotton, died unexpectedly in December 2018, the company waited a month to announce his death. When panicking customers tried to withdraw their cryptocoins, the website went down. Shortly after, the company filed for bankruptcy protection. Evidently, the late Cotton was the only person responsible for moving funds between the company's secure, offline storage and its online server. No one else was able to access the majority of the cryptocoin, which was stored in the former.[55] Later, accounting firm EY, the court-appointed trustee of QuadrigaCX, reported that it was unable to locate most of the cryptocoin reserves held by the exchange, and that the liabilities of the exchange far exceeded its financial assets on hand.[56] Effectively 90 percent of depositors' cryptocoin was reported as lost.[57] It has also been reported that the Royal Canadian Mounted Police (RCMP) and the United States FBI are both investigating the now defunct exchange.[58]

We shall conclude our discussion of risks with a last sobering thought: Contrary to popular belief, the blockchains themselves are not unhackable. Due to the inherent design of a blockchain, all cryptocoins are vulnerable to a so-called *51% attack* in which attackers gain access to 51 percent or more of the nodes in the network. The attacker can use that power to create an alternative version of the blockchain to defraud holders of cryptocoin. In early 2019, such an attack was carried out against Ethereum Classic, a major cryptocoin.[59] This made news because of the prominence of Ethereum, but such attacks had already been made against many of the smaller cryptocoins.

The cryptocoin industry clearly has a long way to go to clean itself up before it can go toe-to-toe with the established financial industry, which has many more controls in place as well as paths to recourse and backstop government guarantees, like those that exist for holders of deposit accounts. If the cryptocoin industry does not clean itself up, government regulators will do it for them. The Financial Action Task Force (FATF) is an intergovernmental organization dedicated to fighting money laundering and terrorist financing. In June 2019, FATF issued a final recommendation that for "virtual asset" (i.e., cryptocoins) payment transmission, the originator's and recipient's names and account details as well as the originator's physical address must be obtained and held on record, and shared between exchanges.[60] This goes against the libertarian spirit of the founders of the cryptocoin industry, but it is a sign that the Wild West days of unregulated cryptocoin trading and transfers are coming to an end.

## Barriers to Success

Cryptocoins face several barriers, including issues of scarcity, scale, and speed; high energy needs; low rates of acceptance; and, last but not least, volatility.

### Scarcity, Scale, and Speed

In some ways, bitcoin and all cryptocoins are like gold: Miners' profits are going down all the time. In a physical gold mine, the ore is initially easy to get to, but after the easy gold has been extracted, the miners have to dig deeper and deeper to get the next ounce. In an old-fashioned gold rush, the first prospectors to get there can almost pick up the gold off the ground, and this privileged group get rich quick, which attracts many more miners (hence the term "gold rush"). But once the easy gold has been taken, the hard digging starts. The mines go deeper and deeper while the cost of extracting each ounce of gold goes up and up. The two rivals for deepest gold mine in the world, the Tautona and Mponeng mines in South Africa, now operate at depths up to 4 kilometers or 2.5 miles below ground.[61]

In a similar way, miners of cryptocoins have continuously had their percentage cut for mining new coin reduced, so the enterprise is not nearly as profitable today as it used to be. And in another similarity, to make enough money out of mining, one now needs a larger-scale operation than in the early days of cryptocoins. This pushes up the capital cost of a coin-mining operation, as you have to buy more and faster servers to run the operation. This also means the cost of entry keeps going up. (The cryptocoin, IOTA, uses a mathematics that is different from the math used by most other cryptocoins, which gives it the advantage of faster transactions than bitcoin or ethereum.[62] This has large companies like Microsoft and Cisco interested in the potential of IOTA for digital transactions.)

The analogy to gold is apt for another very important reason: scarcity of supply. At its inception, bitcoin was set up to only ever allow 21 million bitcoins to be created.[63] Since this limit exists in software, bitcoin's protocol may of course be changed to allow for a larger supply, but making this change was designed to be very hard, requiring an extraordinary level of consensus among the bitcoin community. This restriction is reminiscent of the gold standard (discussed earlier), which ultimately had to be abandoned because having a scarce precious metal of limited supply as a global currency imposes restrictions that become untenable in a growing world economy.

*Bitcoin cash* was created by a group of developers in 2017 to address this problem. This *hard fork* effectively split bitcoin into two different cryptocoins: the conventional bitcoin, subject to the original rules, and the new bitcoin cash, with software that allows eight times the number of transactions per block. (This expansion is somewhat reminiscent of the leap in credit cards from those expecting full payment at the end of the month like the original American Express "gold card," to the more common variety today, extending credit for longer periods or even indefinitely. Like the bitcoin split, that innovation was intended to expand the market to those of lesser means.)

The two bitcoin cryptocoins now trade at different values. However, the hard fork has also split the bitcoin world into two rival camps.[64] A further attempt to speed up bitcoin transactions would involve the rollout of the so-called Bitcoin Lightning Network,[65] which is still in its concept stage. Ethereum's equivalent of the Bitcoin Lightning Network is called the Raiden Network.[66] Both of these networks attempt to engineer fast, low-cost payment processing by bypassing some parts of the cumbersome global consensus process. Neither has yet been proven at scale at the time of writing.

Unlike bills and coins, cryptocoins do not need to be physically transported and can be instantly exchanged around the world. This is a major advantage, and improves upon the current cumbersome process of converting foreign exchange and wiring it through the banking system.

## High Energy Consumption

One inconvenient truth about cryptocurrency mining is that it is essentially a process of turning real physical energy—still generated primarily from burning fossil fuels depending on the location of the servers—into newly minted virtual currency. As mentioned earlier, it takes a great deal of computer power to run the mathematical problems that cryptocurrency miners must solve. The energy consumption of mining bitcoin, the leading cryptocurrency, is spectacularly high, and this environmental sustainability issue is one of the big downsides of the cryptocurrency.

Bitcoin mining's enormous energy expenditure is mostly due to the deliberate, computationally intensive process of cryptographic hashing needed to encode each new block of transactions. The process is wasteful by design: Every miner in the network is tasked with preparing the next batch of transactions to be recorded in the blockchain, but only one of these blocks will be selected. Under bitcoin's proof-of-work algorithm (a consensus-type protocol), the first miner to produce a valid block will get rewarded, but only after the other miners have accepted this block as being in conformance with all the rules. The other miners will then discard their work without getting paid for the quality assurance they did. In order to run the highly computationally intensive cryptographic operations, miners have to be using fast, power-hungry computers, as these are the only machines capable of doing the computations required in a timely fashion. (Remember that it is only the first successful miner that gets paid for processing the transaction.) As a lesser-known fact, bitcoin's holding company is active in the computer hardware business, disclosing in a pre-IPO filing to the Hong Kong Stock Exchange that it sold 2.56 million mining machines to miners in the first half of 2018 alone.[67] Facts like these could ultimately attract the attention of antitrust regulators, who are generally concerned with any transactions that could put a company in a position to have an outsized effect on market pricing.

At the time of writing, the annual electricity consumption of bitcoin is estimated at 73 Terawatt hours (one Terawatt hour equals one billion Kilowatt hours; your monthly energy bill from your electric utility is in Kilowatt hour), equivalent to the annual energy consumption of the entire country of Austria. It takes over 600 Kilowatt hours to do a single bitcoin transaction, compared to less than 200 Kilowatt hours to process 100,000 Visa card transactions! And a last sobering statistic is that each bitcoin transaction has a carbon footprint of 300 kg of $CO_2$.[68]

Even if the energy per transaction has decreased a bit from the early days, the number of bitcoin transactions is going up, so the total energy expended is still rising. At the time of writing, Blockchain.info estimates that the world's bitcoin miners are producing over 70 Terra 256-bit cryptographic hashes each second (TH/s).[69] If bitcoin miners ever manage to reach the consensus required to remove the limit on production of bitcoin beyond its current hardcoded limit of 21 million bitcoins and it becomes more of a global currency, the environmental impact could be severe, especially if similar cryptocoins follow suit.

In a notable recent paper in *Nature Sustainability*, the authors make estimates for the power use of the top four cryptocoins: bitcoin, ether (Ethereum), litecoin, and monero. They arrive at a number of 16.6 TWh/yr, which is a lot lower and more conservative than the other estimates previously mentioned. But even so, the researchers calculated that it shockingly costs more energy to mine an equal value of cryptocoins than to mine real metals from the soil of the earth:

> We estimate that mining bitcoin, Ethereum, Litecoin and Monero consumed an average of 17, 7, 7 and 14 MJ to generate one US$, respectively. Comparatively, conventional mining of aluminium, copper, gold, platinum, and rare earth oxides consumed 122, 4, 5, 7 and 9 MJ to generate one US$, respectively, indicating that (with the exception of aluminium) cryptomining consumed more energy than mineral mining to produce an equivalent market value.[70]

The only hope lies in more efficient algorithms. Proof-of-work à la bitcoin is not the only possible consensus algorithm. More efficient algorithms like *proof-of-stake* have been under development for a number of years, but the industry has not been able to settle on one version of this protocol yet.

## Low Acceptance

A major obstacle to cryptocoins was neatly summarized by the *Wall Street Journal* in the headline, "Bitcoin Is the World's Hottest Currency, But No One's Using It."[71] It points out that the volatility of the cryptocoin, even as it appreciates, makes it unsuitable as a means of payment. Why buy a house in bitcoin today if the currency will be worth 10 percent more next week? With the volatility that cybercurrencies have experienced, people are buying and holding them as speculative, novelty investments instead of using them for payment. That violates the very definition of money, which, as emphasized earlier, includes being a means of payment. This is a central dilemma: in order to be used as a widely-accepted means of payment, cryptocoin needs to have stable value, but then it would not be an attractive investment anymore for those who have fallen in love with the astronomic price appreciations those assets enjoyed until 2017. Already it seems that the bitcoin community has chosen the store-of-value function of money over the means-of-payment function, giving up the idea that everyone will use bitcoin or other cryptocoins to pay for a cup of coffee or buy gasoline or groceries with it.

A related problem with using bitcoin or other cryptocoins as payment is the substantial transaction fee that many vendors demand as part of their acceptance. (This is similar to the situation American Express faces with some vendors, who refuse to take that card due to a relatively high intermediation fee.) And this goes hand in hand with another important distinction of cryptocoins over traditional currency, which operates as a hindrance to growth and gain in the industry, is that there is no interest rate associated with any cryptocurrency. For dollars or euros or pounds, there are quoted interest rates for various classes of investors, but not for any cryptocurrency. There is no such thing as an interest-bearing bitcoin account. This, too, has slowed acceptance of the coin.

## Volatility

But perhaps the greatest barrier to success for cryptocurrency, as mentioned throughout this chapter, is volatility in value. In order to address the volatility problem, a new class of cryptocoin called *stablecoins* now aims to maintain a stable value by pegging the cryptocoin to the U.S. dollar. A number of different stablecoins with names like Tether, TrueUSD, Paxos, Havven and Dai are available. However, the experience with the largest stablecoin, Tether, launched in 2014 demonstrate the difficulties of maintaining a cryptocoin value equal to one U.S. dollar. After quickly gaining popularity and achieving a total market cap of $2.8 billion in August 2014, it experienced a huge crisis of confidence and started trading well below par value with the dollar. After a huge investor sell-off wiped $1 billion off its market cap, Bitfinex, took hundreds of millions of Tether coins off the market. It is believed that the crisis of confidence was driven by the suspicion that the company lacked the dollars on hand to repay people if they sought to redeem their Tether coins en masse.[72]

Indeed, we have seen this story unfold before many times in terms of national currencies and exchange rates. The peg of one currency to another cannot ultimately be dictated by the issuer of the currency, but will be determined by the market. Therefore, many economists believe the concept of stablecoin is flawed at its core. It remains to be seen if the determined efforts by the creators of new stablecoins can prove them wrong.

In June 2019, Facebook's cryptocoin, Libra, was announced as a stablecoin slated for launch in 2020. Libra would be funded by a consortium of more than a dozen companies paying $10 million each, including the payment card giant, Visa and Mastercard, the digital payment pioneer, PayPal, the travel reservation company Booking.com, and the ride-share company, Uber.[73] The capital raised will be used to peg Libra to a *basket* of several government-issued currencies to avoid the volatility associated with cryptocoins. While Libra will not run on the Facebook platform itself, Facebook's access to its 2.4 billion users is what made the other consortium companies want to join. Facebook hopes to address regulatory concerns and build consumer trust by promising to keep its social media and payments data separate. It created a subsidiary, Calibra, to build and maintain all the digital wallet products, including Libra.[74] While many details were unavailable at the time of this writing, it seemed like Libra was intended as cryptocoin that could be used for person-to-person transfers as well as for purchases on Facebook and other websites. With its mammoth user base, Facebook has a lot of market power to get companies and individuals alike to use its cryptocoin and thereby create a market for it. For example, it could offer discounts to Facebook advertisers if they pay in Libra. It could even offer Facebook users Libra to compensate them for revealing more information about themselves.

### Regulatory Actions

What is certain is that Libra will attract new levels of regulatory scrutiny to the cryptocoin industry. In reacting to Facebook's Libra announcement, Mark Carney, the Governor of the Bank of England, was quite clear: "It has to be safe, or it's not going to happen. We, the Fed, all the major global central banks and supervisors, would have direct regulatory (oversight)."[75]

At the G7 meeting in June 2019 the formation of a working group to discuss stable coin was announced. The G7 Stablecoin working group identified four "key considerations":

1. Stablecoin initiatives must ensure public trust by meeting the highest regulatory standards and be subject to prudent supervision and oversight.
2. Stablecoin initiatives should demonstrate a sound legal basis, in all relevant jurisdictions, to ensure adequate protection and guarantees to all stakeholders and users.
3. The governance and risk management framework should ensure operational and cyber resilience.
4. The management of the assets underlying the arrangement must be safe, prudent, transparent and consistent with the nature of obligations to, or reasonable expectations of, coinholders in order to inter alia ensure broad market integrity and coinholder confidence in good times and in bad times.[76]

This is further evidence that the trend we pointed out earlier—that monetary innovations are often made outside the system, only to be eventually incorporated into the system—also applies to today's cryptocoin innovations.

Even cryptocoin skeptics in the cautious world of traditional finance, like Agustín Carstens, head of the Bank of International Settlements (BIS), introduced as a global standard setter in Chapter 4, seem to be coming around to the idea of central bank-issued digital currencies.

In March 2019 Carsten was "not seeing the value," but in June 2019 Carsten said that BIS was supporting the central banks who were already working on such currencies: "It might be that it is sooner than we think that there is a market and we need to be able to provide central bank digital currencies."[77] BIS, owned by 60 central banks, is the central bankers' bank and concerns itself with the stability of the world's financial system. Following up Carsten's remarks, BIS announced the creation of an innovation hub for fintech at central banks.[78]

What may be lighting a fire under slow-moving institutions like BIS is the entry of big-tech into the world of cryptocoin. Carsten's remarks were made days after Facebook's announcement of Libra. In a report[79] in early 2019, BIS had expressed concerns that the amount of data that Facebook, Google, Amazon, and Alibaba are amassing was a threat to consumer privacy and a disadvantage to established financial institutions and banks.

Chris Hughes, a co-founder of Facebook and co-chair of the Economic Security Project, an anti-poverty campaign group, is also concerned that big tech's moves into finance in general (and Libra specifically) could put too much power into the wrong hands. (Earlier, Hughes had famously called for Facebook to be broken up.) Quoted in *The Guardian*, Hughes said: "If even modestly successful, Libra would hand over much of the control of monetary policy from central banks to these private companies. If global regulators don't act now, it could very soon be too late."[80]

★★★

In closing, blockchain and other cryptocoins seem like a new innovation, something truly belonging to the last decade. But maybe they are just a new technological implementation of a very old idea: the creation of private money when people feel that official government currencies are not being managed in their interest. (This is exactly how many people felt in the aftermath of the financial crisis and Great Recession a decade ago.)

As Felix Martin points out in his book on the history of money,[81] private sector actions have often been effective at forcing change on official currencies, but rarely in replacing them. Martin's analysis of monetary history comes down to two fundamental questions: First, *what* are the rules governing the creation of money? Second, *who* makes these rules? In response to the first, bitcoin has very simple rules, as we have seen: There is a fixed, hardcoded limit on the number of bitcoins that can be issued[82]; and the so-called miners create new bitcoin in a highly prescribed way. As to the second question, the answer for bitcoin is that the decision has already been made via the aforementioned hardcode, and the origin of that protocol is traceable only to the incognito Satoshi.

As a social technology, it seems that both these new rules are too restrictive for society at large to accept, and that the evolution of cryptocoins will be in the direction of the controlled relaxation of both these rules, with more power turned over to existing societal institutions like the central banks and established financial institutions. While change is being forced on the established order, the likely future of cryptocoins lies in the old order co-opting the new, and not in a completely new order.

Cryptocoins are very much a work in progress. They were created by libertarian rebels who promised a new monetary utopia, free from the heavy hand of government and the vested corporate interests. But, as we have seen, reality has intruded on the vision of the techno-optimists. Age-old human behavioral flaws, unavoidable regulatory constraints, and the limitations of the new technology, including some nasty negative externalities, all call for a more sober assessment of the potential of cryptocoins to disrupt, much less conquer the financial world.

Part IV: **Beyond Money**

# Chapter 7
# How Blockchains Could Change How Business Is Done

*Now, O king, establish the decree, and sign the writing, that it be not changed, according to the law of the Medes and Persians, which altereth not.* —Officials of Darius the Mede[1]

In the simplest terms, blockchain can be thought of as a new type of database, with *dispersed records* copied among all the database's users rather than being maintained centrally, with *immutable entries* that cannot be altered once written, and with *cryptographic techniques* validating entries instead of a trusted central party. With a blockchain there is no need for a central authority, and no need for the users to trust one another. In the previous chapter we related the intertwined history of bitcoin and blockchain, and explained how blockchain is the technological innovation that enables a digital fiat currency to work without any central authority. We also suggested that blockchain, not bitcoin, may be the more consequential invention in the long run due to its potential applications outside of powering cryptocurrencies. Today, blockchain enthusiasts are identifying all sorts of uses beyond powering cryptocurrencies for their concept of a decentralized, immutable, cryptographically secure database.

Indeed, the potential applications of blockchain go far beyond finance. As the SEC's William Hinman said in a June 2018 speech,[2] the most exciting part of *distributed ledger technology* is, for him, "the potential to share information, transfer value, and record transactions in a decentralized digital environment." Potential applications, he said, include "supply chain management, intellectual property rights licensing, stock ownership transfers, and countless others." And further, "There is real value in creating applications that can be accessed and executed electronically with a public, immutable record and without the need for a trusted third party to verify transactions. Some people believe that this technology will transform e-commerce as we know it."

In this chapter we will consider the most important of those other applications, with an emphasis on the ones related to the role of money and the workings of monetary transactions. In order to appreciate how these applications make use of blockchain and what the technology's constraints are, we shall provide a more detailed explanation of the nuts and bolts of blockchain. We shall go on to explain smart contracts (a major potential application), the industries that could be transformed by blockchain applications, and what challenges remain. But we want to start by first reviewing the major technological and societal

https://doi.org/10.1515/9781547401116-007

trends that have brought us to this point and that explain why there seems to be such widespread receptivity to adopting blockchain in some form or another.

## Blockchain: The Next Big Technology We've Been Waiting For?

Blockchain was introduced to the world as an integral element of the first successful cryptocurrency, bitcoin. As explained in the previous chapter, bitcoin's inception was a reaction to the crisis of confidence caused by the 2008 Great Recession. Its progenitors were the Cypherpunks, a radical movement of tech-savvy libertarians who were distrustful of any central authority. Part of the excitement around blockchain is no doubt simply reflected glory from glittering cryptocoins. But the more substantial excitement is driven by a genuine hunger for a new technology that can solve hitherto unsolved problems. The fact that establishment organizations like banks and governments are pouring millions of dollars into blockchain-related projects seems to indicate that they see this technology as a potentially good solution to real-world problems. Or is it just that everyone is currently overexcited and getting on the blockchain bandwagon too fast?

### The Tech Trends That Got Us Here

Discerning the confluence of technological and societal trends will help us to understand the zeitgeist that makes so many people receptive to blockchain. Let us review how we got here.

Computers started out as mainframes. These were expensive machines that were not affordable for private individuals, and most organizations could only afford one. In some cases, companies could fit only one into their space, as early mainframes were very large. The first mainframe computer to be mass produced, the Univac 1, was the size of a two-car garage: 14 feet wide, 8 feet deep, and 8.5 feet high.[3] In the 1980s, *personal computers* (PCs) were developed. Bill Gates' vision of a "computer on every desk and in every home"[4] quickly became a reality. But the information we had on our first PCs was *localized*, existing only on their hard drives and on removable floppy drives in our physical possession. We could access shared information on our office PCs only within the strict confines of the office's network.

Then, in the 1990s, the *internet* became a massive, popular phenomenon. The internet is a *network of networks* enabled by the invention of a fairly simple, digital communication protocol (Transmission Control Protocol/Internet Protocol, or TCP/IP). It interconnected many existing networks and spawned many new networks. The internet grew and grew, while internet content exploded. People could send one another emails, share files, and access all sorts of information on the *world wide web*. This information is distributed across many different servers worldwide. People who remember the first big internet service providers (ISPs), like AOL, will remember how they started out as walled gardens: When you logged in, you saw a tidily-arranged home page, with menus and content curated by your ISP and hosted on its own network. Your ISP also allowed you to venture out into the wilds of the internet using your own discretion by clicking on another link. That all seems quaint now, but that kind of hybrid solution is typical as society transitions from one technology to the other, like we see with hybrid gasoline-electric cars today. Similarly, as we shall see, the first feasible blockchain applications may not be public, but private.

In the late 1990s and early 2000s, we went from simply being able to access information online, to being able to transact business, whether it was buying from Amazon or doing our banking online. This is now the age of *ecommerce*. This shift into online economics was nothing less than revolutionary—as it revealed for the first time in our generation the nature of money as a true intangible that can exist only in the digital realm. Remember that up to then, consumers either paid by cash, by paper check, or by signing a piece of paper that allowed an electronic funds transfer (EFT), like setting up payment for your car lease or utility bills. All these still have some physical feel to them.

While financial institutions and corporations had been using EFT in the background for a number of decades, the internet made consumers comfortable with the idea of spending virtual money. In the late 2000s, *mobile phones* became powerful enough to fully participate in the internet, which is why we now like to call them *smartphones*. The internet is now completely mobile; you can carry it around in your pocket all day on a powerful, miniaturized computer. And what's more, today you can use your phone as a wallet, and even withdraw cash from an ATM without having an ATM card with you. All these developments prepared us for blockchain, as we shall soon see.

Another big tech trend that arose at the turn of this century and kept on accelerating into our present decade is *cloud computing*.[5] With cloud computing, data are stored and applications are run on a network of servers in data centers that could be anywhere. Individuals, corporations, and governments alike are sending off more and more of our data to external data centers run by providers like Amazon Web Services, Google Cloud, IBM Cloud, and Microsoft Azure. We are so used to doing that now that we don't even notice it. If you buy a Chromebook laptop today, you will find that it has no hard disk drive to store your photos and other big files on, only a small amount of local solid-state memory to help the computer run. This represents the ultimate vision of where the cloud can take us: Everything is stored in the cloud, and all applications run on the cloud and are accessed via a standard web browser.

Salesforce, the cloud-based customer relationship management solution provider, built an empire by betting on this idea early (in 1999). *Software-as-a Service (SaaS)* has since become the dominant way for running large corporate applications. Individuals and businesses don't buy Microsoft Office software that comes with an installation disk and a perpetual license anymore—instead, they subscribe to Microsoft Office 365, which is SaaS. Or, they can use Google Documents, which has nearly equivalent functionality entirely for free. The applications you use daily, like your word processor, spreadsheet, email, and your web browser which make it all possible, all now reside in the cloud.

The cloud is a big part of the next evolution of the internet. The other big internet evolution is the addition of the *Internet of Things (IoT)*, which means that we are now connecting almost everything to the internet, whether those are sensors on a jet engine flying across the ocean, sensors in our appliances at home, or sensors in the wristbands we wear when exercising. The raw data captured from all these devices will soon far exceed all data ever created by human action on this planet. According to estimates by Cisco, a computer network equipment company, the IoT will comprise more than 30 billion connected devices by the year 2020. A staggering 5 Exabyte (quintillion bytes or 10 to the power of 18) of data will be produced every day—that's 5 million Terabytes per day.[6] The cloud and IoT together mean that we now have extremely widely-distributed data generation, storage, and processing.

One last trend to mention is the *open-source* movement, which started back in the late 1980s and was formalized in the late 1990s. The concept of open-source software,[7] which is software that is freely available for use, and for which the programming steps can be inspected (and modified) by anyone, dates back to the earliest days of computers—the 1950s and 1960s—when most software was written by academics. Software only became copyrightable in the United States in 1976, with the passage of a copyright law that year, and even then confusion remained until the 1983 case *Apple Computer, Inc. v. Franklin Computer Corporation.*[8]

Complicating the issue is whether intellectual property protection is best sought through a patent or a copyright: Patents protect the underlying idea, while copyright protects the expression of the idea—namely, the written code.[9] Furthermore, the question of patentability continues to evolve. *In re Beauregard*, 53 F. 3d 1583 (Fed. Cir. 1995) the court said that "computer programs embodied in a tangible medium, such as floppy disks, are patentable," but in the case of *Alice Corp. v. CLS Bank International*, 573 U.S. 208, 134 S. Ct. 2347 (2014), the court narrowed the scope of patentability by saying that the software must be connected to a unique technology.[10]

A famous open-source milestone was the release of Linux[11] by Linus Torvalds in the early 1990s. Linux subsequently became the operating system of choice for many internet servers, drastically reducing the cost of entry for digital start-ups and internet innovators. Linux has since gone mainstream because of its low cost, breadth, and robustness, and today it dominates in the server and supercomputer markets. Another major open-source milestone was the 2008 release of Android, a new smartphone operating system based on Linux, as open-source software by Google. Android has subsequently become the dominant smartphone operating system.

Open-source software is maintained and further developed by a worldwide community of volunteers who also check one another's work and identify bugs in the software. The blockchain originators came from a sub-segment of this community, which is why they were so comfortable with a governance model without a central authority. Today, anyone can download blockchain programs as open-source software, although there are also proprietary software implementations of blockchain.

> In summary, we can discern how technological advances over the last few decades drove societal trends that all represent new levels of personal empowerment, and a weakening of the center, from corporate computers to personal computers; from local to networked computing; from desktop to laptop to mobile; from proprietary software to open-source software; from physical libraries and limited local data to the entire world's knowledge at your fingertips anywhere, anytime; from transacting in person to transacting virtually; from buying and installing software and maintaining your own local storage to renting cloud-based services. Another overarching theme is that we have gone from physical and local to virtual and distributed.

Because many people had already made this transition and adapted their mental models and behavior accordingly, the idea of private yet network-distributed virtual money quickly found receptive soil. And it's the same mindset that has prepared individuals, corporations, and governments for a way of transacting that is more distributed and less centrally controlled. And so, into this environment entered blockchain, where the records are kept by no central authority but by all its users. In addition, blockchain evangelists envision an internet where cryptography empowers users to always remain in control of their data. Contrast this with the situation today in which large technology corporations like Google and Facebook have gained much control over user data after enticing users to give away their data in exchange for free services.

## Putting Blockchain to Use

It bears repeating that blockchain has emerged as a major innovation in computer science because it enables a trusted ledger system without needing a trusted third party (like the old-fashioned banker) in the middle. This is why blockchain has rapidly gone from an insurgent technology enabling the creation of cryptocurrencies to a technology that is being explored and adapted for other purposes by incumbent institutions and their traditional IT solutions providers. If the *use cases* of blockchain proliferate as predicted, it could become a mainstream technology over the next few years. (The slightly annoying term "use case" is beloved by tech-industry insiders. It simply means the way people use a product or technology. One of mankind's first technologies, the axe, already had multiple use cases thousands of years ago. You could, for example, use your axe to chop wood, dismember animal carcasses, or smite your enemies.)

However, at the time of our writing in mid-2019, there are few proven applications of blockchain outside of cryptocurrencies, even though the most cursory web search will review hundreds of *supposed* use cases and lots of excitement and hype surrounding the technology. A closer look at most of the alleged use cases often reveals that they have not passed the exploration or concept phases. This does not necessarily mean that blockchain is going nowhere. It might simply mean that it takes longer to implement at scale than proponents thought.

The long-term success of a transformative new technology—which some believe blockchain is—may not be immediately apparent, especially after initial overhyping followed by disappointment. *Amara's law* is often quoted in this context: "We tend to overestimate the effect of a technology in the short run and underestimate the effect in the long run."[12] But Amara's law cannot apply to all new technologies, as many will never live up to their promise. Blockchain may be more limited in application than its most enthusiastic supporters think it is. The jury is still out, and caution is advised.

## Second Thoughts

In a feverish environment, it gets hard to differentiate hype from real progress. *CoinTelegraph*, an online news site specializing in all things blockchain and cryptocoin, published a list of companies that enjoyed significant growth in stock prices after name changes that added the words *bitcoin* or *blockchain* to their names.[13] In some cases, the name change signified a change in focus, but in others it was only a name change. A famous example is the struggling Long

Island Iced Tea Corporation (NASDAQ: LBCC), which enjoyed a spectacular 458 percent rise after renaming itself as Long Blockchain. *CoinTelegraph*, usually a staunch promoter of the industry, pointed out that this is a worrying trend reminiscent of the dot-com boom, which was followed by a famous bust.

Another thing to bear in mind is that blockchain proponents—or evangelists, as we called cryptocoin fans, given their fervent belief and their desire to convert others—have been very good at making their views known everywhere they can. When you read a positive piece on blockchain, it helps to look at who the author is so that you can calibrate your credulity. A lot of what is published on blockchain (and cryptocurrencies) comes from industry insiders who, although often in a good position to opine, as they are knowledgeable on the topic, also have a commercial interest in puffing up their industry and hyping its technology. Therefore, it's always good to understand from whom and from where an opinion comes before you make your own investment decisions based on it. On the other side, a publication like *The Economist* has generally been skeptical of cryptocurrencies and of blockchain. As with any investment or anything else in life, it is wise to listen to both sides.

The big question to be answered across the next few years is whether blockchain will be the actual mechanism that is adopted at scale, or whether blockchain will only be a catalyst that in the end leads to the adoption of other more robust mechanisms that solve intermediation problems more effectively and efficiently. Specifically in cases where any form of money changes hands, the question is to what extent we can or want to dispense with having a trusted third party in the middle of the process.

## Understanding Blockchain Operation

In this chapter, we are interested in the other non-cryptocoin applications of blockchain. Blockchain explanations often start with an explanation of bitcoin (the first blockchain implementation). However, looking only at the inner workings of bitcoin can cloud our general understanding of how other blockchains (and blockchains in general) operate and what they may be able to do for us. So we shall start with a short, simplified introduction to a generic blockchain.

### Blockchain Basics

Before we can explain the *how* of blockchain, we need to explain the *why* of blockchain. The fundamental point to understand about its purpose is that it is all about *trust* or the lack of it. When you transact with other parties in a network, you cannot necessarily trust them. The conventional way of addressing that issue is to have a trusted central authority, an intermediary between you and your counterparty, that guarantees safe delivery both ways of whatever it is that you and the other party are exchanging.

The central authority also keeps all records in a central ledger that can be audited. The technology we use for this, double-entry bookkeeping, has been available at least since the fifteenth century, but earlier versions could be much older.[14] With double-entry bookkeeping, two accounting entries are required to record each financial transaction. Every credit has to have a corresponding debit, and every debit has to have a credit, as we all learned in Accounting 101. Over the last few decades we have kept our ledgers in computer databases and not on paper, but otherwise, nothing fundamentally changed until blockchain came along. (One can think of blockchain as a whole new type of ledger.)

But what if you cannot trust the central authority? Maybe you are concerned that it might go rogue, or that it might get hacked by an attacker who steals all its data, including your precious assets? Or maybe you are concerned that the central authority is incompetent or corrupt and would not do a good job protecting you from getting cheated by your counterparty. Or what if it is simply impractical to have a central authority because participants are scattered across many nations and they cannot agree on who should be in charge? Or what if the counterparty is totally unknown to you? These are the trust-related problems blockchain was created to solve. Trust, and changing how we think about ensuring trust, is the *why* of blockchain. The latter may also be its enduring legacy, even as the technology evolves.

So how does it work then? The blockchain enables the sharing and exchange of information between *nodes* on a *peer-to-peer (P2P) network*. A P2P network is one where each node can find a connection to another node without a central node acting as the switchboard. When setting up a new printer on your home network, you would typically choose the P2P option and connect it to your secure home Wi-Fi network by providing the network password to the printer. The printer is not connected to some central server that controls who can access it, but it is just another node that any computer logged into your home network has access to. Just like with your home network, any node in blockchain can access another.

Let's follow along the blockchain path, referring to Figure 7.1. In blockchain, a user wishing to complete a new transaction will send that transaction request to the P2P network via his or her computer (a node). This triggers the

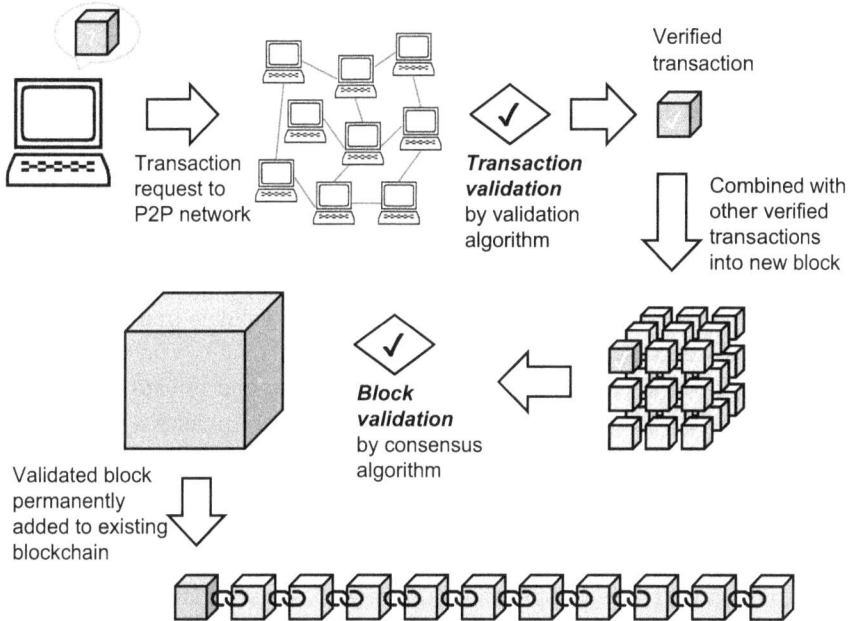

**Figure 7.1:** Simplified blockchain overview (Fig. Note 7.1).

first major trust mechanism as the validation of the transaction and the status of the requesting node are checked by the network of nodes. The validation algorithm is typically *public key cryptography*. The verified transaction is then combined with other verified transactions to create a new "block." This triggers the second major trust mechanism, which is the use of a *consensus algorithm* by the network of nodes to validate the new block. Only after the block is validated by the nodes may it be added to the blockchain, which entails posting the new block to all the nodes in the network so that everyone has the same updated copy of the blockchain.[15]

In bitcoin, the consensus algorithm is solving a tough cryptographic puzzle to find a random value that is referred to as *proof of work*—still a dominant model despite a recent challenge from the Bank of International Settlements, which announced in January 2019 that the formula is not sustainable.[16] There are other consensus algorithms or protocols used by other blockchain platforms (listed at the end of this section). While these algorithms vary, their purpose is the same: requiring nodes on the network to somehow achieve consensus on the validity of the transactions to be added to the blockchain, and making it very hard to falsify a transaction.

## Bitcoin, the Original Blockchain

Blockchain technology is still very new, having been with us for only a decade, and different versions are in the process of evolving. As explained in the previous chapter, the original blockchain was invented by the mysterious Satoshi to make bitcoin work as a purely digital currency without a central authority or the need to trust counterparties. Satoshi's ingenious approach was the first successful attempt at making a cryptocurrency work. It combined a well-understood existing technology, *public key cryptography*, to validate identity with a new *cryptographic hash function* (blockchain's consensus mechanism) to validate transactions and the resulting ledger.

In public key cryptography, there is a public key and private key, which together form a cryptographic key pair. The first person initiates a transaction by signing it with a private key which only he or she knows. The counterparty, or anyone else, can then verify that the message did in fact come from the first person by using the public key, which is visible to everyone. (This technology existed and was used extensively well before the advent of blockchain, but blockchain gave it a new application. Once again, we see that in the realm of money, inventions and subsequent innovations go hand in hand.)

Following counterparty verification, it is the next step (the consensus mechanism) that is the most distinctive aspect of the new blockchain technology. There are a variety of consensus mechanisms in use, but let's look at how this happens in bitcoin, the first blockchain application.

Satoshi Nakamoto proposed block mining as the consensus mechanism to prevent double-spending of bitcoin. Block mining is when miners compete among one another to find the next valid block by solving a computationally intensive mathematical puzzle. It is the miner's job to validate all transactions. The miner at the node that is the first to solve the puzzle gets rewarded with some fraction of a bitcoin. This is also how new bitcoin currency is created—in other words, this is how this new type of money is made. Note that making new money by paying the workers (miners) is reminiscent of using crops like tobacco or seeds as money to pay the farm laborers. It is called *payment in kind*. In Chapter 1 we mentioned that one of the first forms of money was when farm laborers in ancient Sumeria were paid in measures of barley three thousand years ago. Thus, what is old becomes new again.

To solve the puzzle, the miners use a cryptographic hash function which transforms (the verb is "hashes") a collection of data into an alphanumeric string. The string has a fixed length but no fixed value; it is essentially impossible to predict which data collection will produce a specific hash value and therefore add information to the ledger or block. Miners have to run this computation over and over, expending substantial computing resources until the correct value is found by one of them, and the others can check it. The steps are as follows.

Once a bitcoin transaction has been initiated and identities have been confirmed via public key cryptography, the miners get involved. Miners' computers (nodes) bundle transactions of the last 10 minutes into a new transaction block. Then each miner's computer starts to calculate the cryptographic hash function using the transaction block and the previous hash value that contains information about all previous transactions (that is why it is called a "blockchain"), as well as a so-called *nonce*, a random number added to the data by a miner. The bitcoin system requires a very particular form for the acceptable new hash value that comes out of this calculation. To try and get to this value, miners have to keep recalculating the hash value, each time trying out a new nonce until one miner gets it right. The miners have no idea which nonce will work, so they are forced to generate many hash values. That is why bitcoin is so computationally intensive, slow, and, quite frankly, wasteful in energy terms.

The winning miner gets paid in newly minted bitcoin for this *proof of work*, which assures the integrity of the transaction and the bitcoin ledger. With the passage of time, each transaction quickly gets buried under more recent transactions. The database is secure because one can only modify a transaction by redoing all the subsequent proofs of work by the other miners, trying out a dizzying number of new nonces in the process. Such a feat is considered nearly impossible with current technology because of the length of time and amount of energy such computations would take. (What is now virtually impossible may become possible if a large-enough quantum computer[17] could eventually be constructed. But in fairness, this future threat from quantum computing concerns all cryptography currently in use—for example, all passwords for conventional banking accounts, not only for cryptocurrencies.)

## Types of Blockchain

If blockchain is a new species of an accounting system, recognizable by the key traits described in our introduction, we can classify blockchain systems[18] into three subspecies based on who may access and use them.

**Public blockchain**—This is an open platform that people from different organizations can join without restrictions. Every participant has full authority to read and write transactions, and to audit or review any part of the blockchain at any point in time. Since they have no restrictions, these systems are also called *permissionless* blockchains. Each participant has a copy of the entire blockchain, which is synchronized to all nodes. The blockchain is completely decentralized. Its integrity is guaranteed by cryptography and a decentralized consensus mechanism. This is Satoshi's original blockchain concept.

*Private blockchain*—This is a blockchain dedicated to the private sharing and exchange of data either among individuals in one organization or from multiple organizations. Since it does not allow access by unknown users, it is called a *permissioned blockchain*. Nodes are only allowed on to the network according to a set of rules or by some gatekeeper. What they are allowed to write is also restricted. This all means centralized control, and therefore derogates the essence of Satoshi's blockchain idea, which is being open to all without a centralized authority. Furthermore, private blockchain is also not immutable and irreversible because the central authority can tamper with it.

*Consortium blockchain*—This is a hybrid between a public and private blockchain. It is partially private and permissioned, but without any one organization or gatekeeper deciding who is allowed to join. Instead, a predetermined set of validator nodes make that decision. Block validation requires sign-off from these validator nodes too. The consortium decides whether read-write permissions will be public or limited to existing participants. It is not immutable and irreversible because a majority of the consortium can potentially agree to make changes to the blockchain.

Various types of consensus models are at the heart of different blockchain systems. They have been created to meet different design criteria like permissioned or permissionless, the desired transaction rate (proof of work is notoriously slow), desired scalability, whether participation charges are to be levied, and the degree of trust that exist between the nodes—high in private and consortium blockchains, and low in permissionless blockchains.[19]

Achieving consensus in a distributed system like blockchain is obviously quite tricky. The main types of consensus models in use, and examples of the blockchains that use them, are: *proof-of-work* used by bitcoin, *proof-of-stake* used by Ethereum, *proof-of-elapsed-time* used by Intel SawToothLake (now under Linux HyperLedger), Byzantine Fault Tolerance used by HyperLedger Fabric (the most popular permissioned blockchain platform), and *federated byzantine agreement* used by the Ripple and Stellar blockchain platforms.[20]

## Smart Contracts: The Problems They Solve and Create

We enter into contracts every day without thinking about them. When you stop your car and push the button at the entrance to a public parking garage, you enter into a contract to pay a certain hourly rate for parking. When you order coffee at the coffee shop, you are agreeing to pay the posted rate for your beverage, and the coffee shop is agreeing to deliver that beverage. The ability to enter into contracts with others, the *freedom of contract*, is the foundation of our free-market economy. Any exchange of money for something else is effectively being done in compliance with a contract, whether explicit or implicit, and whether complex or simple. Traditional forms of contract have underpinned commerce for thousands of years. As the familiar aphorism says, a contract is "a promise that the law will enforce."

However, the days when the contracting parties could look each other in the eyes are long gone. Thanks to digital technologies like the internet, commerce today is more decentralized than ever. Everyone can find anyone and do business with them. But trust still has to be maintained and risks have to be managed. Traditionally, intermediaries like banks were responsible for coordinating between parties, maintaining money exchanges and other contract protocols, and thereby reducing risks. As the marketplace decentralizes, we need new mechanisms to accomplish these goals. The three main pillars[21] of a future decentralized economy are:

- Liquidity: the expectation of a party that he or she can complete a trade within a reasonably short period of time
- Discovery: the ability of buyers and sellers to find one another at low cost
- Trust: the belief, based on shared understandings and protocols, that a transaction will occur

Fortunately, the digital revolution is also offering us technologies like blockchain, IoT, and advanced forms of automation (like artificial intelligence) from which to construct our new trust mechanisms.

### Introducing Smart Contracts

Smart contracts are self-executing contracts where the terms of agreement between the parties are directly encoded in software. In short, smart contracts are computer protocols. In principle, any blockchain can support smart contracts, but the Ethereum blockchain is often preferred because it was designed to host smart contracts and has the capacity to include smart contract code as well as other files. Bitcoin, on the other hand, is a lean cryptocurrency with strict limitations, which makes it much less suitable for smart contract implementations.

The term "smart contracts" was coined by technologist Nick Szabo in 1994. He defined a smart contract as "a computerized transaction protocol that executes terms of a contract."[22] The idea did not gain much traction absent the right technology to implement it, and lay dormant for years until blockchain came around.

In 2017, Nick Szabo reprised and updated his concept of a smart contract for the blockchain age, in a white paper for the Blockchain Research Institute.[23] Szabo calls a smart application that runs on a secure blockchain consensus protocol, a *decentralized application* or "Dapp." Dapps are considered *trust-minimized* if we can trust the code that runs the transaction feature without necessarily trusting the owners of the computers on which the code runs. According to Szabo, smart contracts are best run on public blockchains, which have the highest security, and can also support their negotiation. Szabo sees three major benefits that smart contracts have over traditional contracts. The first is relieving humans of the mental burden of complex arithmetic, like Uber's complex price algorithm, a kind of smart contract that determines the costs of driving a particular route at a particular time. Drivers and passengers would never be able to agree on a price by factoring in all the variables included in the Uber algorithm. The second benefit is increased predictability and decreased risk in applications like cross-border transactions where legal and other uncertainties are high. The third benefit is a reduction in risks related to trust and security—for example, counterparty risks in financial transactions.

In the digital era, successful companies have typically used the new technology to improve at least one of the main phases of a contract or deal. The first phase, *search*, is where buyers and sellers find and assess one another. This is where the internet has been a boon, with its powerful search engines like Google able to find vendors—anyone selling anything anywhere online—and for such vendors to publish massive online catalogs with illustrations—even videos—and all sorts of other information about their products. The second phase, *negotiation*, is where the terms of the contract are determined, as in the aforementioned case of the Uber algorithm that prices rides. Online auctions like eBay's are other innovations of the negotiation phase. The third phase, *performance*, is where the terms of the contract are performed. Delivery is an example. Automation in Amazon's warehouses, and further integration with third-party-logistics providers like UPS, reduce the delivery times of packages. Yet for contracts that require more complex performance, little new has been achieved with respect to the performance. This phase of the contract probably has the most potential for new advances with the implementation of technologies like blockchain, advanced sensors, IoT, and 5G wireless connectivity.[24] Szabo calls the last contract phase *post-performance incentivization*. This includes the now ubiquitous ratings systems that are intended to provide incentives for good behavior.

In strictly legal terms, the term smart contract may be a bit misleading, since the legally binding contract does not exist within the software designed to execute it. If there were ever a legal dispute, it would still be necessary to go back to the good old fine print of the terms and conditions. Therefore, what is communicated at the user interface will go along with any other existing documents and will be interpreted in the light of existing commercial custom and contract law in order to adjudicate any dispute.[25]

## Scalable, Secure Computer Architectures

The computer architectures that morphed into the internet have a fundamental vulnerability that needs constant patching and vigilance through massively expensive cybersecurity projects, which never seem to end. This is a huge cost of doing business today. All the networks that are now interconnected operate on the paradigm of a central administrator with all-powerful access to the root of each of these systems. This is the conventional client/server architecture where unquestioning full trust is placed in the central administrator of the server, who can read, change, or delete any data without the user even knowing. The vulnerability is that there is no stopping a rogue system administrator.

Many external attacks launched via the internet into these local networks aim to give the hacker control of as many of the systems administrator's privileges as possible. This is akin to successfully disguising yourself as the bank manager and asking your bank subordinates to open the safe for you. These attacks work because techniques for guessing usernames and passwords, together with large numbers of persistent attempts, will succeed in a certain percentage of cases. It is a constant bombardment aided by automation. (Hackers do not personally attack systems one at a time; they set up programs to do that.) A recent University of Maryland study estimates that computers connected to the internet each suffer an attack every 39 seconds on average, or 2,244 attacks per day.[26] This is the twenty-first century version of the highway robbery of old which made roads unsafe for travel in the Middle Ages. If you have money, there is always someone who wants to lighten your purse.

When it comes to the cost of malware and virus attacks, perpetration and protection are asymmetrical—like email spam, these attacks cost very little to execute, while the cost to defend against them is orders of magnitude more. Fortunately, the modern cryptography (also used in blockchain) flips this equation: an encryption operation that takes a fraction of a second can take billions of years to crack (that is, it is practically impossible). Public blockchains offer security benefits that conventional computer networks cannot, because of their different architecture underpinned by cryptography and consensus mechanisms. But this high-level security currently comes at a price of much slower response and transaction times, and higher transaction fees. Blockchains are secure at scale, but not fast enough at scale to take over transactions that are routinely performed by our conventional servers and networks. But if the value of the transaction is large enough, split-second speed is not a requirement, and security is paramount, the blockchain may be the better solution. These are the practical criteria that determine when it will or won't make sense to implement smart contracts on blockchain.

As far back as 2016, *The Economist* columnist writing as Schumpeter pointed out several serious concerns with the concept of using blockchain in smart contracts.[27] Schumpeter questions whether a "techno Utopia" concept that involves bypassing human decision-making altogether can ever work in the real world, and points out the perverse legal outcome it may have. "A blockchain is meant to be immutable. Once contracts are set in cryptographic stone, the whole idea is that they cannot be changed, even though updates are usually how software matures … if code is law, so are bugs in the code—and correcting them may itself mean a breach of contract." On the other hand, humans, flawed as they are, are much better equipped to adjust when things inevitably go wrong. This human flexibility greases the functioning of the economy in so many ways and in so many places that we literally could not live well without it. Relentless, unforgiving, immutable code with bugs may leave everyone worse off.

## Industries That Could Be Transformed

### The Blockchain Bandwagon

We have commented throughout this book on how inventions and innovations in the world of money often start on the fringes with the intent to disrupt the status quo, but then get co-opted by the establishment. A new normal is reached, which is not nearly as radical as what the outsiders had in mind, but represents a more evolutionary change to the system.

We can expect a consolidation of the trendsetting players and a standardization of blockchain platforms as the technology matures. Three leading blockchain consortia, the Enterprise Ethereum Alliance (EEA),[28] Hyperledger from the Linux Foundation, which includes Microsoft and Salesforce.com,[29] and R3 (Corda platform) which includes several large financial companies[30] all currently provide established companies with a way to pool their resources and get assistance in figuring out how to benefit from blockchain. And of course, the whole ecosystem of the usual technology vendors is active in this fast-expanding space, eagerly helping their clients with blockchain pilots and experiments.

There is a much longer list of industries and business models that could be transformed by blockchain than we have space for below. In fact, blockchain enthusiasts would probably claim that any and all industries are open to disruption by blockchain. Therefore, we have selected but a few interesting examples based loosely on the magnitude and likelihood of a blockchain-driven industry transformation.

## Asset Registers

The shared-ledger architecture of blockchain could increase the utility of asset registers, which are public by nature, need to be accessed by many parties, and require secure mechanisms for transferring asset ownership. Asset registers are used to register a variety of assets, whether tangible, such as real estate or works of art, or intangible, such as music or software rights.

For example, blockchain is being looked at as a solution for land registration in several parts of the world. It is especially attractive in countries that do not currently have a robust paper-based system. Georgia, Sweden, and the Ukraine have been testing the technology for land management. Transactions in real estate also involve a lot of middlemen, like brokers, government property offices, title companies, escrow companies, inspectors, appraisers, and notaries public, which makes them cumbersome. A property with a digital address that contains all its essential physical, legal, financial, and other attributes can easily be conveyed via blockchain. The blockchain can also keep historical records and make them visible to those who need them.

Instant Property Network, a company backed by blockchain consortium R3, is running a trial to streamline the property buying process. Bloomberg reported in early 2019 that two major UK banks, Barclays and the Royal Bank of Scotland (RBS), were among 40 companies participating.[31]

Malta recently reformed its rental laws so that every rental contract for property in that Mediterranean island nation will be recorded on a blockchain-based distributed ledger. (Malta is a hub for blockchain with an already blockchain-friendly regulatory environment, an educated workforce and EU membership, all contributing to its strength in the applications of this technology.)[32]

Finally, consider the use of blockchain-powered asset registers for precious gems. Everledger,[33] a distributed ledger system based on blockchain, keeps track of property rights and has registered more than one million diamonds to make it easier to check whether they are stolen or originate from a war zone (and are so-called blood diamonds or conflict minerals). By the same token, the precious metals subject to conflict minerals regulations in the U.S. under the Dodd-Frank Act of 2010 can be traced more easily using blockchain.[34]

### Banking

In a recent post[35] by its blockchain group, IBM, an information technology company that has deep relationships with many financial institutions worldwide, highlights the following three use cases for blockchain in banking:

**Verification of identity:** Banks are bound by "know-your-customer" (KYC) laws and regulations to prevent fraud, money laundering, and use of the banking system by undesirable groups or organizations. But banks don't only have to check identity once. They have to constantly check identity across many systems, and update records accordingly while securing sensitive information. Cryptographic protection could do that by sharing a continually updated record with many parties, thus simplifying the administrative process by reducing unnecessary duplication of information and requests. That is something blockchain could do well.

**Speeding up settlements:** While digital payments are more common these days, the process is still too cumbersome in many cases. Participants do not always have the certainty of receiving payment or of being credited for making a payment. Intermediary financial institutions like clearing houses, regulators, and other banks offer certainty, but they also slow down the process. Payments that cross borders and entail currency conversions can take weeks to clear because of the inefficiencies in reconciling records on separate ledgers from intermediaries. This slowdown is even slower than the blockchain process (which, as we mentioned earlier, is still not rapid). Blockchain's inherent design would provide the required certainty because participants can view the same ledger of transactions—one that is updated through consensus and made immutable through cryptography. At the same time, it could process transactions more quickly than the current network of intermediaries now required for settlement. Government regulators also like this because it makes it easier for them to observe money flows.

For example, early in 2019, J.P. Morgan Chase & Co. announced the launch of JPM Coin, a digital coin that will enable the instantaneous transfer of payments between institutional clients using the banks private blockchain. JPM Coin is not a new cryptocoin, but each digital coin represents the equivalent value in U.S. dollars held in designated accounts at J.P. Morgan.[36] It can be thought of more as a token. In June 2019, Bloomberg reported that clients in the United States, Europe, and Japan have been showing interest in the potential of this digital coin to speed up trading of securities like bonds by enabling near-instant delivery of bonds on the blockchain platform.[37]

**Trade finance:** Obtaining financing and completing trades in global markets is often a lengthy and complex process. Traditional practices, in place for centuries, entail steps like issuing letters of credit, factoring, and insuring the parties. These phases unfold slowly, which means it can take from days up to weeks to complete a single transaction as paper documents (even if in PDF form via email) are sent back and forth to be validated and reconciled. All this ties up capital and slows the conduct of business. Blockchain could assure that everyone accesses the same transaction details, thereby increasing trust and efficiency and lowering the total cost of transactions. Late in 2017, IBM announced that it had formed a consortium with eight major global banks to accomplish exactly that. The group will share a platform for domestic and cross-border commerce built on distributed ledger technology (in other words, blockchain).[38]

## Corporate Structure

One of the most radical potential applications of smart contracts is the idea that they could replace the present corporate structure itself. Some "companies" could theoretically exist only as a bundle of smart contracts, effectively constructing entirely virtual firms that are only bound together in blockchain. In their riskiest form, these might have no human oversight. As computer scientist Roman V. Rampolskiy writes, citing legal scholarship, "Anyone can confer legal personhood on a computer system, by putting it in control of a limited liability corporation in the U.S."[39]

It should be mentioned that the first such attempt, The DAO (for decentralized autonomous organization) ended disastrously when the entity was literally hacked to death by criminals who made off with $60 million of its capital.[40]

## Insurance

Another application of the smart contract is in the insurance realm, where the ability to collect and analyze data is paramount. A *parametric contract* is a contract that has an outcome (e.g., payment) based on measurable data. For example, if it rains less than a certain amount on your farm during a certain period, your drought insurance policy pays out. This form of smart contract lends itself to a variety of insurance types. In the case of business insurance, it can enable paying out for the loss of revenue due to certain weather conditions. Such contracts can be automated as long as the data-input side can be engineered—for example, by creating a so-called data oracle that monitors the books of the insured party for actual revenue losses.

Another application can be with car insurance. With real-time sensors mounted in vehicles, insurance contracts could dynamically adjust to where and how the vehicle is operated. For example, crossing an international border could trigger an add-on premium for additional insurance. Or good driving habits could reduce premiums in real-time.

These examples show how blockchain technology can be adapted to measure contract performance and enforce contract provisions.

## Media

Blockchain can afford media organizations a radical degree of freedom which may or may not be desirable, depending on your perspective on media freedom. A distributed magazine published on blockchain could be impervious to lawsuits (like those faced by *Gawker*) because it is impossible to take down. It could, for example, contain a distributed, immutable record of everyone ever alleged to be a corrupt official or a sexual predator, and it would be virtually impossible for those accused to get redress for libel through the court system, or by the intervention of national authorities on their behalf.

## Stock Trading

While stocks are traded in fractions of a second (making it too fast and voluminous to run trading on current versions of blockchain), the behind-the-scenes process of transferring asset ownership can take a few days. Today, after a broker has sent a transaction to the stock exchange, it needs to be matched with the counterparty. Then the transaction is sent to the Central Counterparty Clearing House and is recorded in the Central Securities Depository (CSD). After that, the transaction is sent to the registrar or transfer agent of the initial trade to update their list or shareholders. This is clearly a cumbersome process because of the need for certainty of ownership and security of transfer. Blockchains could be employed as a secure stock transfer mechanism that will speed up transfers. In 2015 the Nasdaq stock exchange started allowing private companies to use blockchains for share management. The Australian Securities Exchange has announced a similar deal to power its post-trade process.[41]

## Supply Chains and Logistics

Earlier, in our paragraph on asset registers, we mentioned the utility of block-chain in this domain—the same applies to the supply chains that move materials along on a nearly constant basis. In the future, supply chains could track the movement of goods automatically with IoT devices, while recording transactions as well as transacting payments through blockchain. The same blockchain technology that was defined by Satoshi with bitcoin to solve the double-spending problem for money can now be used to solve the double-spending or double-ownership problem for any asset, seamlessly transferring asset ownership one way and credits the other way. All participants—including a product manufacturer in one country, the shipping agent, and the customer in another country, as well as customs officials on both ends—could use the same blockchain-based database to track the product.

The next level for supply chain innovation could be using artificial intelligence to manage such networks autonomously, taking over (at least in part) from the current human operators and their enterprise solutions.

Trillions of dollars flow through global supply chains. The impact of re-shaping supply chains with autonomous and cognitive properties on global financial systems and marketplace participants is hard to imagine, but even harder to exaggerate. We could eventually arrive at a future where robots, as autonomous agents with wallets and purchasing power, transact directly with one another. These agents would know the exact condition of the entire network at any point in time, analyze huge quantities of data, and autonomously execute transactions.[42] This future scenario could not be further from our time-honored experience of exchanging money for goods and services, yet it is around the corner.

## Industries That Will Be Impacted First

Some of the most promising potential applications for blockchain are in areas where existing technology has not succeeded, and where blockchain's unique attributes potentially make it the better solution to an existing problem. Conversely, in areas where blockchain is a solution in search of a problem to solve, we can expect much less traction and much more resistance to adoption.

In early 2017, *Business Insider* reported that "nearly every global bank" was exploring blockchain technology. The banks were exploring the technology themselves, forming partnerships, or joining blockchain consortia to pool their resources. Their primary motive was to drive more efficiencies into bank processes, but they were also looking to enhance their business models and to resist encroachment by fintech competitors.[43]

Compared to these earlier days, banks now have a narrower focus to find tangible use cases for blockchain that solve more immediate real-world problems.[44]

CB Insights, a technology market analysis company, provided an analysis of blockchain trends for 2019.[45] They classify trends in terms of two dimensions: *industry adoption* and *market strength*. Trends scoring high on both dimensions are termed Necessary. These trends are seeing widespread industry and customer implementation and adoption and have market applications that are well understood. Interestingly enough, only three trends are currently in this bucket, and they are all related to various parts of the cryptocurrency value chain. (The trends are bitcoin mining, fiat-crypto exchanges, and custody for digital assets.) Those that are low on both are deemed Experimental. Trends that score high on industry adoption but low on market strength are termed Transitory. Here we see ICOs and smart contract platforms. Trends that are low on adoption but high on market strength are called Threatening. Here we see enterprise distributed ledgers in two applications: first, supply chain; and second, clearance and settlement plus bitcoin and privacy coins.

The state of non-cryptocoin blockchain applications according to CB Insights can be summarized as follows:

- No blockchain applications are currently being adopted in any significant markets.
- Smart contracts are starting to be adopted, but the markets for those applications are still nascent and unproven.
- There are significant markets for enterprise-distributed ledger in supply chain, as well as clearance and settlement processes, but full-scale adoption is still some way off for both.

## Challenges That Remain

*MIT Technology Review* started 2019 with an article titled, "In 2019, blockchains will start to become boring."[46] The *Review* predicts that there will be less hype about blockchain in 2019, but that this will also be the year where we will see more useful applications of the technology. The *Review* offers examples like Walmart's blockchain-based food-supply tracker. Although the retail giant has been testing the tracker for years, it has only recently implemented it, ordering suppliers of leafy greens to be ready to join by September 2019. Another smart-contract example predicted for 2019 is the use of smart contracts to track the rights and obligations in legal agreements on a blockchain, and thereby automate payments in cryptocurrency. Established companies in the online legal agreement space such as LegalZoom and Rocket Lawyer are working with respective partners in the blockchain world to bring these services to the market.

Today, there are several ways of transferring your current business applications to blockchain and building brand new applications on blockchain. Companies can do it in-house, or they can contract their usual IT vendors (all main vendors now claim to be blockchain proficient), or enhance their own capabilities by partnering or joining consortia. Not surprisingly, there are dedicated blockchain-solution vendors out there, most often with origins in the cryptocurrency world. One example of such a blockchain pureplay is Essentia,[47] whose CEO was one of the original bitcoin investors. Essentia claims to have developed a blockchain-based operating system that innovators can use to develop new applications. There are now many creators of such blockchain platforms who make various claims to readiness and maturity, and aggressively market use cases for their products.

## Regulatory Roadblocks

The previously mentioned know-your-customer laws and regulations have long governed the conduct of traditional business, particularly in financial services. Individuals need to provide legitimate proof of who they are, and banks have to check passports and drivers' licenses when new accounts are opened. These laws were originally designed to combat terrorism, money laundering, and other crimes. The decentralized nature of blockchains, and the experience with cryptocurrencies being used by criminals, now have governments insisting that these laws also apply to the new world of blockchain and bitcoin.

The new technology has a particular advantage in the area of recordkeeping. Since records are immutable and stored in a decentralized way, it makes these systems much harder to hack, and it has become virtually impossible to erase your steps.[48]

The fact that blockchain never forgets can also be a problem, not an advantage. For example, European data protection laws, in conformance with the *General Data Protection Regulation* (GDPR) that became effective in May 25, 2018, give individuals the right to ask for their data to be removed from servers. Large penalties can be levied for non-compliance with this so-called "right to be forgotten." This conflicts with the immutable nature of blockchains, which is why we are seeing several *mutable* blockchains being developed—for example, one by Accenture.[49] An even more fundamental problem with data privacy is that blockchain has no privacy *by design*, since every record is replicated to every participant for all to see.

In another twist, government sanctions, such as trade embargoes, can impact the use of blockchain applications internationally. For example, under U.S. law (and similar laws from other countries), blockchain-based software may not be sold to or licensed for use by sanctions targets without a special license.

## Technical Tangles

Blockchain technology has a few internal paradoxes or tangles that are still being worked out. As mentioned earlier, information stored by a blockchain is decentralized. That is, it is not maintained by any central authority, but rather is kept by all the system's users. But there is the tangle. In some cases, those users are participating in an open system. For example, bitcoin and Ethereum blockchains are public and open for anyone to inspect. But businesses do not want all their data to be public and they certainly don't want their back-office functions viewable by anyone. That is why enterprise-level blockchains are permissioned, restricting access only to authorized, known users. Examples of such permissioned blockchains are Corda, a finance-focused blockchain developed by the R3 consortium (a blockchain consortium of banks), and Hyperledger Fabric, originally developed by IBM and Digital Asset.[50]

Another issue is data overload. Blockchain architecture calls for *every* participant to have a copy of *all* the data in the chain. This obviously imposes system overhead, as data have to be sent back and forth between all participants all the time. This is much less efficient than having a centralized database that participants query only for the data they need or wish to update. *The Economist* reports[51] that when the Bank of Canada tried to use blockchain for processing domestic payments, it found no benefit over the existing system, which is already very efficient.

Another set of tangles involves glacially slow transaction speed and monstrously high energy consumption. We discussed these in the previous chapter when discussing cryptocurrencies. These are two very significant real-world drawbacks that will have to be solved in order for blockchain-based systems to take over large-scale financial applications that are currently handled well by conventional information technology.

## Other Limitations

There are things that blockchain simply cannot do and cannot be expected to do, despite the hype. In an article in the *Harvard Business Review*, Tucker and Catalini point out that blockchain has an obvious weak spot in the interface between the physical and the digital world.[52] The authors offer the hypothetical example of tracking babies within a hospital so that they don't get mixed up with one another, an obviously important problem to avoid. But how can one be sure which digital record is associated with which baby? This crucial interface between the digital world and the non-digital world still relies on a trusted intermediary (a nurse in this case), to put the correct tag on every baby and ensure it is not removed until the baby has been discharged in the custody of its parents. When you see claims being made about analogous applications of blockchain, for example, to prevent the trafficking of blood diamonds by tracking the movement of each diamond, keep this issue in mind. No blockchain in the world can overcome the incorrect tagging of an item in the physical world, either by mistake or for nefarious purposes. Therefore, trusted intermediaries are still essential for the integrity of the system in all such applications. Besides, diamonds already come with certificates of authenticity, the old-fashioned way to verify trust.

Even if a blockchain is the best architecture for a particular solution, all the usual realities of implementing large new software solutions remain. Blockchain applications are most often advocated for situations in which there are multiple independent organizations or parties involved who do not fully trust one another, like consortia of companies, or networks of consumers, or some combination of both. But having multiple participants in a major software implementation is in itself a major challenge. It may be no easier to achieve consensus on a blockchain than in a meeting room full of humans arguing about contract terms, system governance, or project milestones!

The first step to implementation is to get consensus on the exact standard to use. This is non-trivial, as potential winners and losers of different standard decisions can fight over them for a long time. Assuming that everyone has agreed on the new standard, the governance issue, who will be in charge, is the next to resolve. Then there are all the typical hardships of contracting and building a system across organizational boundaries, which are compounded by the more unproven technologies the systems contains. Anyone who has been part of or close to a major new IT system implementation in their place of business will appreciate that nothing happens overnight, milestones are often missed, budgets are often exceeded, and there are multiple bugs to be worked out before the promised land is reached. Therefore, any predictions of blockchains scaling up to replace functioning existing systems in the short-term need to be taken with a big pinch of salt.

Lastly, there is good old-fashioned resistance to any major change by humans and their institutions. Where good processes and systems already exist, skepticism of the benefits of change and an attitude of "If it isn't broken, don't fix it" will most often prevail. Many centralized systems are serving us efficiently and with great accuracy and integrity, and are much easier to use than decentralized new blockchain systems.

## Conclusion: Between Promise and Skepticism

At the time of writing, Crunchbase (a provider of business intelligence and tracker of industry investments) has 746 blockchain startups in its databases with a total funding of $3.5 billion.[53] Interestingly, the average founded date for these blockchain startups is August 2016. This coincides with the media attention to blockchain, which reached its fever pitch across 2016 and 2017, only to fall back in volume and get a little more skeptical after the big cryptocoin crash of 2018.

An article in January 2019 by McKinsey & Company, a consultancy, expressed a remarkable degree of skepticism in blockchain's future. The authors make the point that blockchain has not yet become the game changer it was expected to be, and that a big reason for that is that it has often been an overcomplicated solution to the problems it was supposed to solve. It is not for lack of enthusiasm or effort— over 100 blockchain use cases in industries from financial services to healthcare and the arts have been identified.

What is not in doubt is that a lot of work is currently being done on blockchain. Evidence of this can be seen in the booming demand for engineers with blockchain experience together with strong salaries, as reported for the year 2018 by the IEEE.[54] In addition to high levels of venture capital investment in startups, many large and established companies have invested millions in the technology already. For example, IBM has invested more than $200 million in a blockchain-powered data-sharing solution for the IoT. (It is generally believed that blockchain holds great promise for securing the IoT.) According to McKinsey, the financial industry spends around $1.7 billion annually on experimentation. While there is still the sense that blockchain could be a game changer, doubts are setting in because so much has been spent and so little of true substance achieved. Most of the many use cases are still only in the idea phase. Others are in development but with no major output. "The bottom line is that despite billions of dollars of investment, and nearly as many headlines, evidence for a practical scalable use for blockchain is thin on the ground."[55]

Yet, even an ultimate establishment player like the Rockefeller family is moving into cryptocurrencies. In a mix of old and new money, the Rockefeller venture-capital arm Venrock is partnering with the cryptocurrency investor group CoinFund to help entrepreneurs launch blockchain-based businesses. Venrock said it is not looking for a short-term payback, but "making long-term investments to nurture blockchain technology."[56] That may well be the most pragmatic strategy with this technology.

The Gartner Hype Cycle[57] is a useful framework to describe the roller-coaster ride that new technologies—even the ultimately successful ones—typically go through. First, there is some *innovation trigger*, maybe an early proof of concept that captures the imagination and media attention, even though no commercial viability has been proven yet. A frenzy of publicity results in expectations getting overinflated—this is the *peak of inflated expectations*. Then interest wanes as experiments and early attempts at implementations disappoint. There is a shakeout as unsuccessful early adopters drop out. This point is called the *trough of disillusionment*. Persistent survivors keep working on the technology though, and later generation products succeed, with the one successful generation building on the next, the so-called *slope of enlightenment*. Once mainstream adoption takes off and the viability of the technology is generally proven, the *plateau of productivity* is reached.

So where would you think blockchain is on this Gartner Hype Cycle right now? If you guessed that it has passed the peak of inflated expectations and is now on its way down to the trough of disillusionment, you guessed right. That is where Gartner placed blockchain in August 2018 and it is still there. But the question is, will enlightenment and productivity follow? The answer may be yes. Gartner sees blockchain as one of several emerging technologies enabling digitalized ecosystems. In a press release, Mike J. Walker, research vice president at Gartner was quoted as saying, "Blockchain and IoT platforms have crossed the peak by now, and we believe that they will reach maturity in the next five to 10 years."[58]

And that pretty much describes where we are now. Blockchain is a technology that could potentially solve problems for us that are not well-addressed by conventional information technology. On the other hand, blockchain comes with some very real drawbacks of its own. To implement blockchain solutions at scale in the world's financial systems will be disruptive in terms of change, and costly in terms of the technology. Clear eyes are now seeing that. So we are probably looking at a short- to medium-term where some niche applications of blockchain succeed in areas where blockchain has unique benefits, and much noise but little traction in most other areas. Where the benefits of blockchain are not compelling and clear cut, the status quo is likely to prevail. As the old saying in boxing goes, "If you want to be the champion, you have to beat the champion."

# Chapter 8
# The Promises and Perils of a Cashless Realm

*Hence the Ident-I-Eeze. This encoded every single piece of information about you, your body and your life into one all-purpose machine-readable card that you could then carry around in your wallet, and it therefore represented technology's greatest triumph to date over both itself and plain common sense.*

—Douglas Adams, Mostly Harmless *in The Ultimate Hitchhiker's Guide to the Galaxy series*[1]

## The Annoyance of Cash

Have you recently stood at a checkout line behind a person who insisted on paying with cash? Maybe you were in a hurry and you got slightly annoyed because of how much longer it took for that payment transaction to be completed. First, the person dug around for the right mix of notes in his wallet, and maybe even picked out a selection of coins. Then, he had to hand it over to the cashier who had to carefully count the cash, and place it in the right slots in the cash register tray. Maybe the cashier did not have the correct change, and she asked the customer for smaller notes, or she had to ask another cashier for change. Then the cashier had to carefully count out the correct change, and the customer spent time sorting and putting away the notes and coins in his wallet.

Then you stepped forward and swiped or touched your credit card, or touched your mobile phone, and the transaction was done. You breezed through and felt slightly superior. If you are a slightly distrustful person, and particularly if the item involved some large bills, you may have wondered why the previous customer paid for a large purchase with hundreds of dollars of cash. You may have even silently suspected him of running a cash-intensive business and spending cash income he did not declare for income tax purposes.

Then there are, of course, the occasional unpleasant surprises, when we find that only cash is accepted as payment. The store might have a problem with its internet connectivity or some other communication issue that disables their connection to the big card networks. Handwritten "cash only" signs may appear at the door or above the cash registers. This is really inconvenient because many of us don't carry around much cash these days.

https://doi.org/10.1515/9781547401116-008

## Are These the Last Days of Cash?

According to a recent estimate by McKinsey, a global consultancy, cards and mobile payments are gradually replacing cash across the globe, with cash as a share of total payments declining from 92 percent in 2006 to 84 percent in 2016.

Recent surveys of Americans confirm the trend of people carrying less and less cash. In a 2017 U.S. Bank survey, almost half (47 percent) of survey participants said they prefer paying with digital apps over cash. The same survey found that consumers are carrying less cash with them—three-quarters said they carry less than $50 when they go out, and half less than $20. But in contrast, lower-income adults were four times as likely as higher-income adults to make most of their payments in cash.[2] A 2018 survey by Pew Research found that adults with incomes over $75,000 per year are more than twice as likely as those making less than $30,000 a year to report not having used cash to pay for their purchases in a typical week. African Americans were much more likely to rely on cash for all or most of their purchases at 34 percent, compared to 15 percent of whites and 17 percent of Hispanics.[3]

This rich/poor divide on cash usage is even greater between countries: While consumers in wealthier countries generally use less cash in favor of electronic payments, the majority of people still live in countries where 90 percent or more transactions are done in cash.[4]

There are some signs that we may be the last generation that uses cash. Researchers predict that Swedish retailers could stop accepting cash as soon as 2023. Across the globe in China, mobile payments are crowding out cash transactions, having more than doubled in 2016 to over $5 trillion.[5] (The Chinese mobile payment market is dominated by Alipay and WeChat Pay.) The ubiquity of smartphones and the convenience of paying and receiving payments electronically are driving this trend.

In the United States, restaurant chains like Sweetgreen and even some food truck chains like Señor Sisig are going cashless. (See Figure 8.1, licensed under Creative Commons attribution) The convenience and safety of not having to handle cash while preparing food have clear benefits for a food truck operator.

What does the future hold? Are all countries on an inevitable journey to becoming cashless societies, with Sweden leading the way? Not so fast. While Sweden may be the farthest along to a cashless world, it may also be an outlier. To repurpose the old saying, reports of the demise of cash are greatly exaggerated. An extensive study[6] by two Austrian Central Bank economists published in 2017 showed that while currency in circulation as a share of GDP fell over the last 150 years, that decline has not been very large, given the evolution in

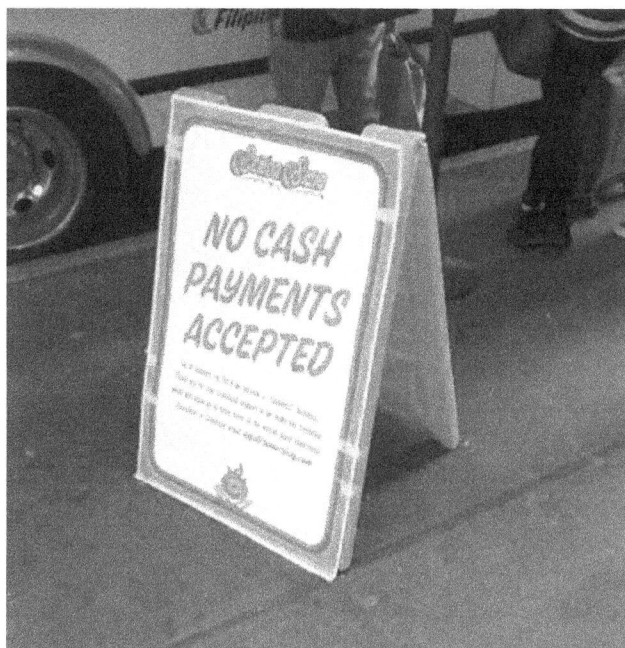

**Figure 8.1:** Cashless sign in front of a Señor Sisig food truck (Fig. Note 8.1).

payment technologies over the same period. They also found that the circulation of cash in many economies has actually *increased* over the last decade.

In the United States, currency demand started rising again after the 1980s. In 2018, Tim Sablik of the Federal Reserve Bank of Richmond published a paper that showed how dollars in circulation as a share of U.S. GDP have nearly doubled from 5 percent to 9 percent over the last decade.[7] This is despite the introduction and growth of new payment technologies, like mobile, over this period. According to the 2016 Survey of Consumer Payment Choice conducted by the Federal Reserve System and cited in this paper, "consumers used cash in 27 percent of transactions in a typical month in 2017, making cash the second most popular payment option after debit cards. That share has held fairly constant since 2008 when the survey began."

So cash is far from dead. How much is still around? According to Sablik,[8] there is $1.6 trillion in U.S. currency in circulation today, about $4,800 for every person in the United States. This seems like a lot, since most of us don't carry around that amount of cash, nor do most of us have thousands of dollars stashed in a safe at home. This poses three questions: Who has the cash, how is it used, and where is all this cash?

Cash is a very important means of payment for low-income households (those earning below $35,000 per year). That means that any program to phase out cash should be carefully designed not to hurt the poor.

Cash is preferred and heavily used by most everyone in small person-to-person transactions, like buying an item at a garage sale or paying a babysitter for a few hours of childcare. In fact, some stores have a minimum amount (such as $10) for credit card transactions. According to the Survey of Consumer Payment Choice, while cash was used in only 8 percent of payments of purchases over $100, it was used in more than half of payments for less than $10.

Consumers still rate cash highly for convenience, cost, and acceptance as a payment medium, but they give it a low rating for record keeping and security. (The latter includes not only the risk of being robbed, but also of being swindled.) Credit cards have desirable features that address these accounting and security concerns. When buying something on a credit card, one enjoys several anti-fraud protections that provide recourse against the vendor after the fact. That's why most people prefer to buy high-value items such as a television set with a credit card. It also explains the growing popularity of online shopping, which by definition is cashless, typically requiring a credit card.

With consumers primarily using cash for small purchases, one would expect that they would not carry much cash on them. The respondents to the aforementioned Fed survey reported that they kept an average of $219 in cash on their person or property. That is still far short of the $4,800 per person previously mentioned. Who, then, holds the bulk of the rest of that money, and for what purpose?

Remember what money is. Beyond being a *unit of account*, it is a *means of exchange*, and we have just seen for what kinds of exchange cash is preferred. Importantly, however, money is also a *store of value*. Maybe people are hoarding cash for this last purpose, the proverbial "stuffing it under the mattress" use of cash? Evidence for this hypothesis may be found in a surprising fact concerning U.S. currency in 2017: For the first time, the number of $100 bills in circulation exceeded the number of $1 bills.[9] What could explain that? With low inflation and still low interest rates, the opportunity cost of keeping cash is low. But if you are going to be holding thousands of dollars in cash, you want to keep it in large denominations. For U.S. currency, that means the $100 bill—or the slang term, "Benjamin," carrying the image of America's famed inventor.

It is also believed that most of the demand for $100 bills comes from outside the United States, driven by the U.S. dollar's status as a safe asset and its nearly universal acceptability for payment. An analysis[10] by another Fed economist, Ruth Judson, concluded that a large amount of U.S. currency was held abroad in $100 bills. But Judson's model also estimates the average amount of cash held by U.S. residents to be around $1,000, which is almost five times the consumer survey estimate. She believes the discrepancy is explained by under-reporting that ignores the needs of the underground economy, where individuals keep large amounts of cash for illicit activities or at the very least to avoid paying taxes.

## The Promise of a Cashless Society

As we have pointed out several times in this book, money keeps evolving to serve the needs of society. Therefore, as society goes digital, money goes digital.

This is just the last step in the continuing evolution of money from the concrete to the abstract. We could argue that money is one of humanity's most important abstractions, on par with mathematics and writing. In the course of human history, we've gone from paying with grain and cattle, to species money made of precious metals, to fiat money made of paper and cheap metals. It was only in 1971 that we finally said goodbye to the gold standard. This means we have been relying on fiat money for less than fifty years.

Will we now take the final step to abstraction and dispense with any physical manifestation of money? If there are good reasons for it, maybe we should. Let's therefore look at some of the advantages of a cashless society.

## The Cost of Cash

High-denomination notes like $100 bills are very attractive to counterfeiters. This requires the treasury to spend more on anti-counterfeiting measures in a never-ending arms race between governments that issue currency and those who would profit from counterfeiting the currency. That is why the U.S. $100 bill (the largest U.S. denomination issued today) is the most expensive U.S. bill to print. It costs the Department of the Treasury (part of the U.S. Federal Reserve System) 14.2 cents to print each $100 note, as compared to about 11.5 cents for the denominations between $5 and $50. The $1 bill is cheapest to print, at only 5.5 cents. To pay for all this, the U.S. Treasury's 2019 currency operation budget is just under $1 billion dollars.[11] Coin in circulation is provided by the U.S. Mint through a separate mechanism.

A government's printing and minting costs are offset by *seigniorage,* the unique form of profit that the issuer of a currency is privileged to collect. Every dollar bill printed and put in circulation makes the government a profit equal to the bill's face-value less its production cost. Of course, some of the new bills replace old bills that are taken out of circulation and destroyed. Every year, the seigniorage will equal the net increase in cash in circulation.

Ironically, given their chartered role as depository institutions, banks do not like cash, because it is a significant cost component for them. For banks, cash operations include cash transportation, sorting, insurance, and holding costs. McKinsey estimates that cash-related operational costs vary between 5 and 10 percent of total bank costs, with mature markets being on the lower end of that spectrum and emerging markets being on the higher end.[12]

Similarly, for retailers, the cost of cash handling can range from 4.7 percent to over 15 percent depending on the retail segment, according to a recent analyst report.[13] Some businesses are more cash intensive than others. The nature of the retail operation determines how often staff has to open cash drawers, close drawers, perform change requests, and handle the pickup of cash during shifts because of too many bills or bills of large denominations accumulating in drawers. Then there is the level of outright theft of cash on the front-end by staff or customers, the fees paid to cash in transit companies, and, of course, bank fees. The costs of managers supervising such activities are also not easy to estimate.

It's not only governments and business that have cash-handling costs. As consumers we pay for access to cash, as we often discover when we are charged fees to make withdrawals at ATMs not in our banking networks. Among individuals, the unbanked have the highest need for cash but also incur the highest costs to access it. According to one estimate, the unbanked in the United States pay four times more in fees to access their money than those with bank accounts, and $4 higher fees per month for cash access on average than those with formal financial services.[14]

Cash, of course, also feeds any "informal" or underground activities. It is well known that there is a substantial underground economy in all countries, even developed countries. A study[15] of the size of the underground economy in the United States estimated that 18 to 23 percent of total reportable income in 2009 was not reported to the Internal Revenue Service. That equals a tax gap in the range of $390 billion to $540 billion. It is believed that much of this lost tax revenue could be clawed back by the government in a cashless economy.

But eradicating the cash used in the underground economy is hard to do. This is a lesson India learned the hard way a few years ago. One evening in November 2016, Prime Minister Narendra Modi made the surprise announcement that the 500 rupee and 1,000 rupee (about $14 U.S.) banknotes would be withdrawn overnight as part of a crackdown on corruption and illicit money hoarding. Banks and ATMs were to be closed the next day. New 500 and

2,000 rupee notes would be issued, and people were given 50 days to exchange their old notes for new, before they would cease to be legal tender.[16]

This drastic measure was supposed to target the rich, who would presumably be stuck with trunks full of illicit money that they could not exchange. Yet, less than a year later, the *Economist* reported that 99 percent (15 trillion rupees) of the old bills were exchanged and accounted for. Presumably, the hoarders and criminals all found ways to legally exchange their cash too. There was no windfall to the Indian government.[17] If anything, the forced bill exchange imposed real hardships on the poor, who had to stand in very long lines for days to exchange their cash while their small businesses suffered. The stress reportedly drove several people to commit suicide. And there was a huge cash shortage, which was a further drag to the economy—to keep the announcement secret, the Indian government had not printed the new bills in advance, and the printing presses took months to catch up with the demand for cash.[18]

## Hard to Say Goodbye

To say that only criminals and tax dodgers like cash would be a gross misstatement and an injustice to the many good people who like using cash for various reasons. After all, the Tooth Fairy almost exclusively makes her payouts in cash. Fundraising groups like the Girl Scouts, the Salvation Army, or your local fire department all collect donations in cash, as do most homeless people. Cash remains the payment medium of choice for many person-to-person transactions, such as children's allowances, contributions to pizza parties, and so on. Generally, the prevalence of cash transactions is centered in the face-to-face consumer economy rather than in business-to-business transactions.

A recent research report by the payments industry journal *PYMNTS* predicts that a full 11.2 percent of the U.S. GDP will still be conducted in cash by 2021, down only a little from 12.6 percent in 2016.[19] While the decline in cash usage is perceptible, it is slow, and cash will retain a big share of our payments in the next few years at least. The same report estimates that a total of $2.36 trillion dollars of cash was withdrawn at U.S. financial institutions in 2016, $700.5 billion dollars of cash at ATMs, and $1,659.9 billion over the counter. That's a whole lot of cash! For comparison, online sales generated only about $360 billion in 2016, and that number is projected to grow to just $638 billion by 2022, according to the report.

What happens if the government actively promotes a cashless society? Earlier we mentioned a bill exchange program in India; that was only part of a larger plan to push the country toward electronic payments. In November 2016, the government of India announced a controversial "demonitization" program called *Cashless India*.[20] The purpose was to drastically shrink the size of the underground or black-market economy in India by driving people to electronic payment methods instead of cash. The program has been met with mixed success. While a target of 25 billion digital transactions was set for 2017 to 2018, only about 16 billion transactions were achieved across all digital payment methods. More than 90 percent of transactions in India still rely on cash. India simply has not built up the digital infrastructure yet to facilitate the total transition, and the informal sector—comprised of a majority of very small stores—remains large.[21]

However, it is estimated that the total cash in circulation in India is one sixth lower than it would have been without the demonitization program. And real progress has been in payment systems innovation. The unified payment interface (UPI) allows easy payments between smartphone owners and is supported by more than 140 Indian banks. Other innovations are in work. Some commentators say that India could become a model for the world. With a population of 1.3 billion, a tenfold increase in digital transactions will be a significant development not just for India but also for the world economy.[22]

Will the whole world go in this same direction? Perhaps so. Part of our enduring affinity for cash is no doubt generational, and simply force of habit. As older generations such as the baby boomers pass, younger generations like the millennials, who are much more comfortable with all-electronic money, will lead us into the cashless future. But even analysts who are bullish about this future caution that it may be more of a "less-cash" future[23] than a 100 percent cashless future. Cash is expected to retain some of its uses, even if these are increasingly niche.

## The Perils of a Cashless Society

In our modern monetary system, cash is gradually becoming less important. There is a philosophical element to this change, along with practical reasons. We have transitioned to seeing money as a method of account (particularly an electronic account) rather than as a physical object we exchange for goods and services.

Even so, there are good reasons we still see the substantial usage of cash we previously outlined. Cash retains its attraction, and it is not only sentimental or a force of habit. For example, cash is robust in a very physical sense of the word. A dollar in your pocket stays a dollar even if you jump into a lake—try that with your mobile phone—or if the power or network goes out. Cash is also safe from hackers and is friendly to the indigent, uneducated, and non-tech-savvy people, as no special hardware or software is required to handle it. It requires only the most rudimentary arithmetic skills because it can physically be counted to see how much you have left after each purchase.

What might we lose if we lose our cash? Saying farewell to cash altogether may mean that we forego very important advantages of cash that we do not think about enough. Indeed, cash offers unique advantages over any electronic form of money. Let's look at a few of the most important.

## Legal Rights

With cash, possession is almost 100 percent of the law. A $20 or other denomination bill is by law a negotiable instrument, which means that whoever holds it has full rights to it—previous holders have no claim. This seemingly arcane legal principle has real-life implications. If someone pays for goods with stolen cash, the person from whom this cash was stolen has no recourse against the vendor who accepted the cash in good faith for his goods. The victim's only recourse is against the thief. Contrast this with the situation where someone sells a stolen car. In this case, the victim of the theft has recourse against the person who bought the stolen car, even if it were bought in good faith. The unfortunate purchaser may lose both the car and the money she paid for it.

These are old legal rules that societies have settled on to balance the sometimes conflicting goals of fairness and certainty in different situations. Cash provides a certainty and finality to our transactions that is very necessary to grease the wheels of the economy by guaranteeing anonymous, arms-length transactions.

## Equity and Inclusion

CNN recently reported on the growing trend for retail businesses to insist on either credit card or smartphone payments instead of cash. Fast food restaurant owners mention speed, efficiency, and safety as the main advantages of going cashless. By speed and efficiency they mean faster-moving checkout lines, and by safety, they mean a lesser chance of their restaurants getting robbed. But because low-income consumers are so much more reliant on cash, local politicians across the United States are considering banning the no-cash-accepted practices. For example, New York City Council member Ritchie Torres says that 25 percent of New Yorkers are underbanked and that there continues to be barriers for lower-income people to access credit in the poorest parts of New York City. He also says cashless policies have a disparate impact on communities of color such as African Americans and Latinos. Torres introduced a bill late in 2018 that would ban cashless business practices and levy fines for offenses. Proponents of cashless payments point to the relative ease with which prepaid cards may be purposed by those who don't have credit or debit cards.[24] However, such prepaid cards all come with fees, unlike cash, which carries no fees.

The tension is between those who favor retail and financial innovation and those who want to ensure access to the marketplace for everyone. As this debate is being conducted in many jurisdictions, the *Wall Street Journal* reported that Philadelphia became the first major U.S. city to ban cashless stores. At the state level, Massachusetts is so far the only state that mandates that all retailers accept cash.[25]

## Privacy

Cash is private and not associated with any person. Our right to privacy is the fundamental right we have to decide how much we reveal about ourselves and our actions, when, and to whom. As humans and citizens of a free society, we want to retain some rights as to what governments, corporations, and other individuals know about us. Everything that passes through electronic bank accounts like checking, savings, and credit card accounts is easily discoverable by the government. Every transaction on any particular account is known to the financial services company that provides you with that convenience. Your shopping patterns are constantly being monitored by retailers online and by brick-and-mortar stores. The reason your grocery store gives you discounts for using your loyalty card is so they can track all your purchase patterns. Your online browsing patterns are being monitored by Google and other internet advertisers all the time.

It is maybe true that terrorists, drug smugglers, and other criminals prefer cash, but so do babysitters, waiters, and dog walkers. The assertion that no one engaged in legal activities should fear a cashless society is ill-informed or downright disingenuous. You might as well say, "Well, if you have nothing to hide, then you won't mind the police coming over to your house at any time, just to look around a bit, will you?" Debates on such fundamental freedoms have been held many times in the history of free societies, in constitutional assemblies and courts of law, in law school classes, and in the press. Just because criminals abuse their rights does not mean that we should take everyone else's rights away. This is a core principle that underpins free societies. In practice it means, for example, that we would rather let a certain percentage of criminals go free than to lock up any innocent people.

There are no really new questions of principle around privacy and a cashless world. Once we find that we still agree on the right to, and need for, privacy in a cashless society, we should proceed to solve the technical and legal problems of how to give effect to that principle. This is, of course, easier said than done.

Aside from possibly cryptocoin, cash is the only truly anonymous form of money and the last vestige of monetary privacy we have left. As mentioned earlier, all electronic transactions are recorded and can be easily tracked by many commercial interests as well as by governments. Cryptocoin evangelists therefore would like to see a future in which cryptocoin takes over cash as a fully electronic but also anonymous payment method. We have extensively commented on the pros and cons of cryptocoin in Chapter 6.[26] We will only add here that cryptocoin is even more dependent on the modern telecommunications and power infrastructure than money in the conventional financial system.

## Freedom

Closely related to privacy is the element of freedom. To understand the connection between cash and freedom, let's look at a couple of scenarios. First, let's say a notorious terrorist is running from the police, who are hot on his heels as he sprints through narrow streets in the capital city. While running, he tosses his mobile phone and wallet into the river to avoid being tracked. Breathless and desperate to avoid the ubiquitous street cameras with instant facial identification, he manages to sneak into a wooded area bordering the city. For days, he hides out there while drinking water from a small stream. He grows a beard and finds a discarded pair of sunglasses to disguise himself. Now famished, the fugitive ventures into the city late one night, where he pickpockets an inebriated man coming out of a bar. He hopes it will take his victim until the next morning to discover the theft and report his wallet stolen.

Elated, the hungry fugitive takes the cashless payment card out of the wallet, and swipes it to buy a large hot dog from a street vendor who barely glances at him. Finally satiated, he realizes that his only hope is to get out of town quickly. He walks to the station, keeping his head down as much as possible. At a ticket kiosk, he selects his destination. The prospect of escaping is now real and a slight smile is coming to his face. He taps the payment card to pay for the ticket. But the instant he does that, the face-recognition camera built into the ticket kiosk identifies a mismatch with the true owner of the payment card, and an earsplitting alarm goes off. Drones appear out of nowhere to incapacitate the fugitive, who is arrested on the spot and dragged away by police.

If you believe the premise of this story—that it is about a notorious runaway terrorist—you may be applauding the way technology makes police work easier, and how it is almost impossible for a fugitive to sustain himself while on the lam in a cashless society.

But what if this story isn't about a terrorist on the run? What if the story is about you, who had the misfortune of growing up in an authoritarian society? Maybe you got yourself in big trouble by merely writing a mildly critical poem about the dear leader. When friends saw your satirical poem, some laughed, but others who turned out to be collaborators of the state security organization reported you. Without due process, the regime immediately declared you to be a terrorist and enemy of the state. You knew that meant at least twenty years of hard labor in a gulag, or worse. That's why you ran.

How do you feel now about the power that a cashless society could give a future government over you?

If you have concerns, you are not alone, and you are not the first. Such concerns predate our modern electronic society by two thousand years (at least). Relating his famous first-century AD apocalyptic vision about a demonic beast that would rule the earth in its final years, controlling people by controlling their commerce, John of Patmos wrote:

> Also it causes all, both small and great, both rich and poor, both free and slave, to be marked on the right hand or the forehead, so that no one can buy or sell who does not have the mark, that is, the name of the beast or the number of its name.[27]

While it was previously hard to imagine exactly how such a draconian scheme would be pulled off in practice, the technology for doing so is readily available today. Microchips can be implanted under the skin and swiped over scanners. NPR recently reported that thousands of Swedes are having microchips the size of a grain of rice implanted in their hands so they can simply swipe their hands to get access to office buildings and gyms, and can carry their emergency contact details as well as railway tickets with them electronically.[28] The European Union's General Data Privacy Regulation (GDPR), which went into effect in May 2018, may or may not reassure people that it is safe to adopt such technologies.[29]

## Corporate Power

Cash may be printed or minted under the control of a central government-owned bank, but once it is distributed to the population, the government effectively loses control over who holds it and for what purposes it is used. That is why cash is a form of freedom from the government. Similarly, cash also means freedom from financial intermediaries and other corporate interests. But any all-digital currency or payment system effectively only moves (i.e., is transferred or used as payment) and retains money at the pleasure of those who may then exercise electronic control over it.

What if you signed a smart contract with your life insurer that you would adopt a healthier lifestyle in return for a major discount on your insurance? What if it is a condition of that agreement that you don't smoke, drink, or eat junk food anymore? Then, the moment you try to make an electronic payment for a cheeseburger with fries and a beer, the transaction is flagged, the payment is declined, and your mere attempt to buy that forbidden meal is logged as a black mark against your credit record. This Orwellian scenario obviously cannot happen as long as there is cash, but when all the cash is gone, there is nothing to stop corporations from acting as in this example, or worse.

A related concern is that a few mega-financial institutions may corner the market on electronic payments and start to charge monopoly-level transaction fees once they gain that power.

## Cyber Attacks

Another reason for keeping cash as a payment option is the threat of cyber-crime against not only individuals but also the financial institutions on which they rely. The financial services industry is the prime target of cyber attacks. It is estimated that financial services firms are attacked 300 times more frequently than companies in other industries. While the typical American company suffers 4 million cyber attacks per year, the typical financial services firm is attacked one billion times a year. Banks lost $16.8 billion to cybercriminals in 2017.[30] This does harm to more than just banks in the abstract; every attack against a bank is also an attack against its customers. Banks spend billions of dollars to fortify their technology infrastructure against such attacks, and they also have to insure themselves against such liabilities. The technology and insurance costs get passed on to customers by way of higher fees and higher interest rate spreads (as banks need to stay in business). Furthermore, bank customers can suffer from the inconvenience and privacy invasion associated with these attacks.

It is not just retail and commercial banks that are under attack. Central banks are being attacked too. The whole banking infrastructure is a target. In 2019 Trend Micro, an IT security company, reported that over the past three years, banks suffered $87 million in combined losses from attacks that compromised their SWIFT (Society for Worldwide Interbank Financial Telecommunication) infrastructures.[31] And of course, we as bank customers are under constant attack too. We have all been cautioned not to fall victim to phishing and other fraudulent schemes that trick us into giving away our contact and security details to cyber criminals. Simply look in your email spam folder to see the frequency of such attacks.

In early 2019, U.S. Federal Reserve Chair Jerome Powell and Japan's central bank chief Haruhiko Kuroda declared that cyber attacks are currently the biggest risk for financial institutions. But it's not just criminals who are attacking the financial industry. Reuters recently reported that an increasing share of attacks are politically motivated and state-sponsored.[32] Cyber attacks are cost-effective and plausibly deniable methods of asymmetrical warfare that are attractive to terrorists and state actors alike.

It is a safe bet that the frequency and intensity of these attacks will only increase, and that in a cashless society, attacks executed by hostile states may become a highly cost-efficient act of war, with the purpose of crippling the economies of their adversaries at a much lower cost than using conventional weapons of war. Such attacks could not only result in the temporary disablement of financial systems, but could permanently destroy financial data. What happens when the bank or investment company totally forgets that you ever had $100,000 in your account with it? What happens when even the backup records are corrupted? Not having any cash to fall back on when the financial system is down will not only greatly increase society's vulnerability to such attacks, but may also be an open invitation to more frequent and ambitious attacks from malign private and state actors. Such attacks could pose existential risks to the global financial system as we know it. We cannot rush toward a cashless society without fully addressing these vulnerabilities.

## What's in Your Doomsday Wallet?

But it is not only malicious acts by cyber criminals or hostile governments that should concern us. Going to a completely cashless society means that we are also putting our full trust in the reliability of our electricity supply and of our telecommunications infrastructure. It means that as individuals, we are fully reliant on whatever device we carry with us which serves as our digital wallet, or on whatever biometric identification system eventually obviates the need to carry a device of any kind. Sooner or later, every one of us will lose or break our mobile phone or wallet. That is a constant personal risk each of us will have to bear in a cashless society, and not hard to understand.

Let us not forget that our electronic devices will only keep working while the electrical supply is on or until their batteries run out. Your cash does not disappear out of your physical wallet when the lights go out—the bills and coins stay in your pocket. But your entire electronic wallet disappears when the phone battery runs out, or the bank servers are down, or the internet goes down.

So let's consider the more systemic risks to entire societies associated with a breakdown in our electrical and communication infrastructure. What happens when the power goes down?

On August 14, 2003, shortly after 2pm Eastern Daylight Time, a high-voltage power line in Ohio brushed against a tree branch and shut down. This type of electrical fault occurs all the time, but what happened next on that fateful afternoon was far from routine. Additional faults, overloaded infrastructure, and human error led to a cascade of faults that took down the entire power grid across the northeastern part of North America. The massive blackout stretched across southeastern Canada, including the province of Ontario, and eight northeastern U.S. states, including New York. Over 50 million people were without power for two days. Eleven deaths were attributed to this incident and the economic cost was estimated at $6 billion.

One of your authors lived through that event in Toronto, Ontario, and can offer a firsthand account of what happened. It was an early Wednesday afternoon on a bright late-summer day. Most people were at work when the power went off abruptly. During the first few minutes of the blackout, everyone wondered whether it was local or more widespread, and whether the power would be restored soon. Emergency lights came on in offices and commercial buildings, and backup power kept the internet working for a while. There was a certain nervousness, as this event came only two years after the September 11, 2001 terrorist attacks. It didn't take long for people to find out on the internet that it was a widespread power outage and that fortunately, no foul play was involved.

At around mid-afternoon, people started streaming out of office buildings and looking for ways to get home. The Toronto subway system and streetcars were not operational. Traffic lights were out, and there were traffic jams everywhere. Ordinary citizens stepped in to direct traffic at intersections. Many people walked home. Some could not. In New York City, photographs taken during the event show throngs of people walking across the Brooklyn Bridge to leave the city, and stranded commuters sleeping on the steps of the Central Post Office.[33]

Mobile phones kept working for a while after the power went out, but it was hard to get through to anyone because the high volume of attempted calls swamped the system. Cell phone tower battery back-ups only kept the wireless system running for a while before it went down later that afternoon. Mobile phones were useless even before they ran out of power.

It was very hard to get gasoline for your car, as gas station pumps all needed electricity. Even if a gas station had a back-up generator for the pumps, you needed cash on hand to buy gasoline. All electronic points of sale were inoperative for more than a day. Cash was king again, but many people did not have the cash they needed. ATMs were offline and banks were closed. There was no way to get cash unless you already had it or could get it from someone else who had it.

The moral of the story is clear. There are still times when only cash will do. The Great Northeast Blackout of 2003 demonstrated how fragile our technological society is, and how we are one major blackout or other catastrophe away from being back in the eighteenth or nineteenth century. But it will even be worse for us than our ancestors, because we are not used to operating this way. The big blackout taught your author to always keep an envelope marked "emergency cash" with a few $20 bills in it. (Few will accept $100 bills in such a situation.)

### What Happens When the Big One Comes?

While there were several inquiries into the 2003 blackout and numerous new measures were adopted to make the power grid more reliable, there is no guarantee that there will not be any major blackouts in future.

Wind, hurricanes, and winter storms often result in local or regional power blackouts. And there is always the possibility of natural disasters with an even larger effect on modern electronics. Giant solar magnetic storms may sound like something from science fiction, but they are real and have the potential to wreak havoc on our technologically driven society. The largest magnetic storm ever recorded (consider that we did not have the equipment to record earlier events) struck the earth in 1859. It is called the Carrington Event. The telecommunications infrastructure at the time comprised only of telegraph networks. Telegraph systems failed across North America and Europe and telegraph operators got electric shocks from the equipment, as the sparks literally flew.[34] (This is all the more notable because unlike all modern electronics, these old telegraph systems contained no semiconductors, which are much more vulnerable to such voltage spikes.)

We know with certainty that rare but massive solar super storms will happen from time to time. We know that our power and communications infrastructure is not only highly vulnerable to them, but will also take a long time to repair after a damaging event. It is estimated that another storm of the magnitude of the Carrington Event could result in planet-wide economic costs in the trillions of dollars, and a recovery time of upward of four years, as critical infrastructures like large power transformers would have to be rebuilt and replaced. A much smaller event in March 1989 took down the Hydro-Quebec power grid in eastern Canada, with a resulting loss of electricity to 6 million people for up to nine hours. And in 2012, we dodged a bullet when the earth barely missed being hit with a sizable magnetic superstorm on par with the Carrington Event.[35]

In the previous section, we discussed cyber attacks. It is, of course, entirely possible that our power grids could be taken down by cyber attacks on the energy infrastructure before they are destroyed by natural phenomena. That may be even more likely in the short term. In the spring of 2019, it came to light that the United States had deployed dormant malware in Russia's energy grid as a counterweight to previously reported Russian insertion of dormant malware in U.S. systems that would allow it to sabotage power plants, oil and gas pipelines, or water supplies in any future conflict with the United States. While fortunately neither side has activated the malware, the threat is now there.[36] This is reminiscent of the doctrine of mutually assured destruction that typified the nuclear standoff between the old USSR and the United States during the Cold War. Knowing that both sides would be devastated in a nuclear conflict was supposed to keep the peace by making conflict unthinkable.

Speaking of nuclear attacks, the electromagnetic pulse (EMP) from a nuclear attack will "fry" electronics within a large range of the nuclear detonations, literally causing planes to drop from the sky, satellites to die, and of course, mass electrical and communications blackouts.[37] (One of the reasons the United States and the Soviet Union stopped atmospheric tests of nuclear bombs in the sixties was because they killed their own satellites in orbit.) EMP attacks may also be launched by non-nuclear means, by so-called "e-bombs" that are high-energy microwave transmitters. It is thought that both the United States and Russia have e-bomb technology.

The more dependent we as a society are on our electrical and electronic infrastructure—and going cashless would greatly increase that dependence—the more vulnerable we are to such attacks. Attacking the money that a society uses is a very effective attack on that society itself.

Our twenty-first-century technological society is a lot more fragile than we care to admit. We don't need a once-in-a-hundred- or two-hundred-year event to show us that. Hurricanes and earthquakes are much more common than solar super storms, and have the demonstrated ability to knock out entire cities or regions for days or even weeks. We are vulnerable to the potential of human-made disasters like cyber warfare or thermo-nuclear war to incapacitate all our modern infrastructure. Are we really ready to say goodbye to cash?

People who like to prepare for doomsday scenarios have options that are superior to stashing large quantities of fiat cash. Government paper notes like U.S. dollars are the easiest way to exchange for goods during short-term emergencies. But an emergency of longer duration, which is also accompanied by a breakdown in social order and trust of the government, calls for a form of money that is a more reliable store of value than fiat money issued by a national government.

For some, good, old-fashioned gold will never lose its glitter, especially in calamitous times. Modern gold bullion coins like the South African Krugerrand, American Eagle, or Canadian Maple Leaf come in various sizes, but the most popular coin size for each contains exactly one troy ounce of gold. Such coins trade at dollar values that track the gold price per ounce closely (which is around $1,400 at the time of this writing). These well-known gold coins are minted by their respective national mints and are legal tender. They have attractive designs and are easily traded because they can be trusted to contain the correct amount of gold. If you are so inclined, bullion coins are a convenient way of storing some of your wealth in the precious yellow metal. One can imagine that they would retain their value in some futuristic, post-apocalyptic society, if this were a major concern of yours. Specie money still exists for those who see a need for it.

## A Last Word on Cash

It should be clear by now that there are risks in rushing headlong into cashlessness. At the very least, we need to address some significant concerns before we can transition to a future cashless society. First, is the technology ready? We have seen that though it appears to be ready, it does not have the robustness and all the convenience of cash. There is much technical work still to be done.

Second, is society ready? The time it takes for widespread societal changes to be absorbed by society is usually driven not so much by technological readiness but by the willingness of humans to adopt a new way of doing things. So the adjustment to a cashless society may take a generation or more. Baby boomers and others from older generations will likely cling to cash long after the millennial and Gen Z generations have switched to being cashless.

Finally, there are important questions to be answered about the equity, fairness, and security of cashless societies:

- How will we extend the benefits of a cashless society to all of its members, including the poorest members of society?
- How can we prevent governments or large corporations from using the unique new power that 100 percent cashless money will give them to infringe on basic human rights and freedoms?
- How do we safeguard our society and its economic system against the inherent vulnerabilities of all-electronic money to various attacks and natural disasters?

As citizens and consumers, we need satisfactory answers to all of these questions before we can commit to taking our society cashless. The future of society's most important technology depends on the choices we make today.

# Closing Thoughts

We have come full circle: We started this book by describing a primitive cash-less society, and how we would need to reinvent money if we suddenly lost it in order to keep track of our mutual obligations. We ended by describing what a cashless society based on twenty-first-century technology may look like, and why there are good reasons to pause before we rush into it.

We described the development of money and the accompanying economic theories. We saw that money keeps evolving to serve the needs of an evolving human society. Though it is a very successful technology, money—like the eco-nomic and political systems it supports—is far from perfect. We discussed why some people make and have so much more money than others.

Banks need to put new money into circulation daily, and we looked at how that happens. We also looked at how the global financial system is set up to allow money to move between different parties in the economy. Turning to technology, we reported on fintech, an ever-expanding frontier of financial in-novations. We noted the long-term impact of some of the earlier fintech innova-tions, from the introduction of ATMs to mobile banking. By looking at today's fintech, we got a glimpse over the horizon and saw how our latest technologies could change the way we as a society interact with our money.

The fintech innovations that are currently most in the news are cryptocoin and blockchain. We considered whether cryptocoins are money yet, and whether blockchain—with the many financial applications it can support—may be even more consequential in the long run.

We shall conclude by reminding ourselves that money is a societal innova-tion. It is not some force of nature, or a species of plant or animal that evolves by itself. We humans make it, and we control it. We cannot abdicate that responsibil-ity. Money always needs to serve its society, not society its money. This is a fine line to walk, and one that is so easy to cross.

Money may be something abstract, a necessary fiction, but it has very real life consequences. Those who don't have it suffer real hardships. Those who have too much of it can grow aloof and arrogant. Ultimately, we, the people, have to take responsibility for the type of money that we use and how it impacts people's lives.

In order to take on that responsibility, it is important that citizens have a good working understanding of what money is, and what it isn't; what it can do, and what it cannot do; what it should do, and what it shouldn't do. We hope that this book has contributed to that understanding.

https://doi.org/10.1515/9781547401116-009

# Figure Notes

**Fig. Note 1.1:** Yap island stone money, Wikimedia Commons, https://commons.wikimedia.org/wiki/File:StoneMoney.JPG, licensed under Creative Commons attribution.

**Fig. Note 1.2:** The Ishango bone. Wikimedia Commons, https://commons.wikimedia.org/wiki/File:Os_d%27Hishango_%C2%A9dada2009_b_103.jpg, licensed under Creative Commons attribution.

**Fig. Note 1.3:** Medieval tally sticks, Wikimedia Commons, https://commons.wikimedia.org/wiki/File:Medieval_tally_sticks.jpg, licensed under Creative Commons attribution. This image was originally posted to Flickr by Hampshire Museums at https://www.flickr.com/photos/106445670@N03/14169002135. It was reviewed on 28 March 2015 by FlickreviewR and was confirmed to be licensed under the terms of the cc-by-sa-2.0.

**Fig. Note 1.4:** Various Roman coins. Free for commercial use Pixabay license, https://pixabay.com/photos/coins-roman-coinsmoney-roman-3298260/.

**Fig. Note 1.5:** Zimbabwean one hundred trillion dollar note (2008). Wikimedia Commons, https://commons.wikimedia.org/wiki/File:Zimbabwe_$100_trillion_2009_Obverse.jpg, licensed under Creative Commons attribution.

**Fig. Note 2.1:** Transformative economic revolutions, Peet van Biljon, 2019.

**Fig. Note 2.2:** Replacement of horses by automobiles in the United States. Analysis and chart by Peet van Biljon. Data sources: Kilby/Ensminger, US DOT.

**Fig. Note 2.3:** IBM Personal Computer Model 5150 (launched in 1981). By Ruben de Rijcke—Own work, CC BY-SA 3.0 U.S., https://commons.wikimedia.org/w/index.php?curid=9561543.

**Fig. Note 2.4:** World GDP per capita 1960–2017, Peet van Biljon 2019. Data source: The World Bank national accounts data, Creative Commons attribution, CC BY-SA 4.0.

**Fig. Note 2.5:** Jobs involving routine tasks aren't growing. Maximiliano Dvorkin, "Jobs Involving Routine Tasks Aren't Growing," On the Economy Blog, Federal Reserve Bank of St. Louis, Jan. 4, 2016, https://www.stlouisfed.org/on-theeconomy/2016/january/jobs-involving-routine-tasks-arent-growing.

Following Dvorkin's nomenclature and methodology, the latest U.S. Bureau of Labor Statistics data series were mapped as follows:
- *Non-routine cognitive* = Management, Professional, and Related Occupations [LNU02032201]
- *Routine cognitive* = Sales and Office Occupations [LNU02032205]
- *Routine manual* = Construction and Extraction Occupations [LNU02032210]; Installation, Maintenance, and Repair Occupations [LNU02032211]; Production, Transportation and Material Moving Occupations [LNU02032212]
- *Non-routine manual* = Service Occupations [LNU02032204]

**Fig. Note 2.6:** Pre-tax national income share of the top 1 percent from 1913 to 2013.[AL1] Data source: World Inequality Database, 2019. https://wid.world/data/#countriestimeseries/sptinc_p99p100_z/US/1930/2017/eu/k/p/yearly/s

https://doi.org/10.1515/9781547401116-010

**Fig. Note 2.7:** Productivity growth and hourly compensation growth, 1948 -2017. Data source: Economic Policy Institute, "The importance of locking in full employment for the long haul," August 21, 2018. Figure B, https://www.epi.org/publication/the-importance-of-locking-in-full-employment-for-the-long-haul/.

**Fig. Note 3.1:** Neon sign for a payday loan store. https://commons.wikimedia.org/wiki/File: Payday-loan-store.jpg

**Fig. Note 3.2:** Currency images, TaxRebate.org.uk, https://www.flickr.com/photos/ 59937401@N07/5857220614.

**Fig. Note 3.3:** Chart conceptualized by Alexandra R. Lajoux based on various categories at FederalReserve.gov, as of 8/6/2019.

**Fig. Note 4.1:** Key players of global finance. Chart conceptualized by Alexandra R. Lajoux and designed by Chris Smith of Quarternative.com.

**Fig. Note 4.2:** One view of intermarket dependencies. Based on data from the Corporate Finance Institute at this link: https://corporatefinanceinstitute.com/resources/knowledge/ trading-investing/intermarket-analysis/. Graphic conceptualized by Alexandra Lajoux and designed by Chris Smith of Quarternative.com.

**Fig. Note 5.1:** WEF's functions of financial services (simplified). From "Beyond Fintech: A Pragmatic Assessment Of Disruptive Potential In Financial Services", World Economic Forum, Aug. 2017, www3.weforum.org/ ... /Beyond_Fintech_- _A_Pragmatic_Assessment_ of_ Disruptive_Potential_in_Financial_Services.pdf

**Fig. Note 6.1:** Bitcoin closing price per Coindesk. Data from https://www.coindesk.com/ price/bitcoin

**Fig. Note 7.1:** Simplified blockchain overview, Peet van Biljon, 2019.

**Fig. Note 8.1:** Cashless sign in front of a Señor Sisig food truck. Picture by Gary Stevens, Flickr, https://www.flickr.com/photos/garysoup/39060927525/in/photostream/, Attribution 2.0 Generic (CC BY 2.0)

# Endnotes

## Chapter 1

1. John Adams, letter to Thomas Jefferson, Aug. 25, 1787, https://founders.archives.gov/documents/Jefferson/01-12-02-0064.
2. Felix Martin, *Money: The Unauthorized Biography, From Coinage to Cryptocurrency*, 2013, New York: Vintage Books.
3. William Henry Furness, *The Island of Stone Money, Uap of the Carolines*, Philadelphia and London: J.B. Lippincott Company, 1910, Available at https://books.google.com/books?id=zoIcAAAAMAAJ.
4. Felix Martin, *Money: The Unauthorized Biography, From Coinage to Cryptocurrency*, New York: Vintage Books, 2013, pp. 4–8.
5. Milton Friedman, *Money Mischief: Episodes in Monetary History*, New York: Harcourt Brace, 1994.
6. S. Fitzpatrick. Banking on stone money: the influence of traditional "currencies" on blockchain technology. Society for American Archaeology annual meeting, Washington, D.C., April 13, 2018. Available at https://www.academia.edu/3944491/Banking_on_Stone_Money.
7. Ross Pomeroy, "Is the 20,000-Year-Old Ishango Bone the Earliest Evidence of Logical Reasoning?" *RealClearScience*, Nov. 23, 2016, https://www.realclearscience.com/blog/2015/11/the_earliest_evidence_of_logical_reasoning.html.
8. Tim Harford, "What tally sticks tell us about how money works," BBC Radio World Service, Jul 10, 2017, https://www.bbc.com/news/business-40189959.
9. "Bart Sells His Soul," *The Simpsons*, Fox Broadcasting Corporation, 4th episode, 7th season, Oct. 8, 1995. Plot available on https://en.wikipedia.org/wiki/Bart_Sells_His_Soul.
10. Ibid.
11. David Graeber, *Debt—The First 5,000 Years*, 2011, New York: Melville House.
12. Other words tracing etymology to the Latin *finire* include *la finance* (French), *die* Finanz (German), and *las finanzas* (Spanish).
13. As the Oxford English Dictionary states,"Late Middle English: from Old French, from finer 'make an end, settle a debt', from fin 'end' (see fine). The original sense was 'payment of a debt, compensation, or ransom' ..." https://en.oxforddictionaries.com/definition/finance.
14. World Bank, GDP data, https://data.worldbank.org/indicator/NY.GDP.MKTP.CD?view=map.
15. J.P. Smit, Filip Bueken, and Stan du Plessis, "Cigarettes, Dollars, and Bitcoins: An Essay on the Ontology of Money," *Journal of Institutional Economics*, Volume 12, Issue 2 *(2016)*, pp. 327–347.
16. J.P. Smit, Filip Bueken, and Stan du Plessis., "Cigarettes, Dollars, and Bitcoins: An Essay on the Ontology of Money," *Journal of Institutional Economics*, Volume 12, Issue 2 *(2016)*, pp. 327–347.
17. Gold's industrial utility is however much more recent, and associated with the age of electronics.

https://doi.org/10.1515/9781547401116-011

18. The belief that money only has value because of the commodity it is based on, is called metallism. Proponents of the gold standard come from this school.
19. Genesis 17:12.
20. Herodotus: Volume 1, January 1, 1830, L. Hansard & Sons.
21. Mike Markowitz, "Medieval Numismatics: Coins of the Crusaders," Coin Week, October 27, 2018. https://coinweek.com/world-coins/medieval-numismatics-coins-of-the -crusaders/.
22. See for example https://www.computersmiths.com/chineseinvention/papermoney.htm.
23. John Kenneth Galbraith, *Money*, Princeton University Press. Kindle Edition, pp. 55–57.
24. Ibid., pp. 55–57.
25. Ibid., pp. 67.
26. Ibid., p. 73.
27. Ibid., pp. 42–43.
28. Ibid., pp. 49–50.
29. John Kenneth Galbraith, *Money*, Princeton University Press. Kindle Edition, pp. 159–160.
30. https://www.gold.org/sites/default/files/documents/1925apr28.pdf.
31. The IS-LM model inspired by John Hicks's insightful interpretation of J.M. Keynes's *General Theory* is a staple of economic textbooks and the most widely taught model.
32. Milton Friedman, "The Counter-Revolution in Monetary Theory," IEA Occasional Paper, no. 33, Institute of Economic Affairs. First published by the Institute of Economic Affairs, London, 1970. Available at https://miltonfriedman.hoover.org/friedman_images/ Collections/2016c21/IEA_1970.pdf.
33. It should be apparent from this example that the liquidity of an asset may vary from time to time. Houses are more liquid during sellers' markets when multiple competitive offers may be solicited in a matter of days.
34. This is standard textbook monetary theory. See for example David Gowland, *Money, Inflation & Unemployment: The Role of Money in the Economy*, Harvester Press Group: Sussex, England, 1985.

## Chapter 2

1. John Kenneth Galbraith, "Money: Whence It Came, Where It Went," new edition 2017 (originally published 1975), Princeton University Press, p. 4.
2. The difference between what issued money like a new banknote is worth, and what it costs to produce it, is called *seigniorage*. This is the government's "profit" when it issues money, whether note or coin. It is the seigniorage which is stolen by counterfeiters, proving that printing counterfeit money is never a victimless crime, even if the fake money is never detected in circulation. Counterfeiting money means stealing from the government.
3. See for example Nick Bontis," Intellectual capital: an exploratory study that develops measures and models," Management Decision 36, no. 2 (1998): pp. 63–76. Available at https://www.researchgate.net/profile/Zeeshan_Hamid/post/I_need_questionnaires_on_ Human_Capital_HRM_Practices_and_Organizational_Performance/attachment/ 59dd4533b53d2f3449523692/AS:548036097314816@1507673395802/download/2.+HC_and_ FP.pdf.

4. Gross Domestic Product (GDP) is the most frequently used measure for the total level of economic activity in a country. GDP is defined as the market value of the goods, services, and structures produced by the economy in a given period. It can be calculated in three different ways: as the sum of goods and services sold to final users, as the sum of income payments and other costs incurred in the production of goods and services, and as the sum of the value added at each stage of production. For more details on U.S. GDP measurement, see the *NIPA Handbook* published by the Bureau of Economic Analysis at http://www.bea.gov/resources/methodologies/nipa-handbook.

5. John Kenneth Galbraith, "Money: Whence It Came, Where It Went," new edition 2017 (originally published 1975), Princeton University Press, p. 4.

6. George Soros, *The Alchemy of Finance* (New York: Wiley), p. 24.

7. Yuval Noah Harari, *Sapiens: A Brief History of Humankind*, 2014, HarperCollins.

8. C.W., "Plagued by dear labour," *The Economist*, Oct. 21, 2013, https://www.economist.com/free-exchange/2013/10/21/plagued-by-dear-labour.

9. "Digital Feudalism," by Zach Scott, Towards Data Science.com, October 23, 2018. https://towardsdatascience.com/digital-feudalism-b9858f7f9be5.

10. https://www.nobelprize.org/prizes/lists/all-prizes-in-economic-sciences/.

11. Yuval Noah Harari, *Sapiens: A Brief History of Humankind,* 2014, HarperCollins.

12. Ibid.

13. Ibid.

14. Ibid.

15. "Historical Estimates of World Population," United States Census Bureau, https://www.census.gov/data/tables/time-series/demo/international-programs/historical-est-worldpop.html.

16. Yuval Noah Harari, *Sapiens: A Brief History of Humankind*, 2014, HarperCollins.

17. "A brief history of numbers and counting, Part 1: Mathematics advanced with civilization," by Steven Law, Deseret News, August 5, 2012. See https://www.deseretnews.com/article/865560110/A-brief-history-of-numbers-and-counting-Part-1-Mathematics-advanced-with-civilization. html

18. "Historical Estimates of World Population," United States Census Bureau, https://www.census.gov/data/tables/time-series/demo/international-programs/historical-est-worldpop.html.

19. These and other historical economic numbers stated in modern currency equivalents that we can understand are the result of the life work of the British economic historian, Angus Maddison (1926–2010). His work is being continued by the Growth and Development Centre at the University of Groningen in the Netherlands, where Madison was an emeritus professor. For an assessment of Maddison's life work, see "Maddison Counting," *The Economist*, April 29, 2010, https://www.economist.com/finance-and-economics/2010/04/29/maddison-counting?story_id=16004937. The original Maddison Database 2010 is available at https://www.rug.nl/ggdc/historicaldevelopment/maddison/releases/maddison-database-2010.

20. Angus Maddison, Maddison Database 2010, available at https://www.rug.nl/ggdc/historicaldevelopment/maddison/releases/maddison-database-2010.

21. Klaus Schwab, *The Fourth Industrial Revolution*, 2016, Crown Business Books: New York.

22. In his book, Schwab acknowledges that the term *Industry 4.0* was coined at the Hannover Fair in Germany in 2011, where it was meant to refer to smart factories. Schwab has a broader definition.

23. Ibid.

24. "Fast Facts About Agriculture," https://www.fb.org/newsroom/fast-facts.

25. See "Agricultural Value Added per Worker 2017," https://ourworldindata.org/employ ment-in-agriculture

26. https://www.iea.org/energyaccess/database/.

27. See "Smart Greenhouse Changing Agriculture: Next Hot Trend in Smart Farming," February 19, 2019. https://www.agritechtomorrow.com/article/2019/02/smart-greenhouse-changing-agriculture-next-hot-trend-in-smart-farming/11253.

28. Hans-Joachim Voth, "Living standards during the industrial revolution: An economist's guide," *The American Economic Review*, 2003, 93(2), 221.

29. https://en.wikipedia.org/wiki/Thomas_Robert_Malthus.

30. Jakob B. Madsen, James B. Ang and Rajabrata Banerjee, "Four centuries of British economic growth: the roles of technology and population," *Journal of Economic Growth*, 2010, 15:263–290.

31. Adam Smith, *An Inquiry into the Nature and Causes of The Wealth of Nations*, 1776, Book 1, Chapter V.

32. Anyone who has been a buyer or seller of a house has vividly experienced these effects, and was probably educated by their real estate agent on whether they were operating in a seller's market or a buyer's market at the time.

33. This is called *sustaining innovation*, because it is innovation needed to keep the competition at bay, but not to create a truly new market for a new product.

34. To recap micro-economic theory: In perfect competition, price and quantity is determined by the intersection of the market (aggregate) supply and demand curves. However, there is no supply curve for a monopolist. For a monopolist, the demand curve is also the average revenue curve, and the marginal revenue is twice as steep as the demand curve. A monopolist's profit is maximized at the point where the marginal revenue curve is intersected by the rising marginal cost of production curve.

35. Jeanna Smialek, "The business of equality," *Bloomberg Businessweek*, March 25, 2019.

36. Note, however, that because money is a *social* invention, its economic principles can get distorted through *social biases*. In some cases, a certain job in a company—say, a "receptionist"—can be incorrectly perceived as requiring lower skills than a certain other job in that same company—say, a "sales associate"—when in fact the skill levels required in the two jobs at that company are equivalent. This is a problem tackled by H.R. 2039. The Fair Pay Act of 2019, sponsored by Rep. Eleanor Holmes Norton (D-DC-At-Large), a pending bill that would prohibit "paying wages to employees … in a job that is dominated by employees of a particular sex, race, or national origin at a rate less than the rate at which the employer pays wages to employees …. in another job that is dominated by employees of the opposite sex or of a different race or national origin, respectively, for work on equivalent jobs." The bill states that the term "equivalent jobs" means "jobs that may be dissimilar, but whose requirements are equivalent, when viewed as a composite of skills, effort, responsibility, and working conditions." The bill allows differential pay for equivalent jobs if the difference it is based on a qualifying factor such as merit or seniority.

37. Walter Scheidel, *The Great Leveler* (The Princeton Economic History of the Western World), 2017, Princeton University Press.

38. Ibid.

39. Ibid.

40.  Alvaredo, F., Atkinson, A. B., Piketty, T., Saez, E., "The top 1 percent in international and historical perspective." *Journal of Economic Perspectives*, 27(3), pp. 3–20, 2013.

41.  "Poverty and Shared Prosperity 2018: Piecing Together the Poverty Puzzle," World Bank, 2018, Washington, DC: World Bank. License: Creative Commons Attribution. CC BY 3.0 IGO.

42.  Homi Kharas and Kristofer Hamel, "A global tipping point: Half the world is now iddle class or wealthier," Sept. 27, 2018, Brookings, https://www.brookings.edu/blog/future-development/2018/09/27/a-global-tipping-point-half-the-world-is-now-middle-class-or -wealthier/.

43.  Ibid.

44.  Economists have developed measures such as the widely used Gini coefficient, to represent the income or wealth distribution in particular societies.

45.  Colin Drury, "Mark Carney warns robots taking jobs could lead to rise of Marxism," *The Independent*, April 14, 2018, https://www.independent.co.uk/news/uk/home-news /mark-carney-marxism-automation-bank-of-england-governor-job-losses-capitalism -a8304706.html.

46.  Ibid.

47.  Morris A. Davis et al., "The Price of Residential Land for Counties, ZIP Codes, and Census Tracts in the United States," Federal Housing Finance Agency, Working Paper 19-01, Jan. 2019. https://www.fhfa.gov/PolicyProgramsResearch/Research/Pages/wp1901.aspx.

48.  Estelle Sommeiller and Mark Price, "The new gilded age: Income inequality in the U.S. by state, metropolitan area, and county," The Economic Policy Institute, July 19, 2018, https://www.epi.org/publication/the-new-gilded-age-income-inequality-in-the-u-s-by-state-metropolitan-area-and-county/.

49.  "Local Area Personal Income: New Estimates for 2017; Comprehensive Updates for 2001–2016," Bureau of Economic Analysis, Nov. 15, 2018, https://www.bea.gov/system/files/2018-11/lapi1118_0.pdf

50.  The surplus of what a company earns over its cost of capital.

51.  Sree Ramaswamy, Michael Birshan, James Manyika, Jacques Bughin, and Jonathan Woetzel, "What every CEO needs to know about 'superstar' companies," McKinsey Global Institute, April 2019. https://www.mckinsey.com/featured-insights/innovation-and-growth/what-every-ceo-needs-to-know-about-superstar-companies.

52.  http://www.pewinternet.org/fact-sheet/mobile/.

53.  Kyle Taylor and Laura Silver, "Smartphone Ownership Is Growing Rapidly Around the World, but Not Always Equally," Pew Research Center, Feb. 5, 2019, https://www.pewglo bal.org/2019/02/05/smartphone-ownership-is-growing-rapidly-around-the-world-but-not -always-equally/.

54.  "The Mobile Economy 2018," GSMA, https://www.gsma.com/mobileeconomy/wp-content /uploads/2018/05/The-Mobile-Economy-2018.pdf.

55.  David H. Autor and David Dorn, "The Growth of Low-Skill Service Jobs and the Polarization of the U.S. Labor Market," *The American Economic Review*, 2013, Vol. 103, No. 5, pp. 1553–97.

56.  David H. Autor, "Work of the Past, Work of the Future," February 27, 2019, American Economic Association: Papers and Proceeding, May 2019, https://economics.mit.edu/files/16724.

57.  Maximiliano Dvorkin, "Jobs Involving Routine Tasks Aren't Growing," On the Economy Blog, Federal Reserve Bank of St. Louis, Jan. 4, 2016, https://www.stlouisfed.org/on-the-economy/2016/january/jobs-involving-routine-tasks-arent-growing.

58. https://www.census.gov/data/tables/2018/demo/income-poverty/p60-263.html.

59. Gary Stoller, "39 Million Americans Can't Afford a Vacation This Summer," *Forbes*, April 25, 2019, https://www.forbes.com/sites/garystoller/2019/04/25/39-million-americans-cant-afford-a-vacation-this-summer/#68101339107c.

60. Adrian D. Garcia, "Survey: Most Americans wouldn't cover a $1K emergency with savings," Bankrate.com, Jan. 16, 2019, https://www.bankrate.com/banking/savings/financial-security-january-2019/.

61. https://data.worldbank.org/indicator/SI.POV.GINI?.

62. https://obamawhitehouse.archives.gov/blog/2013/06/11/what-great-gatsby-curve.

63. Miles Corak, "Income Inequality, Equality of Opportunity, and Intergenerational Mobility," *Journal of Economic Perspectives*, Vol. 27, No. 3, 2013, pp. 79–102.

64. OECD (2019), *Under Pressure: The Squeezed Middle Class*, OECD Publishing, Paris, https://doi.org/10.1787/689afed1-en.

65. Richard V. Reeves, "The dangerous separation of the American upper middle class," The Brookings Institute, September 3, 2015, https://www.brookings.edu/research/the-dangerous-separation-of-the-american-upper-middle-class/.

66. Matthew Stewart, "The 9.9 Percent Is the New American Aristocracy," *The Atlantic*, June 2018, https://www.theatlantic.com/magazine/archive/2018/06/the-birth-of-a-new-american-aristocracy/559130/.

67. Thomas A. Hirschl and Mark R. Rank, "The Life Course Dynamics of Affluence," *PLOS ONE*, 10(1): e0116370, 2015. https://doi.org/10.1371/journal.pone.0116370.

68. Thomas Piketty, *Capital in the Twenty-First Century*, translated by Arthur Goldhammer, 2014, Harvard University Press: Massachusetts.

69. "A modern Marx," *The Economist*, May 3, 2014, https://www.economist.com/leaders/2014/05/03/a-modern-marx.

70. Adam Smith, *An Inquiry into the Nature and Causes of the Wealth of Nations* (Methuen & Company, 1776), 35.

71. See 2 Chronicles 36:22–23, and Ezra 1, in the Hebrew Bible.

## Chapter 3

1. The banks identified in this chapter as the world's oldest central banks are drawn from a list that appears at https://www.jagranjosh.com/articles/10-oldestcentral-bank-in-the-world-1494419021-1.

2. https://www.bankofengland.co.uk/knowledgebank/who-owns-the-bank-of-england

3. https://www.bankofengland.co.uk/knowledgebank/who-owns-the-bank-of-england

4. "A Brief Account of the Intended Bank of England," by William Paterson, 1695. https://quod.lib.umich.edu/e/eebo/A56581.0001.001/1:2?rgn=div1;view=fulltext

5. "One pretended Patriot comes and tells us, This Design will make the King Absolute, by becoming Master thereof, nor is there any way to prevent it; *For*, says he, *Rich and Money'd Men, we find by experience, are naturally timerous and fearful, and are easily brought to comply with the Times to save what they have. And the keeping of this Fund being of necessity committed to such, the prospect of their Profit, in conjunction with their natural Easiness, will of course induce them to joyn with the Prince, who is always

best able to encourage and support them." https://quod.lib.umich.edu/e/eebo/A56581.0001.001/1:2?rgn=div1;view=fulltext

6. "Another comes Cock-a-hoop, and tells ye, … That the very establishing of a *Bank* in *England*, will of course alter the Government, for that is to entrust the Fund of the Nation in the Hands of Subjects, who naturally are, and will always be sure to be of the popular side, and will insensibly influence the Church and State." https://quod.lib.umich.edu/e/eebo/A56581.0001.001/1:2?rgn=div1;view=fulltext

7. "The Bank of England and the State," by Felix Schuster, Manchester at the University State 1905. https://en.wikisource.org/wiki/The_Bank_of_England_and_the_State

8. Given the popular tendency to believe in conspiracies, these two quotations have captured the imagination of central banking opponents, from whom has arisen a famously spurious quote that includes anachronistic references to inflation and deflation, well before the coinage of those terms. The attribution of the two verifiable quotes and the reference to the spurious quote all come from "Private Banks (Spurious Quotation)." Thomas Jefferson Encyclopedia cited at https://www.monticello.org/site/jefferson/private-banks-spurious-quotation#footnoteref4_ud8unx7

9. https://www.federalreserve.gov/faqs/about_14986.htm

10. https://www.boj.or.jp/en/about/outline/history/index.htm/

11. http://www.boc.cn/en/aboutboc/ab7/200809/t20080926_1601882.html

12. https://www.ecb.europa.eu/ecb/orga/escb/html/index.en.html and the European Central Bank.

13. https://www.https://www.boj.or.jp/en/about/outline/history/index.htm/riksbank.se/en-gb/about-the-riksbank/

14. https://www.bankofengland.co.uk/

15. https://www.bankofscotland.co.uk/

16. https://www.bde.es/bde/en/

17. https://www.bde.es/bde/en/secciones/sobreelbanco/patrimonios/La_coleccion_de_/La_coleccion_de_arte.html

18. https://www.banque-france.fr/en/banque-de-france/history/institution

19. https://www.banque-france.fr/en/banque-de-france/about-banque-de-france/missions

20. https://www.norges-bank.no/en/

21. A description of the fund appears here: https://www.nbim.no/en/the-fund/about-the-fund/. "Countries with a structural surplus of cash, such as from natural resources, may hold it in the central bank, but outside the TSA in some form of sovereign wealth fund." Government Cash Management: Relationship between the Treasury and the Central Bank Mario Pessoa and Mike Williams Fiscal Affairs Department International Monetary Fund, November 2012. https://www.imf.org/external/pubs/ft/tnm/2012/tnm1202.pdf

22. https://www.suomenpankki.fi/en/bank-of-finland/

23. "Countries with a structural surplus of cash, such as from natural resources, may hold it in the central bank, but outside the [treasury single account] in some form of sovereign wealth fund. The rules to create and operate these accounts should be clearly defined, particularly in relation to the treasury's ownership of the resources, even if, in practice, the management of the account is provided by the central bank." Government Cash Management: Relationship between the Treasury and the Central Bank, by Mario Pessoa and Mike Williams Fiscal Affairs Department International Monetary Fund, November 2012, p. 17. https://www.imf.org/external/pubs/ft/tnm/2012/tnm1202.pdf

24. https://www.oenb.at/en/About-Us.html

25. Total asset figures are from Yardeni Research https://www.yardeni.com/pub/peacock fedecbassets.pdf

26. https://www.fbi.gov/news/testimony/combating-money-laundering-and-other-forms-of-illicit-finance

27. https://www.bis.org/publ/othp04_2.pdf

28. http://english.gov.cn/state_council/2014/09/09/content_281474986284115.htm

29. https://www.mof.go.jp/english/about_mof/functions/

30. See https://www.yardeni.com/pub/peacockfedecbassets.pdf Note that this amount has been declining in recent years due to the Federal Open Market Committee's balance sheet normalization program. See https://www.federalreserve.gov/monetarypolicy/bst_recenttrends.htm

31. https://www.treasury.gov/about/organizational-structure/ig/pages/fraud-alerts_index2.aspx

32. https://www.ceicdata.com/en/germany/balance-sheet-deutsche-bundesbank/deutsche-bundesbank-db-assets

33. This power to issue banknotes is pursuant to Article 106, paragraph I, of the Treaty establishing the European Community. See Article Article L. 141–5 in https://www.banque-france.fr/sites/default/files/media/2017/03/27/statutes-of-banque-de-france.pdf

34. https://www.bundesbank.de/en/bundesbank/organisation/mission-statement-and-strategy/the-bundesbank-s-mission-statement-618248

35. https://www.bundesfinanzministerium.de/Web/EN/About/Minister_and_State_Secretaries/minister_and_state_secretaries.html

36. The audit firm PWC sponsors a Central Bank Financial Reporting Working Group. https://www.pwc.com/gx/en/industries/financial-services/banking-capital-markets/central-bank-advisory-group.html

37. The National Geographic Society, a highly reputable institution founded in 1888, considers there to be seven continents: Asia, Africa, North America, South America, Antarctica, Europe, and Oceania. (Other sources count Europe and Asia as a single continent (Eurasia) due to a shared land mass.) https://www.nationalgeographic.org/encyclopedia/continent/.

38. https://www.atmia.com/news/association-of-african-central-banks-%28aacb%29-40th-ordinary-meeting-of-the-assembly-of-governors/5139/

39. Statutes of the Association of African Central Banks (AACB) http://www.aacb.org/sites/default/files/STATUTES%20AACB%20WITH%20AMENDMENTS.pdf

40. https://beac.int/

41. https://www.bceao.int/en/content/presentation-bceao

42. https://www.cepal.org/en

43. http://www.asbasupervision.com/en/who-we-are

44. https://www.ecb.europa.eu/ecb/orga/escb/eurosystem-mission/html/index.en.html

45. https://www.ecb.europa.eu/ecb/orga/capital/html/index.en.html

46. In addition, functions include setting exchange rate policy, prudential policy development (how much reserve capital banks must have), supervision/oversight, foreign exchange intervention, foreign exchange reserves, liquidity management, lender of last resort, banking/account management services, payment systems (inter-bank), settlement systems for central bank money, other settlement systems, debt management, asset management, economic development, research, statistics, and consumer services.

47. https://en.oxforddictionaries.com/definition/credit

48. https://www.accountingcoach.com/blog/short-term-bank-loan-recorded

49. See "Can banks individually create money out of nothing?—The theories and the empirical evidence," by Richard A. Werner, *International Review of Financial Analysis*, Vol. 36, December 2014, pp. 1–19. https://www.sciencedirect.com/science/article/pii/S1057521914001070#s3000

50. Ibid. [Werner (2014) op. cit. note 1.]

51. See "Bank Runs in the Digital Era," by Thomas Hale, Financial Times, March 29, 2019. https://ftalphaville.ft.com/2019/03/29/1553854256000/Bank-runs-in-the-digital-era/

52. *Naked Money: A Revealing Look at What It Is and Why It Matters* by Charles Wheelan (New York: WW Norton & Company, 2017), xiv.

53. This is referred to as the equity definition of insolvency. The alternate definition is the balance sheet definition, in which the debtor's liabilities exceed the debtor's assets. See https://www.britannica.com/topic/insolvency

54. "Subprime Mortgage Crisis, Its Timeline and Effect," by Kimberly Amadeo, updated June 25, 2019. https://www.thebalance.com/subprime-mortgage-crisis-effect-and-timeline-3305745

55. See "Interest Rate Risk in the Banking Book," from the Bank of International Settlements, "Changes in interest rates also affect a bank's earnings by altering interest rate-sensitive income and expenses, affecting its net interest income." Basel Committee on Banking Supervision, March 25, 2019.

56. See http://www.finra.org/investors/mortgage-backed-securities

57. *The Financial Crisis Inquiry Report: Final Report of the National Commission on the Causes of the Financial and Economic Crisis in the United States* (2011) ISBN 978–0-16–087727-8 Economic Crisis in the United States, https://www.govinfo.gov/content/pkg/GPO-FCIC/pdf/GPO-FCIC.pdf

58. Ibid. (https://www.govinfo.gov/content/pkg/GPO-FCIC/pdf/GPO-FCIC.pdf).

59. See https://www.federalreserve.gov/pubs/feds/2008/200859/200859pap.pdf

60. https://www.frbsf.org/economic-research/publications/economic-letter/2006/december/mortgage-innovation-and-consumer-choice/

61. http://w4.stern.nyu.edu/economics/docs/workingpapers/2018/CRAsforOUPhandbook Revised.pdf

62. https://www.sec.gov/page/ocr-section-landing

63. "The three credit rating agencies were key enablers of the financial meltdown. The mortgage-related securities at the heart of the crisis could not have been marketed and sold without their seal of approval. Investors relied on them, often blindly. In some cases, they were obligated to use them, or regulatory capital standards were hinged on them. This crisis could not have happened without the rating agencies. Their ratings helped the market soar and their downgrades through 2007 and 2008 wreaked havoc across markets and firms." https://www.govinfo.gov/content/pkg/GPO-FCIC/pdf/GPO-FCIC.pdf For the counter view, see the minority report https://promarket.org/blame-2008-financial-crisis/

64. https://www.experian.com/blogs/ask-experian/credit-education/score-basics/what-is-a-good-credit-score/

65. For a good overview of consumer credit regulation affecting a U.S. multinational, see p. 10 of the annual report of Equifax. https://investor.equifax.com/~/media/Files/E/Equifax-IR/Annual%20Reports/2018-annual-report.pdf

66. The Consumer Financial Protection Bureau has published a comprehensive list for the United States. https://files.consumerfinance.gov/f/documents/cfpb_consumer-reporting-companies-list.pdf

67. https://www.linkedin.com/pulse/credit-bureau-around-world-raymond-anderson/

68. https://www.creditkarma.com/credit-cards/i/fico-score-vs-credit-score/

69. This refers to section 54(1) of the UK Modern Slavery Act 2015. See https://www.experianplc.com/media/3557/slavery-and-human-trafficking-statement-2018-19.pdf, referring to: http://www.legislation.gov.uk/ukpga/2015/30/section/1/enacted

70. https://investor.equifax.com/~/media/Files/E/Equifax-IR/Annual%20Reports/2017-annual-report.pdf

71. https://investors.transunion.com/~/media/Files/T/Transunion-IR/annual-reports/2017/tru-2017-annual-report.pdf

72. https://www.newyorkfed.org/medialibrary/interactives/householdcredit/data/pdf/HHDC_2019Q1.pdf see also "Total Household Debt Rises for 16th Straight Quarter," Federal Reserve Bank Of New York, Aug. 14, 2018, https://www.newyorkfed.org/newsevents/news/research/2018/rp180814

73. https://ycharts.com/indicators/us_auto_loan_debt

74. "Total Household Debt Rises for 16th Straight Quarter," Federal Reserve Bank Of New York, Aug. 14, 2018, https://www.newyorkfed.org/newsevents/news/research/2018/rp180814

75. https://www.newyorkfed.org/medialibrary/interactives/householdcredit/data/pdf/HHDC_2019Q1.pdf see also "Total Household Debt Rises for 16th Straight Quarter," Federal Reserve Bank Of New York, Aug. 14, 2018, https://www.newyorkfed.org/newsevents/news/research/2018/rp180814

76. The original report is here: https://www.ftc.gov/sites/default/files/documents/reports/section-319-fair-and-accurate-credit-transactions-act-2003-fifth-interim-federal-trade-commission/130211factareport.pdf A 2015 follow-up report is here: https://www.ftc.gov/news-events/press-releases/2015/01/ftc-issues-follow-study-credit-report-accuracy

77. "Credit Errors Upend Lives of Thousands of Consumers." Atlanta Journal and Constitution, February 7, 2019. https://www.ajc.com/news/state–regional/credit-errors-upend-lives-thousands-consumers/UrgLhTkNsv8VNbWEFpZi7O/

78. https://www.esma.europa.eu/sites/default/files/library/esma33-9-320_final_report_guidelines_on_disclosure_requirements_applicable_to_credit_rating_agencies.pdf

79. https://www.fsb.org/wp-content/uploads/P040219.pdf

80. See p. 4 of https://www.fsb.org/wp-content/uploads/P040219.pdf

81. https://www.fdic.gov/bank/analytical/qbp/2018mar/qbpnot.html

82. "Nonbanks eat up lending market share with 40% increase in loan origination," The Real Deal: New York Real Estate News, August 22, 2018. https://therealdeal.com/2018/08/22/nonbanks-eat-up-lending-market-share-with-40-increase-in-loan-origination/

83. In the United States, for example, in recent years, nonbanks crossed the 50 percent threshold to become the dominant providers of mortgage loans under federal programs Fannie Mae, Freddie Mac, and Ginnie Mae. Housing Finance at a Glance: A Monthly Chartbook (June 2018). https://www.urban.org/sites/default/files/publication/98669/housing_finance_at_a_glance_a_monthly_chartbook_june_2018_0.pdf. See also https://www.fhfa.gov/SupervisionRegulation/FannieMaeandFreddieMac/Pages/About-Fannie-Mae—Freddie-Mac.aspx

84. See "Fannie Mae, Freddie Mac, and the 2008 Credit Crisis," Investopedia, May 2019. https://www.investopedia.com/articles/economics/08/fannie-mae-freddie-mac-credit-cri sis.asp

85. https://www.sofi.com/blog/how-top-countries-university-education-handle-student-loan-debt-repayment/

86. https://www.theguardian.com/money/2016/aug/25/financial-slavery-play-new-york-fringe-festival

87. https://mediacentral.princeton.edu/media/Breaking+Free+From+Financial+Slavery/0_aeb0zwr6

88. https://www.amazon.com/dfree-Breaking-Free-Financial-Slavery/dp/B004JNKISI

89. https://www.amazon.com/Debt-Slavery-Other-Things-Taught/dp/0978545702

90. Jeanna Smialek, "The business of equality," *Bloomberg Businessweek*, March 25, 2019.

91. https://www.bls.gov/careeroutlook/2018/data-on-display/education-pays.htm

92. Adam Tempkin and Christopher Maloney, "Expensive Loans to Desperate People Built This $90 Billion Industry," Bloomberg Businessweek, Feb. 14, 2019, https://www.bloom berg.com/news/articles/2019-02-14/expensive-loans-to-desperate-people-built-this-90-billion-industry

93. https://www.bis.org/publ/othp04_2.pdf

94. https://www.federalreserve.gov/faqs/how-does-the-federal-reserve-board-determine-how-much-currency-to-order-each-year.htm

95. https://www.federalreserve.gov/faqs/currency_12773.htm

96. https://ec.europa.eu/info/about-european-commission/euro/euro-coins-and-notes/euro-banknotes

97. http://mentalfloss.com/article/52759/15-international-banknotes-show-queen-elizabeth%E2%80%99s-aging-process

98. "The Faces of Britain's Banknotes in Pictures." jehehttps://www.theguardian.com/busi ness/gallery/2013/apr/26/banknotes-winston-churchill-predecessors-in-pictures

99. https://www.itv.com/news/2019-04-02/new-50-note-should-feature-someone-from-mi nority-background/

100. "The Great Seal was first used on the reverse of the one-dollar Federal Reserve note in 1935. The Department of State is the official keeper of the Seal. They believe that the most accurate explanation of a pyramid on the Great Seal is that it symbolizes strength and durability. The unfinished pyramid means that the United States will always grow, improve and build. In addition, the 'all-seeing eye' located above the pyramid suggests the importance of divine guidance in favor of the American cause. The inscription ANNUIT COEPTIS translates as 'He (God) has favored our undertakings,' and refers to the many instances of Divine Providence during our Government's formation. In addition, the inscription NOVUS ORDO SECLORUM translates as 'A new order of the ages,' and signifies a new American era." https://www.treasury.gov/resource-center/faqs/Currency/Pages/edu_faq_currency_portraits.aspx

101. http://uscode.house.gov/view.xhtml?req=(title:12%20section:225a%20edition:prelim)

102. See Table 1 at Roles and Objectives of Modern Central Banks. Bank of International Settlements (XXXX). https://www.bis.org/publ/othp04_2.pdf

103. http://english.gov.cn/archive/laws_regulations/2014/08/23/content_281474983043640.htm

104. Maurice Obstfeld, Jay C. Shambaugh, and Alan M. Taylor "The Trilemma in History: Tradeoffs Among Exchange Rates, Monetary Policies, and Capital Mobility," Review of

Economics and Statistics, 2005, 87 (3): pp. 423–438. https://www.mitpressjournals.org/doi/10.1162/0034653054638300. Another source provides this explanation:

- **Side A:** A country can choose to fix exchange rates with one or more countries and have a free flow of capital with others. If it chooses this scenario, independent monetary policy is not achievable because interest rate fluctuations would create currency arbitrage stressing the currency pegs and causing them to break.
- **Side B:** The country can choose to have a free flow of capital among all foreign nations and also have an autonomous monetary policy. Fixed exchange rates among all nations and the free flow of capital are mutually exclusive. As a result, only one can be chosen at a time. So, if there is a free flow of capital among all nations, there cannot be fixed exchange rates.
- **Side C:** If a country chooses fixed exchange rates and independent monetary policy, it cannot have a free flow of capital. Again, in this instance, fixed exchange rates and the free flow of capital are mutually exclusive.

105. If a country chooses fixed exchange rates and independent monetary policy it cannot have a free flow of capital. Again, in this instance, fixed exchange rates and the free flow of capital are mutually exclusive.

106. Hasan Comert, "From Trilemma to Dilemma," Working Paper, University of Massachusetts, Amherst, March 5, 2019. https://www.peri.umass.edu/publication/item/1158-from-trilemma-to-dilemma-monetary-policy-effectiveness-after-the-bretton-woods-world See also "Trilemma Definition," by Christina Majaski, March 13, 2019. https://www.investopedia.com/terms/t/trilemma.asp

107. "Roles and objectives of modern central banks," by David Archer, Chapter 2 in a publication entitled Issues in the Governance of Central Banks (Bank of International Settlements: May 2009) https://www.bis.org/publ/othp04.htm

108. For a detailed explanation of how central banks affect money supply, see https://www.britannica.com/topic/central-bank

109. http://lexicon.ft.com/Term?term=m0,-m1,-m2,-m3,-m4

110. The Encyclopedia Britannica editors explain why: "Open-market sales of securities by the central bank drain cash reserves from the commercial banks. This loss of reserves tends to force some banks to borrow from the central bank, at least temporarily. ... Open-market sales, by reducing the capacity of the banking system to extend credit and by tending to drive down the prices of the securities sold, also tend to raise the interest rates charged and paid by banks." https://www.britannica.com/topic/central-bank

111. https://www.newyorkfed.org/markets/pomo_landing.html

112. In France, the High Council for Financial Stability, headed by the minister of finance and which also includes the central bank governor, has issued a rule effective July 2018 that precludes them from lending to certain highly leveraged companies. See "France sets limit for bank exposure to corporate debt," Reuters, May 11, 2018.

113. For a detailed account of the role of central banks in the mitigation of the 2009 to 2010 financial crisis, see Payment Systems: Design, Governance and Oversight, by Bruce J. Sommers (Risk Books, 2012). http://riskbooks.com/payment-systems-design-governance-and-oversight

114. https://www.bis.org/about/index.htm

115. A chart in the BIS study (op cit., note18) shows China as an example.

116. https://www.congress.gov/bill/115th-congress/house-bill/7095/text

117. Eugene F. Fama, Does the Fed Control Interest Rates? (June 29, 2013). The Review of Asset Pricing Studies, Forthcoming; Chicago Booth Research Paper No. 12–23; Fama-Miller Working Paper. Available at SSRN: https://ssrn.com/abstract=2124039 or http://dx.doi.org/10.2139/ssrn.2124039. This paper points to irregular patterns in the spread of commercial paper rate (e.g., corporate notes) and the federal funds target rate 1982–2011, showing both negative and positive spreads. The negative spreads, when the corporate notes paid interest lower than the federal target rate, were up to 1 point lower, and the positive spreads in some cases exceeded 2 points. https://www.adam smith.org/blog/economics/central-banks-dont-control-interest-rates

118. https://research.stlouisfed.org/publications/economic-synopses/2019/04/19/factors-be hind-the-decline-in-the-u-s-natural-rate-of-interest?

119. "How the U.S. Federal Reserve Sets Interest Rates," by John Mervin, BBC, November 28, 2017. http://www.source.ly/110DP#.XTpbXndFzIU

120. "LIBOR is due to die in 2021. Hurry up and drop it, say regulators," *The Economist*, June 8, 2019. See for example https://www.economist.com/finance-and-economics/2019/06/08/libor-is-due-to-die-in-2021-hurry-up-and-drop-it-say-regulators

121. See https://www.theice.com/iba/libor For the story behind this, see "This Man Wants to Mend, Not End, LIBOR," Daniel Kruger, Wall Street Journal May 2019 https://www.wsj.com/articles/this-man-wants-to-mend-notend-libor-11557054043. At issue is the risk-free rate for https://www.theice.com/publicdocs/IBA_ICE_Term_Risk_Free_Rates_October_2018.pdf

122. "New Frontier: Monetary Policy with Ample Reserves," by Scott A. Wolla, May 2019. https://research.stlouisfed.org/publications/page1-econ/2019/05/03/a-new-frontier-mon etary-policy-with-ample-reserves?

123. "The Verdict on Ten Years of Quantitative Easing," https://www.theguardian.com/busi ness/2019/mar/08/the-verdict-on-10-years-of-quantitative-easing

124. Ibid. See also https://corporatefinanceinstitute.com/resources/knowledge/economics/quantitative-easing/.

125. "All Around the World, Central Bank Independence Is Under Threat," by Anirban Nag, Rene Vollgraaff, and Walter Brandimarte, *Bloomberg*, December 6, 2018; updated December 10, 2018. https://www.bloomberg.com/news/articles/2018-12-07/the-political-heat-is-on-for-central-banks-from-u-s-to-europe

126. https://finance.yahoo.com/news/role-shadow-banking-cryptocurrency-industry-080028409.html

127. https://finance.yahoo.com/news/role-shadow-banking-cryptocurrency-industry-080028409.html

128. "Central Bank Warnings on the Global Economy Are Getting Louder," by Howard Davies, December 6, 2018. https://www.theguardian.com/business/2018/dec/06/central-bank-warn ings-are-getting-louder-and-more-frequent-howard-davies

129. The study covered 1,200 bank leaders from institutions of varying type and size in the U.S. in 2019. See https://www.bai.org/bai-news/2018/11/28/bai-uncovers-top-trends-in-financial-services-for-2019. For infographic details see https://www.bai.org/research/bai-banking-out look/top-2019-trends-infographic.

130. "Crypto vs. Fiat: The Battle is On." https://www.aier.org/article/crypto-vs-fiat-battle

131. "Enable, Empower, Ensure: A New Finance for the New Economy," Speech given by Mark Carney, Governor of the Bank of England at the Lord Mayor's Banquet for Bankers and Merchants of the City of London at the Mansion House, London 20 June 2019.

https://www.bankofengland.co.uk/-/media/boe/files/speech/2019/enable-empower-en
sure-a-new-finance-for-the-new-economy-speech-by-mark-carney

132. https://www.theguardian.com/business/2018/nov/19/why-central-bank-digital-currencies-
will-destroy-bitcoin

133. As Christopher Smart of the Carnegie Endowment for International Peace has noted,
"The risks for the existing global order are not that another power will displace
Washington on these issues, but that there will be no leadership in areas that have
become increasingly important to global commerce. Worse, the response to the next
financial crisis will be uncoordinated and disastrous." See "Future of the Dollar and Its
Role in Financial Diplomacy," by Christopher Smart, Carnegie Endowment for
International Peace, December 16, 2018. https://carnegieendowment.org/2018/12/16/fu
ture-of-dollar-and-its-role-in-financial-diplomacy-pub-77986

# Chapter 4

1. https://www.cnbc.com/2019/04/11/shadow-banking-is-now-a-52-trillion-industry-and-
posing-risks.html

2. Most modern democracies have three branches of government—legislative, executive, and
judicial—and most policy-setting power lies within the executive function through a
central bank and, separately, a minister of finance or treasury, as explained in Chapter 3.

3. *EC v. W.J. Howey Co.*, 328 U.S. 293 (1946) https://www.law.cornell.edu/supremecourt/
text/328/293#fn4_ref For a recent SEC speech citing the case, see "When Howey Met
Gary (Plastic)," by William Hinman, Director, Corporate Finance, U.S. Securities and
Exchange Commission, June 14, 2018. https://www.sec.gov/news/speech/speech-hin
man-061418#_ftn4

4. https://data.worldbank.org/indicator/CM.MKT.LDOM.NO

5. https://data.worldbank.org/indicator/CM.MKT.TRAD.CD

6. See ragm.com

7. See "Wall Street firms take aim at America's stock-exchange oligopoly: *Their new
platform promises low costs and transparency*," The Economist, January 10, 2019.

8. See https://www.nyse.com/trade

9. "Bond Yields and Market Pricing," Morningstar (undated). https://news.morningstar.
com/classroom2/course.asp?docId=5375&page=3

10. To give a simplified, generic example (using an interest rate that represents an historic
average per https://fred.stlouisfed.org/series/FEDFUNDS), consider that if interest rates
have risen from 5 percent to 6.25 percent, this means that investors can now buy a bond
with a face value of $1,000 and a coupon rate of 5 percent ($50 per year) for $800 (a
price that is $200 less than its coupon value), making the bond's yield higher now,
consistent with current interest rates (50/800 x 100 = 6.25 percent); and the reverse is
also true.

11. https://www.fidelity.com/fixed-income-bonds/individual-bonds/overview

12. https://www.forbes.com/sites/kevinmcpartland/2018/10/11/understanding-us-bond-
market/#2a4bd98d1caf

13. https://www.nyse.com/markets/bonds

14. https://www.spglobal.com/en/research-insights/articles/whats-next-for-us-municipal-green-bonds

15. https://www.fidelity.com/fixed-income-bonds/individual-bonds/overview

16. https://www.treasurydirect.gov/news/pressroom/pressroom_comotcend0711.htm

17. Ibid. (Fidelity overview)

18. https://www.sec.gov/Archives/edgar/data/70858/000119312518209014/d597183d424b3.htm#toc597183_13

19. See for example https://www.treasurydirect.gov/indiv/products/prod_auctions_glance.htm

20. As explained by the Corporate Finance Institute, "The yield-to-maturity only equals the coupon rate when the bond sells at face value. The bond sells at a discount if its market price is below the par value, and in such a situation, the yield-to-maturity is higher than the coupon rate. A premium bond sells at a higher price than the face value, and its yield is lower than the coupon rate." https://corporatefinanceinstitute.com/resources/knowledge/finance/coupon-rate/ For rates in recent auctions, see the following: https://www.treasurydirect.gov/instit/annceresult/annceresult.htm

21. The value of the bond is the present value of the sum of contractual payments its issuer must make from the current time until the bond matures. The formula for the value of a bond with a single annual payment is

$$B_o = I \times \left[ \sum_{t=1}^{n} 1/(1+k_d)^t \right] + M[1/(1+k_d)^n] \text{ where}$$

$B_o$ is the value of the bond, I is the annual amount of interest it pays, n is the years to, maturity, M is the face value of the bond, and $k_d$ is the required return.

The discount rate by which the contractual rates are discounted to get the present value of these payments is also known as the required return. The required return depends on the prevailing interest rates and the risk of default. The higher the risk of default, the higher the premium over the prevailing interest rate.

22. Spriha Srivastava, "The US bond yield curve has inverted. Here's what it means," Forbes, March 25, 2019. https://www.cnbc.com/2019/03/25/the-us-bond-yield-curve-has-inverted-heres-what-it-means.html See also "$11 Trillion In Bonds Yield Less Than Zero. Does It Matter?" by Raoul Elizalde, Forbes, June 22, 2019. https://www.forbes.com/sites/raulelizalde/2019/06/22/11-trillion-in-bonds-yield-less-than-zero-does-it-matter/#5c57a7ae5075

23. https://www.thebalance.com/inverted-yield-curve-3305856

24. "The Inverted Yield Curve: Facts and Fictions," Frank Armstrong III, Forbes, June 30, 2019.

25. The term "electronification" is used in "The Foreign Currency Market: What it is and How It Works," by Francisco Javier Fernandez, May 26, 2017, at https://www.bbva.com/en/foreign-currency-market-work/

26. As of early 2018, the number was $5.1 trillion. See https://www.bloomberg.com/news/articles/2018-03-29/fx-platforms-banning-last-look-bet-buy-side-wants-transparency

27. See for example the introduction to *World Bank Group Commodity Markets Outlook*, October. World Bank, Washington, D.C., 2018 License: Creative Commons Attribution CC BY 3.0 IGO.

28. http://pubdocs.worldbank.org/en/921301546633915027/CMO-Pink-Sheet-January-2019.pdf

29. Commodities Heat Map, Nasdaq (perpetual). https://www.nasdaq.com/markets/heat-maps.aspx

30. "AI in Agriculture," Neuromation, October 1, 2018. https://medium.com/neuromation-blog/ai-in-agriculture-49c0ea0e2b48

31. "Table 2: Major Exporters of Agricultural Products: Share of Total Export Value, 2000 and 2016," in *The State of Agricultural Commodities Markets*, 2018. Food and Agricultural Organization of the United Nations, October 2018, showing that the European Union has a 41.1 percent share, the U.S. an 11 percent share, and others lower than 6 percent. http://www.fao.org/3/I9542EN/i9542en.pdf

32. See for example https://onlinelibrary.wiley.com/doi/full/10.1111/fire.12182

33. For a detailed account of the role of central banks in the mitigation of the 2009–2010 financial crisis, see *Payment Systems: Design, Governance and Oversight* by Bruce J. Sommers (Risk Books, 2012). http://riskbooks.com/payment-systems-design-governance-and-oversight

34. https://www.swift.com/about-us/discover-swift/technology-operations

35. See for example Ehab Yamani, The Endogeneity of Trading Volume in Stock and Bond Returns: An Instrumental Variable Approach, *The Financial Review: Eastern Finance Association*, May 2019.
https://www.swift.com/news-events/news/payments-standards-changes-for-2020-and-why-you-should-act-now

36. Reinventing International Clearing and Settlement: How Distributed Ledger Technology Could Transform Our Global Payment System, by Bob Tapscott, The Tapscott Group, January 2018.

37. https://www.fca.org.uk/

38. https://www.iosco.org/

39. Source: Fact Sheet OICU-IOSCO October 2018 https://www.iosco.org/about/pdf/IOSCO-Fact-Sheet.pdf

40. https://www.elysee.fr/en/g7

41. https://g20.org/en/

42. "The Effect of G20 Summits on Global Financial Markets," by Marco Lo Duca and Livio Stracca, European Central Bank, Eurosystem, Working Paper 1668, 2014 "We focus on the period from 2007 to 2013, looking at equity returns, bond yields and measures of market risk such as implied volatility, skewness and kurtosis. Our main finding is that G20 summits have not had a strong, consistent and durable effect on any of the markets that we consider," https://www.ecb.europa.eu/pub/pdf/scpwps/ecbwp1668.pdf

43. https://www.fsb.org/

44. https://www.ifc.org/wps/wcm/connect/corp_ext_content/ifc_external_corporate_site/home. The World Bank includes the International Bank of Reconstruction and Development to assist in the reconstruction and development of territories of members by facilitating the investment of capital for productive purposes, including the restoration of economies destroyed or disrupted by war, the reconversion of productive facilities to peacetime needs and the encouragement of the development of productive facilities and resources in less developed countries.

45. https://www.imf.org/en/About

46. https://www.imf.org/en/About/Key-Issues/Fintech

47. http://www.worldbank.org/en/about/what-we-do. The World Bank includes the International Bank of Reconstruction and Development to assist in the reconstruction and

development of territories of members by facilitating the investment of capital for productive purposes, including the restoration of economies destroyed or disrupted by war, the reconversion of productive facilities to peacetime needs and the encouragement of the development of productive facilities and resources in less developed countries. https://www.worldbank.org/en/who-we-are/ibrd

48. http://www3.weforum.org/docs/WEF_Institutional_Brochure_2016.pdf

49. https://www.weforum.org/about/world-economic-forum

50. The idea that businesses are not just responsible to their shareholders but also other stakeholders like employees, governments, and customers.

51. As an example, consider what happens when multiple nations, out of self-interest, set tariffs. This sets off a chain reaction that can have both positive and negative results. For example, consider tariffs, which can be seen automatically as "good" or "bad" depending on one's status as an exporter or an importer. Many companies are both, so, as a study from the International Monetary Fund has observed, effects are complex—"for example, a country may see trade volumes decrease due to higher tariffs levied on some of its imports and exports but, at the same time, benefit from trade diverted in its direction as tariffs are raised elsewhere." G20 Surveillance Note G-20 Finance Ministers and Central Bank Governors' Meetings July 21–22, 2018 Buenos Aires, Argentina, by the International Monetary Fund 2018. https://www.imf.org/external/np/g20/pdf/2018/071818.pdf

52. See this article by economist Daniel Cohen in his essay on the "Panglossian World of Finance," citing economist Paul Krugmanhttps://economistsview.typepad.com/economists view/2008/06/the-panglossian.html

53. "Self-interest: Defining and understanding a human by Russell Cropanzano et al. Journal of Organizational Behavior 26(8), December 2005, pp. 985–991. https://www.re searchgate.net/publication/229802551_Self-interest_Defining_and_understanding_a_ human_motive

54. "Clearly, sustained low inflation implies less uncertainty about the future, and lower risk premiums imply higher prices of stocks and other earning assets. We can see that in the inverse relationship exhibited by price/earnings ratios and the rate of inflation in the past. But how do we know when irrational exuberance has unduly escalated asset values, which then become subject to unexpected and prolonged contractions as they have in Japan over the past decade?" "The Challenge of Central Banking in a Democratic Society," a speech before the American Enterprise Institute December 5, 1996.

55. First Nat'l Bank of Boston v. Bellotti, 435 U.S. 765 (1978); Citizens United v. Federal Election Commission (U.S. Supreme Court, 2010).

56. A global value chain occurs when firms "split up production processes into various stages and locate them around the world to exploit differences in factor endowments and comparative advantage," notes the Bank of International Settlements. This has resulted in "long production chains that span multiple sectors over many countries, with intermediate goods shipped several times before finally becoming embodied in final goods for consumption." BIS Papers No. 100 Globalisation *and deglobalisation* (BIS Monetary and Economic Department, December 2018).

57. For the U.S. example, see https://www.treasurydirect.gov/indiv/research/indepth/ tbonds/res_tbond_rates.htm.

    The authority to run an auction is found in the Code of Federal Regulations, Section 31. See "Sale and Entry of Marketable Book Entry Treasury Bills, Notes, and Bonds,"

Department of Treasury Circular, Fiscal Services Series 1–96. https://www.treasurydir ect.gov/instit/statreg/auctreg/31CFRPart356.pdf

58. "Globally, privately-financed projects comprise a relatively small share (estimated at around 5 to 10 percent) of total infrastructure spending.... Infrastructure is, by nature, a public good, and the bulk of infrastructure assets is financed from public sources." Source: Evaluation of the effects of financial regulatory reforms on infrastructure finance, by the Financial Stability Board (November 2018). http://www.fsb.org/wp-content/uploads/ P201118-1.pdf

59. FDI investment outflows can have a major impact on the foreign exchange rate of the recipient country, as the investing company may need to buy a lot of currency of the host country to make that investment, or conversely selling a lot of that country's currency if it divests.

60. "Contrary to the hopes of national-populist movements' that nation states will win back their former status as sovereign actors, in reality, the process of dissolution of physical and non-physical borders continues at great speed," says Volker Stanzel of the German Institute for International and Security Affairs, a think tank based in Berlin. "New Realities in Foreign Affairs: Diplomacy in the 21st Century," by Volker Stanzel, SWP Research Paper 2018/RP 11, November 2018.

61. Notably, even a function as narrow as budgeting can vary greatly from country to country. An OECD study comparing the United Kingdom, the Netherlands, and Slovenia found differences. OECD Journal on Budgeting, Volume 18 Issue 2 (2018).
    *Recent developments in the work of the Budget Office*
    https://read.oecd-ilibrary.org/governance/recent-developments-in-the-work-of-the-bud get-office_budget-18-5j8fz1k92gvh#page11

62. "Gross Capital Flows by Banks, Corporates and Sovereigns," by Stefan Avdjiev et al. (Bank of International Settlements Working Paper). https://www.bis.org/publ/work760. pdf

63. "Globalization and the Increasing Correlation between Capital Inflows and Outflows," by J. S. Davis, J. S., and E. van Wincoop, NBER Working Paper, No. 23671. (2017). https:// www.nber.org/papers/w23671

64. For a helpful illustration of this point involving a cup of coffee, see the Science Education Resource Center at Carleton College. https://serc.carleton.edu/introgeo/mod els/loops.html

65. "Developing Student Understanding of Complex Systems in the Geosciences," by Steven Hurst, University of Illinois, posted at https://serc.carleton.edu/NAGTWorkshops/complex systems/workshop2010/participants/hurst.html

66. "Currency All-Time Highs and Lows" by Stephen D. Simpson, January 18, 2012, blog on Investopedia's Forex page, https://www.investopedia.com/articles/forex/12/currency-all-time-highs-lows.asp.

67. For Soros's explanation of the theory, see https://www.ft.com/content/0ca06172-bfe9-11de-aed2-00144feab49a

68. This pattern is called "three-line-strike" in candlestick charting, a kind of technical investing (that is, investing that is not based on company fundamentals but rather on stock market patterns). Candlestick charts present stock price data to show the open, high, low, and close price for a stock for the time frame the trader has chosen—for example, day by day. The X axis shows time and the Y axis shows price. The data for each day is presented to look like a candlestick. The high is the wick, the low is the tail.

The candlestick is colored one way (for example green) to show a rise in value and another way (for example red) to show a drop. How candlesticks appear over time is then analyzed for patterns in length (distance between high and low price for the time period) and in color (red-vs.-green). For an explanation of these patterns, see https://www.investopedia.com/articles/active-trading/092315/5-most-powerful-candlestick-patterns.asp

69. For ample proof that Smith believed God to be behind economic principles see "God and the Economists," by Jerry Bowyer, Forbes, August 17, 2011.

70. "God and the Market: Adam Smith's Invisible Hand," by Paul Oslingen, Journal of Business Ethics (2012) 108, pp. 429 ff, in https://www.jstor.org/stable/23259282?seq=1#page_scan_tab_contents and see "Why Is the 'Invisible Hand' in the Middle of Smith's Works? Coincidence or subtle statement?" by Mark Skousen, Foundation for Economic Education, March 9, 2011. See "God and the Market: Adam Smith's Invisible Hand," by Paul Oslingen, Journal of Business Ethics (2012) 108, pp. 429 ff, in https://www.jstor.org/stable/23259282?seq=1#page_scan_tab_contents

71. See *More Heat than Light: Economics as Social Physics, Physics as Nature's Economics* (Historical Perspectives on Modern Economics). Cambridge: Cambridge University Press. For example, see the appendix pp. 402–403, "The Mathematics of the Langrangian and Hamiltonian Formalisms." First, he presents a formula called the Langrangian equation of motion used in neoclassical economics to explain the behavior of markets. He then introduces the Hamiltonian formula used in physics for to explain the conservation of energy xx. He concludes, "The Langrangian equation of motion may be derived from the Hamiltonian, and vice versa," providing yet another equation to prove it.

72. SEC rules say that at least 80 percent of a fund's investment must follow its name. Source FINRA. http://www.finra.org/investors/mutual-funds

73. Source, Morningstar, cited in "Spoilt Rotten: Are There Too Many Mutual Funds & ETFs?," by Simon Constable, Forbes, May 2018. https://www.forbes.com/sites/simonconstable/2018/05/16/spoilt-for-choice-are-there-too-many-mutual-fund-etf-choices/#1402cff92f37

74. *Collusion: How Central Bankers Rigged the World* by Nomi Prince (Nation Books: 2018).

75. *Giants: The Global Power Elite* by Peter Phillips (Seven Stories Press, 2018).

76. *Road to Ruin: The Global Elites' Secret Plan for the Next Financial Crisis* by Jim Rickert (Penguin: 2016) follows his books *The New Case for Gold* (Penguin, 2016) and *The Death of Money: The Coming Collapse of the International Monetary System* (Portfolio, 2014), which predicted immanent failure at the hands of "the world's major financial players—national governments, big banks, multilateral institutions."

77. *What They Do with Your Money: How the Financial System Fails Us, and How to Fix It* by Stephen Davis, John Lukomnik, and David Pitt-Watson (Yale University Press, 2016).

78. For example, one drug used to treat psoriasis and other conditions, comes with the following warning from the TV announced: "Humira can lower your ability to fight infections including tuberculosis. Serious, sometimes fatal infections and cancers, including lymphoma, have happened, as have blood, liver and nervous system problems, serious allergic reactions and new or worsening heart failure..." Voiceover transcribed courtesy of this blogger: https://www.peoplespharmacy.com/2019/03/04/fda-boss-infuriates-patients-with-drug-safety-tweet/

79. Global Enforcement Review: Exploring the Impact of Regulatory Enforcement on the Global Financial Services Industry (Duff & Phelps, 2018). https://www.duffandphelps.com/-/media/assets/pdfs/publications/compliance-and-regulatory-consulting/global-enforcement-review-2018.ashx?la=en

80. The U.S. percentage was slightly lower in 2017 and could be lower for subsequent years due to financial deregulation under the Trump administration. For a discussion of how different U.S. administrations have regulated the financial sector, see "Financial regulation in the US: as the world turns and the pendulum swings," by Alexandra Lajoux, *Financier Worldwide,* September, 2018. https://www.financierworldwide.com/financial-regulation-in-the-us-as-the-world-turns-and-the-pendulum-swings#.XQG2bIhKjIU

81. "Apple's Stock Market Scam," by Alex Shepherd, *The New Republic,* August 3, 2018. https://newrepublic.com/article/150382/apples-stock-market-scam

82. "New Bond Market Scandal," S&P Global Market Intelligence, December 21, 2018. https://www.spglobal.com/marketintelligence/en/news-insights/trending/is-SfqgZ4EMSYBaJWdgERA2

83. https://www.britannica.com/topic/Silver-Thursday

84. https://www.cftc.gov/ConsumerProtection/FraudAwarenessPrevention/CFTCFraudAdvisories/fraudadv_commoditypool.html

85. See for example "CFTC Orders Commodity Trading Firm and Principal to Pay a $315,000 Civil Monetary Penalty for 'Cherry-Picking' Scheme." https://www.cftc.gov/PressRoom/PressReleases/7862-18

86. https://www.bloombergquint.com/onweb/fx-platforms-banning-last-look-bet-buy-side-wants-transparency

87. "Winds of Change in $5 Trillion FX Market," by Joel Weber and Jason Kelly, Bloomberg, March 29, 2018. https://www.bloomberg.com/news/articles/2018-03-29/fx-platforms-banning-last-look-bet-buy-side-wants-transparency

88. Exchange Rate Mechanism, Adam Hayes, January 28, 2019, under Investing at Investopedia. https://www.investopedia.com/terms/e/exchange-rate-mechanism.asp

89. https://www.fatf-gafi.org/about/

90. https://www.worldfinance.com/markets/five-lesser-known-financial-bubbles

91. For a more complete list, see http://www.thebubblebubble.com/historic-crashes/.

92. See "Sir Isaac Newton: Monumental Scientist, Terrible Investor," Blog of July 6, 2017. https://nstarcapital.com/2017/07/sir-isaac-newton-monumental-scientist-terrible-investor-2/

93. http://www.mshistorynow.mdah.ms.gov/articles/70/john-law-and-the-mississippi-bubble-1718-1720

94. "Yep, Bitcoin was a Bubble. And it Popped." https://www.bloomberg.com/crypto

95. Shoshanna Delventhal, "How Crypto Coin Sales are Rebounding After ICO Bubble Collapse," Investopedia, April 2019. https://www.investopedia.com/how-crypto-coin-sales-are-rebounding-after-ico-bubble-collapse-4684625

96. New Data Shed Light on Mutual Fund Time Horizons, by Anne M. Tucker. http://clsbluesky.law.columbia.edu/2018/07/02/new-data-shed-light-on-mutual-fund-time-horizons/

97. https://www.amazon.com/Irrational-Exuberance-Robert-J-Shiller/dp/0767923634

98. "Investing: How Market Cycles Drive Emotions," Anne Kates Smith, Chicago Tribune, December 31, 2018. https://www.chicagotribune.com/business/sns-201812131235–tms–kplngmpctnkm-a20181231-20181231-story.html

99. For the GRIPS typology see The Behavioral Economics Guide, 2018. https://www.behavioraleconomics.com/the-be-guide/the-behavioral-economics-guide-2018/ p. 110.

100. For a more complete list, see https://www.visualcapitalist.com/wp-content/uploads/2017/09/cognitive-bias-infographic.html.

101. For an example of a mathematics professor who played the market and lost his shirt (and elbow-patched jacket too, no doubt) see: John Allen Paulose, *A Mathematician Plays the Stock Market* (New York: Basic Books, 2003). https://www.amazon.com/Mathematician-Plays-Stock-Market/dp/0465054811

102. https://www.valuewalk.com/2018/07/number-of-us-public-companies-fall-50/

103. https://www.sec.gov/smallbusiness/goingpublic/exchangeactreporting

104. https://www.investor.gov/additional-resources/news-alerts/alerts-bulletins/updated-investor-bulletin-accredited-investors

105. For a summary of a November 2018 roundtable on the topic, see https://blogs.cfainstitute.org/marketintegrity/2018/11/30/sec-holds-proxy-process-roundtable-will-reforms-follow/

106. https://www.federalregister.gov/documents/2018/08/07/2018-15896/regulation-of-nms-stock-alternative-trading-systems

107. https://www.sec.gov/comments/s7-26-18/s72618-5180407-183530.pdf For reflections on comments by Warren Buffet and Jamie Dimond, see "As Bells Toll for Earnings Guidance, We Ponder Progress," by Peter R. Gleason, June 18, 2018.

108. "Just 10 Percent of Trading Is Regular Stock Picking," by Evelyn Cheng, https://www.cnbc.com/2017/06/13/death-of-the-human-investor-just-10-percent-of-trading-is-regular-stock-picking-jpmorgan-estimates.html

109. "Idiosyncrasies and challenges of data driven learning in electronic trading," by https://arxiv.org/pdf/1811.09549.pdf

110. In Chapter 6, we note, "While stocks are traded in fractions of a second (making it too fast and voluminous to run trading on current versions of blockchain), the behind-the-scenes process of transferring asset ownership can take a few days."

111. See "Idiosyncrasies and challenges of data driven learning in electronic trading," JP Morgan, 2018. https://arxiv.org/pdf/1811.09549.pdf

112. https://www.amazon.com/Heretics-Guide-Global-Finance-Hacking/dp/0745333508

113. See "Stock Trading Apps Lure Novice Investors," Wall Street Journal, January 23, 2019. http://www.profjournal.com/mail/wrkfiles/Entrepreneurship20195.html

114. "The EU is right to refuse legal personality for Artificial Intelligence," by Thomas Burra, EU Interactiv.com, May 31, 2018.

115. The Implications of Modern Business-Entity Law for the Regulation of Autonomous Systems, by Shawn Bayern, Stanford Technology Law Review Vol. X. No. X (2015), revised May 13, 2017. https://papers.ssrn.com/sol3/papers.cfm?abstract_id=2758222

116. "Company Law and Autonomous Systems: A Blueprint for Lawyers, Entrepreneurs, and Regulators" Shawn Bayern et al., *Hastings Science and Technology Law Journal*, Vol. 9, No. 2 (Summer 2017). https://papers.ssrn.com/sol3/papers.cfm?abstract_id=2850514

117. Raffaele Sava—Co-Chief Investment Officer of BlackRock Active Equity https://www.blackrock.com/investing/literature/whitepaper/bii-2019-investment-outlook.pdf

## Chapter 5

1. Linda Rodriguez McRobbie, "The ATM is Dead. Long Live the ATM!," *Smithsonian Magazine*, Jan. 8, 2015, https://www.smithsonianmag.com/history/atm-dead-long-live-atm-180953838/
2. https://www.pymnts.com/cash/2017/atmia-says-us-atms-finally-see-growth/
3. "The History of Credit Cards." Creditcards.com
4. https://www.dinersclub.com/about-us/history
5. Clari Tsosie, "The History of the Credit Card," Nerdwallet.com, Feb. 9, 2017, https://www.nerdwallet.com/blog/credit-cards/history-credit-card/
6. "Total Household Debt Rises for 16th Straight Quarter," Federal Reserve Bank Of New York, Aug. 14, 2018, https://www.newyorkfed.org/newsevents/news/research/2018/rp180814
7. W. Scott Frame, Larry Wall, and Lawrence J. White, "Technological Change and Financial Innovation in Banking: Some Implications for Fintech," Federal Reserve Bank of Atlanta, Working Paper 2018–11, October 2018, https://doi.org/10.29338/wp2018-11.
8. https://www.gobankingrates.com/banking/banks/history-online-banking/
9. https://www.fool.com/investing/2017/01/03/what-percent-of-bank-of-americas-customers-uses-it.aspx
10. https://www.gobankingrates.com/banking/banks/history-online-banking/
11. For a contemporaneous account, see "Bells and Whistles," by Ronaleen R. Roha, Kiplinger Personal Finance Magazine, September 1999, pp. 90–91.
12. https://www.vodafone.com/content/index/what/m-pesa.html
13. https://www.linkedin.com/feed/update/urn:li:activity:6474357894744666112
14. Stan Sienkiewicz, "The Evolution of EFT Networks from ATMs to New On-Line Debit Payment Products," Discussion Paper Payment Cards Center, Federal Reserve Bank of Philadelphia, April 2002, https://www.philadelphiafed.org/-/media/consumer-finance-institute/payment-cards-center/publications/discussion-papers/2002/eftnetworks_042002.pdf
15. Bharath Kumar, "The Story of PayPal," Medium.com, May 21, 2017, https://medium.com/@bharath.bkj/the-story-of-paypal-b708efe83064
16. https://www.paypal.com/stories/us/paypals-fourth-quarter-and-full-year-2017-results
17. https://www.statista.com/outlook/296/100/digital-payments/worldwide
18. Jeff Muskus, "Europe's Quiet Tech Success," *Bloomberg Businessweek*, Feb. 18, 2019, pp. 17–20.
19. "Beyond Fintech: A Pragmatic Assessment Of Disruptive Potential In Financial Services", World Economic Forum, Aug. 2017, www3.weforum.org/ .../Beyond_Fintech_-_A_Pragmatic_ Assessment_of_Disruptive_Potential_in_Financial_Services.pdf
20. "Inside NFC: How Near Field Communication Works." APC Magazine. August 17, 2011. http://www.apcmag.com/inside-nfc-how-near-field-communication-works.htm/
21. Lisa Gerstner, "A New Way to Tap and Pay," *Kiplinger's Personal Finance*, April 2019, p. 44.
22. Alak Majumder et al., "Pay-Cloak: A Biometric Back Cover for Smartphones: Facilitating secure contactless payments and identity virtualization at low cost to end users," *IEEE Consumer Electronics Magazine*, Vol. 6, Issue 2, April 2017, DOI: 10.1109/MCE.2016.2640739.
23. Chanyaporn Chanjaroen and Joyce Koh, "Singapore's Biggest Bank Takes on China Giants in Fintech Battle," *Bloomberg BusinessWeek*, May 14, 2018, https://www.bloom

berg.com/news/articles/2018-05-14/fintech-battle-pits-biggest-singapore-bank-against-china-giants.

24. "China's digital-payments giant keeps bank chiefs up at night," *The Economist*, Aug. 19, 2017, https://www.economist.com/business/2017/08/19/chinas-digital-payments-giant-keeps-bank-chiefs-up-at-night

25. "China's digital-payments giant keeps bank chiefs up at night," *The Economist*, Aug. 19, 2017, https://www.economist.com/business/2017/08/19/chinas-digital-payments-giant-keeps-bank-chiefs-up-at-night

26. "A bank in your pocket," *The Economist*, May 4th, 2019, Special report—Banking, pp. 3–4.

27. https://expandedramblings.com/index.php/taobao-statistics/

28. https://bankinnovation.net/2018/07/square-will-reapply-for-banking-license-with-the-fdic-after-last-weeks-withdrawal/

29. Andy Medici, "Bye-bye, Banker," Washington Business Journal, Nov. 23, 2018, pp. 18–22.

30. W. Scott Frame, Larry Wall, and Lawrence J. White, "Technological Change and Financial Innovation in Banking: Some Implications for Fintech," Federal Reserve Bank of Atlanta, Working Paper 2018–11, October 2018, https://doi.org/10.29338/wp2018-11.

31. Zeke Faux and Shaheen Nasiripour, "Why Goldman Sachs Is Lending to the Middle Class," *Bloomberg BusinessWeek*, June 29, 2018, https://www.bloomberg.com/news/articles/2018-06-29/why-goldman-sachs-is-lending-to-the-middle-class.

32. See *The Story of Lemonade*, by Ty Sagalow (New York: Outskirts Press, 2019).

33. https://intelligent.schwab.com/

34. https://www.wealthfront.com/

35. https://robinhood.com/

36. https://www.forbes.com/sites/investor/2017/04/18/the-stock-picking-robots-are-coming/#6eccb0555d93

37. "Registered investment companies typically do not have employees—instead, they contract with other businesses to provide services to the fund." Source: 2018 Investment Company Fact Book: A Review of Trends and Activities in the Investment Company Industry (Washington, DC: Investment Company Institute, 2018).

38. Note: Investment Company Factbooks from the past two decades do not show significant any change in the percentage of employment in administrative functions since turn of century—it's been flat at about 10 percent, and they are counting only employees of investment managers, which should go down if outsourcing is occurring. However, this indicator may change in the future.

39. https://www.kickstarter.com

40. https://www.investopedia.com/terms/n/nonaccreditedinvestor.asp

41. https://www.sec.gov/smallbusiness/exemptofferings/regcrowdfunding

42. https://www.sec.gov/smallbusiness/exemptofferings/rega

43. https://www.seedrs.com/

44. https://www.algomi.com/about-us

45. Billy Bambrough, "Global Fintech Warning to Traditional Banks—The Threat Is 'Real and Growing'," *Forbes*, Oct. 17, 2018, https://www.forbes.com/sites/billybambrough/2018/10/17/global-fintech-warning-to-tradional-banks-the-threat-is-real-and-growing/#6efddcc12c71

46. https://www.biometricupdate.com/201808/voice-and-speech-recognition-predicted-to-reach-6-9b-by-2025-as-alexa-powered-banking-trials-launch

47. Meg Conlan-Donnely, "How Will Biometrics Affect the Future of Banking Security?", BizTech, March 19, 2018, https://biztechmagazine.com/article/2018/03/how-will-biometrics-affect-the-future-of-banking-security

48. https://standards.ieee.org/industry-connections/ec/autonomous-systems.html

49. Peter High, "Carnegie Mellon Dean of Computer Science on the Future of AI," Forbes, Oct. 13, 2017, https://www.forbes.com/sites/peterhigh/2017/10/30/carnegie-mellon-dean-of-computer-science-on-the-future-of-ai/#5bb455cb2197

50. Research at the Connectome project at Harvard indicates that each human has "tens of billions of neurons connected through perhaps one hundred trillion synapses." http://cbs.fas.harvard.edu/science/connectome-project

51. Dan Philps, "Artificial Intelligence-Driven Investing: High Alpha behind the Buzz," Enterprising Investor, May 17, 2018. https://blogs.cfainstitute.org/investor/2018/05/17/artificial-intelligence-driven-investing-high-alpha-behind-the-buzz/

52. Suman Bhattacharyya, "Canada-based Manulife Bank is betting on conversational AI to hook customers," bank innovation, July 3, 2019, https://bankinnovation.net/2019/07/canada-based-manulife-bank-is-betting-on-conversational-ai-to-hook-customers/

53. https://www.kryptographe.com/blockchain-quotes-from-successful-leaders/

54. https://www.theregister.co.uk/2018/08/14/distributed_ledger_technology_system_cambridge_university_report/

55. Tom Serres and Bettina Warburg, "Introducing Asset Chains: The Cognitive, Friction-free, and Blockchain-enabled Future of Supply Chains," foreword by Don Tapscott, Blockchain Research Institute, Nov. 28, 2017.

56. Camilo Maldonado, "Apple and Goldman Sachs Are Launching a New Credit Card. Here Is What We Know," Forbes, March 21, 2019, https://www.forbes.com/sites/camilomaldonado/2019/03/21/apple-goldman-new-credit-card/

57. Camilo Maldonado, "Apple Just Released New Details About The Apple Card With Goldman Sachs," Forbes, March 25, 2019, https://www.forbes.com/sites/camilomaldonado/2019/03/25/apple-just-released-new-details-about-the-apple-card-with-goldman-sachs/#34515839644b

58. Jennifer Surane, "The Apple Card Is a Big Step for Goldman Too," Bloomberg Businessweek, April 1, 2019, p.29.

59. Ilias Louis Hatzis, "Blockchain Front Page: Are Apple, Amazon, Google and Facebook the future of banking?," Daily Fintech, March 4, 2019, https://dailyfintech.com/2019/03/04/blockchain-front-page-are-apple-amazon-google-and-facebook-the-future-of-banking/

60. https://www.politico.com/story/2019/07/08/facebook-cryptocurrency-maxine-waters-1571234

61. https://online.maryville.edu/blog/the-future-of-finance/

62. "Gerard du Toit and Maureen Burns, "Evolving the Customer Experience in Banking," Bain & Company, Nov. 20, 2017. https://www.bain.com/insights/evolving-the-customer-experience-in-banking/

63. Janna Herron, "Cash deposited in Robinhood's 3% checking and savings isn't insured, SIPC says," USA Today, Dec. 14, 2018, https://www.usatoday.com/story/money/2018/12/14/robinhood-checking-and-savings-features-not-insured-says-sipc/2310208002/

64. "Why Fintech May Not Be Fit For Public Consumption," Seeking Alpha, June 18, 2019, https://seekingalpha.com/article/4270733-fintech-may-fit-public-consumption

65. Joshua Mayers, "Where are all the fintech IPOs?," Pitchbook, June 3, 2019, https://pitchbook.com/news/articles/where-are-all-the-fintech-ipos

66. Ron Shevlin, "The Solution To The Fintech IPO Shortage," *Forbes*, July 1, 2019, https://www.forbes.com/sites/ronshevlin/2019/07/01/solution-to-fintech-ipo-shortage/#743cc50e3491

67. "Tech's raid on the banks," *The Economist*, May 4th, 2019, Special report—Banking, p. 9.

68. Michelle F. Davis, "Where the Branches Aren't," *Bloomberg Businessweek*, March 11, 2019, pp. 24–25.

## Chapter 6

1. We also note that McKinsey & Company have started to use the word *crypto-asset* in their reports, implying a broader asset class based on crypto technologies.

2. In the U.S., the Federal Deposit Insurance Corporation (FDIC) closed 465 "failed" banks—that is, banks FDIC deemed to be insolvent—from 2008 to 2012. By contrast, in the five years prior to 2008, the FDIC closed on ten banks. Furthermore, the Dodd-Frank Act of 2010 requires banks to claw back compensation paid to directors and officers deemed responsible for bank failure.

3. See "Europe's Tea Party" The Economist, January 2014. https://www.economist.com/leaders/2014/01/02/europes-tea-parties

4. Petri Basson, "The untold history of bitcoin: Enter the Cypherpunks," *Medium*, Jan 26, 2018, https://medium.com/swlh/the-untold-history-of-bitcoin-enter-the-cypherpunks-f764dee962a1

5. Sadly, now that cryptocurrencies exist, they have spawned radical constituencies actively cheering for the collapse of stock markets and the established financial order.

6. Satoshi Nakamoto, "Bitcoin: A Peer-to-Peer Electronic Cash System," 2018. Available at https://bitcoin.org/bitcoin.pdf

7. Math note: In a white paper dated January 23, 2018, titled, "Block Arrivals in the Bitcoin Blockchain," R. Bowden et al. explain and critique the mathematics of the original paper as follows: "Bitcoin is an electronic payment system where payment transactions are verified and stored in a data structure called the blockchain. Bitcoin miners work individually to solve a computationally intensive problem, and with each solution a bitcoin block is generated, resulting in a new arrival to the blockchain … . In the original bitcoin paper, it was suggested that the blockchain arrivals occur according to a homogeneous Poisson process. Based on blockchain block arrival data and stochastic analysis of the block arrival process, we demonstrate that this is not the case." Instead, the authors offer a non-homogenous Poisson process, pointing out that average arrival times for blockchain transactions vary over time. https://arxiv.org/pdf/1801.07447.pdf

8. Nathanial Popper, *Digital Gold: Bitcoin and the Inside Story of the Misfits and Millionaires Trying to Reinvent Money*, Harper: New York, 2015.

9. Alexander Muse, "How the NSA identified Satoshi Nakamoto," Medium.com, Aug. 26, 2017. https://medium.com/cryptomuse/how-the-nsa-caught-satoshi-nakamoto-868affcef595

10. Laura Saunders, "Make the Most of Your Failed Bitcoin Gamble: Sell Now," *The Wall Street Journal*, Dec. 21, 2018, https://www.wsj.com/articles/make-the-most-of-your-failed-bitcoin-gamble-sell-now-11545388207

11. Michael J. Casey, "Crypto Winter Is Here and We Only Have Ourselves to Blame," Coindesk.com, Dec. 3, 2018, https://www.coindesk.com/the-crypto-winter-is-here-and-we-only-have-ourselves-to-blame?

12. Ali Montag, "This crypto-millionaire bought a Lamborghini for $115 thanks to bitcoin," CNBC.com, Feb. 7, 2018, https://www.cnbc.com/2018/02/07/bitcoin-millionaires-are-buying-lamborghinis-with-cryptocurrency.html

13. "Steven Russolillo and Paul Vigna, "Bitcoin Is Back Above $10,000 and Investors Say This Rally Is Different," *The Wall Street Journal*, June 22, 2019, https://www.wsj.com/articles/bitcoin-is-back-above-10-000-and-investors-say-this-rally-is-different-11561201454?

14. "Remarks by Chairman Alan Greenspan At the Annual Dinner and Francis Boyer Lecture of The American Enterprise Institute for Public Policy Research, Washington, D.C.," Dec. 5, 1996, The Federal Reserve Board, https://www.federalreserve.gov/boarddocs/speeches/1996/19961205.htm

15. George Soros expounded this theory in a book titled *The Alchemy of Finance* in 1987, following the market crash of that year. The book continues to be relevant. See *The Alchemy of Finance*, Second Edition, by George Soros (Wiley, 2015), https://www.wiley.com/en-us/The+Alchemy+of+Finance%2C+2nd+Edition-p-9780471445494

16. George Soros, "General Theory of Reflexivity," *The Financial Times*, Oct. 26, 2009, https://www.ft.com/content/0ca06172-bfe9-11de-aed2-00144feab49a

17. Vikram Mansharamani, "bitcoin: Boom or Bust?" LinkedIn.com, March 1, 2017, https://www.linkedin.com/pulse/bitcoin-boom-bust-vikram-mansharamani/?mod=article_inline

18. Spencer Jakab, "Bitcoin Wasn't a Bubble Until It Was," *The Wall Street Journal*, Dec. 14, 2018, https://www.wsj.com/articles/bitcoin-wasnt-a-bubble-until-it-was-11544783400?

19. Richard Nieva, "Ashes to ashes, peer to peer: An oral history of Napster," *Fortune*, Sept. 5, 2013, http://fortune.com/2013/09/05/ashes-to-ashes-peer-to-peer-an-oral-history-of-napster/

20. Brian Chen, "April 28, 2003: Apple opens iTunes Store," *Wired*, April 28, 2010, https://www.wired.com/2010/04/0428itunes-music-store-opens/.

21. https://losangeles.cbslocal.com/2019/06/03/apple-likely-to-end-itunes-report-says/

22. https://www.spotify.com/us/ For Spotify's story as a public company, see also https://www.inc.com/guadalupe-gonzalez/spotify-cfo-direct-listing-ipo-slack.html

23. https://cryptocoincharts.info/markets/info

24. https://www.coinbase.com/

25. https://gemini.com/

26. https://www.binance.com/en

27. "What's Next In Blockchain," CB Insights, 2019, https://www.cbinsights.com/research/report/blockchain-trends-2019/

28. Paul Vigna, "Most Bitcoin Trading Faked by Unregulated Exchanges, Study Finds," *The Wall Street Journal*, March 22, 2019, https://www.wsj.com/articles/most-bitcoin-trading-faked-by-unregulated-exchanges-study-finds-11553259600?

29. "Financial Aid Funding Cryptocurrency Investments," *The Student Loan Report*, March 22, 2018, https://studentloans.net/financial-aid-funding-cryptocurrency-investments/

30. Helen Partz, "Confirmed: Travel Booking Giant Expedia Has Quietly Removed bitcoin Payment Option," *Cointelegraph.com*, Jun. 28, 2018, https://cointelegraph.com/news/confirmed-travel-booking-giant-expedia-has-quietly-removed-bitcoin-payment-option

31. https://www.binance.vision/economics/what-is-ripple. See also Reinventing International Clearing and Settlement: *How Distributed Ledger Technology Could Transform Our Global Payment System*, *by* Bob Tapscott (The Blockchain Research Institute, 2018).

32. Lubomir Tassev, "Maduro's Promotion of the Petro Yet to Yield Results," *bitcoin.com*, Dec. 27, 2018, https://news.bitcoin.com/maduros-promotion-of-the-petro-yet-to-yield-results/

33. Tommaso Mancini Griffoli et al., "Casting Light on Central Bank Digital Currency," IMF Staff Discussion Note, SDN18/08, Nov. 2018, https://www.imf.org/en/Publications/Staff-Discussion-Notes/Issues/2018/11/13/Casting-Light-on-Central-Bank-Digital-Currencies-46233

34. Mike Orcutt, "At least 15 central banks are serious about getting into digital currency," *MIT Technology Review*, Dec. 14, 2018, https://www.technologyreview.com/s/612573/at-least-15-central-banks-are-serious-about-getting-into-digital-currency/

35. "Winds of Change: The Case for New Digital Currency," speech by Christine Lagarde, IMF Managing Director, Singapore Fintech Festival, November 14, 2018, https://www.imf.org/en/News/Articles/2018/11/13/sp111418-winds-of-change-the-case-for-new-digital-currency

36. Michael Pearl, "Exclusive: NASDAQ-Powered Crypto Exchange DX Set to Launch Next Month," *Finance Magnates*, May 5, 2018, https://www.financemagnates.com/cryptocurrency/exchange/exclusive-nasdaq-powered-crypto-exchange-dx-set-to-launch-next-month/

37. "Goldman drops bitcoin trading plans for now: Business Insider," Sept. 5, 2018, *Reuters*, https://www.reuters.com/article/us-goldman-sachs-cryptocurrency/goldman-drops-bitcoin-trading-plans-for-now-business-insider-idUSKCN1LL1M0

38. Wayne Duggan, "The U.S. Dollar Is Crushing bitcoin," *U.S. News & World Report*, Sept. 7, 2018, https://money.usnews.com/investing/cryptocurrency/articles/2018-09-07/the-us-dollar-is-crushing-bitcoin

39. Shawn Tully, "The NYSE's Owner Wants to Bring Bitcoin to Your 401(k). Are Crypto Credit Cards Next?" *Fortune*, Aug. 3, 2018, http://fortune.com/longform/nyse-owner-bitcoin-exchange-startup/

40. Justin Baer, "Fidelity Says It Will Trade Bitcoin for Hedge Funds," *The Wall Street Journal*, Oct. 15, 2018, https://www.wsj.com/articles/fidelity-offers-professional-investors-access-to-a-new-world-trading-bitcoin-1539621000

41. James Faucette et al., "Bitcoin Decrypted: A Brief Teach-in and Implications," Morgan Stanley Research, Dec. 18, 2017, available at https://fa.morganstanley.com/robert.emple/mediahandler/media/113362/BitCoin%20Blockchain%20MS%20paper.pdf

42. "Pro-Crypto SEC Commissioner: Don't Wait on bitcoin ETF, Could Take Days or Years," Dec. 6, 2018, https://www.ccn.com/pro-crypto-sec-commissioner-dont-wait-on-bitcoin-etf-could-take-days-or-years/

43. Laura Saunders, "Make The Most of Your Failed bitcoin Gamble: Sell Now," *The Wall Street Journal*, Dec. 21, 2018, https://www.wsj.com/articles/make-the-most-of-your-failed-bitcoin-gamble-sell-now-11545388207

44. IRS Sending Warning Letters to More Than 10,000 Cryptocurrency Holders, *The Wall Street Journal*, July 26, 2019, https://www.wsj.com/articles/irs-sending-warning-letters-to-more-than-10-000-cryptocurrency-holders-11564159523

45. "Digital Asset Transactions: When Howey Met Gary (Plastic), William Hinman, Director, Division of Corporate Finance, U.S. Securities and Exchange Commission, June 14, 2018.

Remarks at the Yahoo Finance All Markets Summit: Crypto. https://www.sec.gov/news/speech/speech-hinman-061418

46. https://www.congress.gov/bill/116th-congress/house-bill/2144/text

47. Kate Rooney, "Lawmakers look to change SEC's 72-year-old securities definition to exclude cryptocurrencies," CNBC.com, Dec. 20, 2018, https://www.cnbc.com/amp/2018/12/20/lawmakers-look-to-change-secs-72-year-old-securities-definition-to-exclude-crypto currencies.html?

48. https://www.acfe.com/fraud-triangle.aspx

49. Wilma woo, "China escalates cryptocurrency ban blocking 124 offshore exchanges," Bitcoinist.com, Aug. 23, 2018, https://bitcoinist.com/china-escalates-cryptocurrency-ban-will-block-124-offshore-exchanges/

50. Gabriel T. Rubin, Dave Michaels and Alexander Osipovich "U.S. Regulator Demands Trading Data from Bitcoin Exchanges in Manipulation Probe," *The Wall Street Journal*, June 8, 2018. https://www.wsj.com/articles/u-s-regulators-demand-trading-data-from-bitcoin-ex changes-in-manipulation-probe-1528492835

51. Peter Tchir, "I Would Be Shocked If Bitcoin Prices Weren't Manipulated," *Forbes*, May 28, 2018, https://www.forbes.com/sites/petertchir/2018/05/28/i-would-be-shocked-if-bitcoin-pri ces-werent-manipulated/#30fc90452be9

52. Daniel Shane, "Billions in cryptocurrency wealth wiped out after hack," *CNN Business*, June 18, 2018, https://money.cnn.com/2018/06/11/investing/coinrail-hack-bitcoin-ex change/index.html

53. Paul Vigna, "Two Groups Account for $1 Billion in Cryptocurrency Hacks, New Report Says," *The Wall Street Journal*, Jan. 28, 2019, https://www.wsj.com/articles/two-groups-account-for-1-billion-in-cryptocurrency-hacks-new-report-says-11548676800?mod=hp_lista_pos2

54. Justin Scheck and Bradley Hope, "The Man Who Solved bitcoin's Most Notorious Heist," *The Wall Street Journal*, Aug. 10, 2018, https://www.wsj.com/articles/the-man-who-solved-bitcoins-most-notorious-heist-1533917805?mod=hp_lead_pos5

55. Taylor Telford, "After founder's sudden death, cryptocurrency exchange can't access $190 million in holdings," *Washington Post*, Feb 4., 2019, https://www.washingtonpost.com/busi ness/2019/02/04/cryptocurrency-company-owes-customers-million-it-cant-repay-because-owner-died-with-only-password/?utm_term=.b43024aec8f4

56. Ernst & Young Inc, "IN THE MATTER OF THE BANKRUPTCIES OF QUADRIGA FINTECH SOLUTIONS CORP.; WHITESIDE CAPITAL CORPORATION AND 0984750 B.C. LTD. OF THE CITY OF HALIFAX, IN THE PROVINCE OF NOVA SCOTIA, TRUSTEE'S PRELIMINARY REPORT," Estate File No's.: 51–2499072; 51–2498985 and 51–2498986, Court File No's.: 43213; 43211 and 43212, https://www.scribd.com/document/409470435/Trustee-Report-FINAL?campaign=SkimbitLtd&ad_group=100652X1574425X096e3f7b5b188662519927006085746f&keyword=660149026&

57. Nikhilesh De, "QuadrigaCX Has $21 Million in Assets and Owes $160 Million: EY Report," Coindesk.com, May 10, 2019, https://www.coindesk.com/quadrigacx-has-21-mil lion-in-assets-and-owes-160-million-ey-report

58. Jeff John Roberts, "FBI Probing Bitcoin Exchange Quadriga Over Missing $136 Million, Source Alleges," *Fortune*, March 4, 2019, http://fortune.com/2019/03/04/quadriga-fbi-bitcoin/

59. Mike Orcutt, "Once hailed as unhackable, blockchains are now getting hacked," *MIT Technology Review*, Feb. 19, 2019, https://www.technologyreview.com/s/612974/once-hailed-as-unhackable-blockchains-are-now-getting-hacked/?

60. Anna Baydakova and Nikhilesh De, "All Global Crypto Exchanges Must Now Share Customer Data, FATF Rules," Coindsek.com, June 21, 2019, https://www.coindesk.com/fatf-crypto-travel-rule?

61. Praveen Dudu, "The top ten deepest mines in the world," *Mining Technology*, Sept. 11, 2013, https://www.mining-technology.com/features/feature-top-ten-deepest-mines-world-south-africa/

62. This type of crypto coin is cryptocurrency designed to enable data exchange between sensor-equipped machines that populate the Internet of Things (IoT). https://www.investopedia.com/news/closer-look-iota/

63. For a discussion of this limit, currently estimated to be just under 21 million (20999999.9769 BTC). Predictions vary on when this endpoint will be reached, and whether or not there could be changes to the system. See https://bitcoin.stackexchange.com/questions/161/how-many-bitcoins-will-there-eventually-be

64. Timothy B. Lee, "bitcoin rival bitcoin Cash soars as Coinbase adds support," arstechnica.com, Dec. 12, 2017, https://arstechnica.com/tech-policy/2017/12/bitcoin-rival-bitcoin-cash-soars-as-coinbase-adds-support/

65. "What Is Lightning Network and How It Works," CooinTelegraph.com, https://cointelegraph.com/lightning-network-101/what-is-lightning-network-and-how-it-works#what-is-the-lightning-network

66. https://raiden.network/101.html

67. http://www.hkexnews.hk/APP/SEHK/2018/2018092406/Documents/SEHK201809260017.pdf

68. https://digiconomist.net/bitcoin-energy-consumption, accessed Dec. 31, 2018.

69. "Hash Rate," https://blockchain.info/charts/hash-rate, accessed Dec. 31, 2018.

70. "Quantification of energy and carbon costs for mining cryptocurrencies," *Nature Sustainability*, Volume 1, pp. 711–718, 2018, available at https://www.nature.com/articles/s41893-018-0152-7

71. Georgi Kantchev et al., "bitcoin Is the World's Hottest Currency, but No One's Using It," *The Wall Street Journal*, Dec. 2, 2017, https://www.wsj.com/articles/bitcoin-is-the-worlds-hottest-currency-but-no-ones-using-it-1512142187?

72. Brian Fung, "One of the hottest things in cryptocurrency right now: Stablecoins," *The Washington Post*, Nov. 1, 2018, https://www.washingtonpost.com/technology/2018/11/01/one-hottest-things-cryptocurrency-right-now-stablecoins/?utm_term=.9cbd8307bfd5

73. "Facebook's New Cryptocurrency, Libra, Gets Big Backers," *Wall Street Journal*, June 13, 2019. https://www.wsj.com/articles/facebooks-new-cryptocurrency-gets-big-backers-11560463312

74. Dimitra Kessenides and Madeleine Lim, "Can You Trust Libra?" *Bloomberg Businessweek*, June 24, 2019, pp. 26–29.

75. "Central banks will want oversight of Facebook's Libra: Bank of England's Carney," Reuters, June 21, 2019, https://www.reuters.com/article/us-britain-boe-carney-facebook/central-banks-will-want-oversight-of-facebooks-libra-bank-of-englands-carney-idUSKCN1TM0RW

76. JD Alois, "G7 Update on Stablecoins: Working Group has Identified Some Key Considerations for Critical Issues to be Solved," Crowdfund Insider, July 21, 2019, https://www.crowdfundinsider.com/2019/07/149722-g7-update-on-stablecoins-working-group-has-identified-some-key-considerations-for-critical-issues-to-be-solved/

77. "Ephrat Livni, Facebook's Libra is spurring central banks' interest in issuing cryptocurrency," *Quartz*, June 30, 2019, https://qz.com/1655896/facebooks-libra-forces-central-banks-to-tackle-cryptocurrencies/

78. "Abhishek Vishnoi, "BIS to Set Up Financial Tech Innovation Hub for Central Banks," Bloomberg, June 20, 3019, https://www.bloomberg.com/news/articles/2019-06-30/bis-to-set-up-financial-tech-innovation-hub-for-central-banks

79. Big Tech in Finance Opportunities and Risks, Bank of International Settlements, https://www.bis.org/publ/arpdf/ar2019e3.pdf

80. Phillip Inman and Angela Monaghan, "Facebook's Libra cryptocurrency 'poses risks to global banking,'" *The Guardian*, June 23, 2019, https://www.theguardian.com/technology/2019/jun/23/facebook-libra-cryptocurrency-poses-risks-to-global-banking

81. Felix Martin, "Money: The Unauthorized Biography, From Coinage to Cryptocurrency," New York: Vintage Books, 2013.

82. For a discussion of this limit, currently estimated to be just under 21 million (20999999.9769 BTC). Predictions vary on when this endpoint will be reached, and whether or not there could be changes to the system. See https://bitcoin.stackexchange.com/questions/161/how-many-bitcoins-will-there-eventually-be

# Chapter 7

1. Daniel 6:8, KJV.

2. "Digital Asset Transactions: When Howey Met Gary (Plastic)," William Hinman, Director, Division of Corporate Finance, U.S. Securities and Exchange Commission, June 14, 2018. Remarks at the Yahoo Finance All Markets Summit: Crypto. https://www.sec.gov/news/speech/speech-hinman-061418

3. Source: The History of Computing Project, sponsored by a consortium of museums. See https://www.thocp.net/hardware/mainframe.htm#introduction

4. https://www.quora.com/Did-Bill-Gates-really-say-he-wanted-a-computer-in-every-home-and-when-did-he-say-that

5. For the origins of cloud computing, see Antonio Regalado, "Who Coined 'Cloud Computing'?" *MIT Technology Review*, Oct. 31, 2011, https://www.technologyreview.com/s/425970/who-coined-cloud-computing/

6. Tim Stack, "Internet of Things (IoT) Data Continues to Explode Exponentially. Who Is Using That Data and How?" Cisco blogs, Feb.5, 2018, https://blogs.cisco.com/datacenter/internet-of-things-iot-data-continues-to-explode-exponentially-who-is-using-that-data-and-how

7. "Source" means the source code, which are the programming commands in various programming languages that knowledgeable humans can easily understand and compose software in. Ultimately software can be executed by computer hardware only in binary form, but is written in source code form for human convenience. Binaries cannot readily be understood or modified by humans, so access to source code is essential in order to change the software. The open-source model gives users of binary code access to the source code for the binaries they are using so that they can examine, understand, and modify or fix that software.

8. Jan L. Nussbaum, "*Apple Computer, Inc. v. Franklin Computer Corporation* Puts the Byte Back into Copyright Protection for Computer Programs," Golden Gate University Law Review, Volume 14, Issue 2, Article 3, Jan. 1984, http://digitalcommons.law.ggu.edu/cgi/viewcontent.cgi?article=1344&context=ggulrev

9. For an excellent discussion including extensive case citations, see "Software Patent or Copyright: Everything You Need to Know, https://www.upcounsel.com/software-patent-or-copyright

10. For guidance on a global level, see https://www.wipo.int/edocs/mdocs/aspac/en/wipo_ip_phl_16/wipo_ip_phl_16_t5.pdf. For U.S. guidance, see https://www.uspto.gov/web/offices/pac/mpep/s2106.html#ch2100_d29a1b_139b2_397.

11. Linux was written from scratch to closely resemble Unix, a proprietary operating system originally developed at AT&T's famous Bell Laboratories.

12. http://www.oxfordreference.com/view/10.1093/acref/9780191826719.001.0001/q-oro-ed4-00018679

13. Darryn Pollock, "Wonders of Naming the Company 'Blockchain' or 'Bitcoin'," *Cointelegraph*, Jan. 14, 2018, https://cointelegraph.com/news/wonders-of-naming-the-company-blockchain-or-bitcoin

14. Tim Arford, "Is this the most influential work in the history of capitalism?" BBC News, Oct. 23, 2017, https://www.bbc.com/news/business-41582244

15. For a detailed and more technical explanation of blockchain operation, see Deepak Puthal et al., "Everything you wanted to know about the blockchain," *IEEE Consumer Electronics Magazine*, Vol.7, No.4, July 2018, pp. 6–14.

16. *Beyond the Doomsday Economics of "Proof-of-Work" In Cryptocurrencies* by Ralph Auer, BIS Working Papers January 2019. https://www.bis.org/publ/work765.pdf, See also https://www.coindesk.com/bitcoins-proof-of-work-algorithm-needs-replacing-argues-bis-study

17. https://royalsocietypublishing.org/doi/full/10.1098/rsos.180410

18. Deepak Puthal et al., "Everything you wanted to know about the blockchain," *IEEE Consumer Electronics Magazine*, Vol. 7, No.4, July 2018, pp. 11–12.

19. Ibid.

20. Arati Baliga, "Understanding Blockchain Consensus Models," Persistent Systems Ltd., Apr. 2017, available at https://www.persistent.com/wp-content/uploads/2017/04/WP-Understanding-Blockchain-Consensus-Models.pdf

21. Sangeet Paul Chaudary, "How to win with marketplaces: The three success factors," The Next Web, 4 May 2013. thenextweb.com/entrepreneur/2013/05/04/how-to-winwith-marketplaces-the-three-success-factors/#.tnw_B0Mz6ej5

22. Nick Szabo, "Smart Contracts," Hacker News, 1994. www.tuicool.com/articles/U7veauY

23. Nick Szabo, "Winning Strategies for Smart Contracts," foreword by Don Tapscott, Blockchain Research Institute, Dec. 4, 2017. https://www.blockchainresearchinstitute.org/project/smart-contracts/

24. A next-generation wireless technology with a high data transmission rate. For more details, see https://www.verizon.com/about/our-company/5g/what-5g

25. For a thoughtful article on the continuing need for "dumb" contracts, including a demonstration of limitations on how natural language in a contract can be converted into program language, see "The Persistence of "Dumb" Contracts," by Jeffrey M. Lipshaw Stanford University January 21, 2019. https://stanford-jblp.pubpub.org/pub/persistence-dumb-contracts

26. "Hackers Attack Every 39 Seconds," *Security Magazine*, Feb. 10, 2017, https://www.securi tymagazine.com/articles/87787-hackers-attack-every-39-seconds

27. Schumpeter, "Not-so-clever contracts," *The Economist*, Jul. 28, 2016, https://www.econo mist.com/business/2016/07/28/not-so-clever-contracts

28. https://entethalliance.org/

29. https://www.hyperledger.org/

30. https://www.r3.com/

31. "Alastair Marsh, "Barclays, RBS Join Blockchain Trial to Speed Property Sales," Bloomberg, April 4, 2019, https://www.bloomberg.com/news/articles/2019-04-04/bar clays-rbs-join-blockchain-trial-to-speed-property-sales

32. Daniel Kuhn, "Malta to Register All Rent Contracts on Blockchain," Coindesk.com, June 24, 2019, https://www.coindesk.com/malta-to-register-all-rent-contracts-on-blockchain?

33. https://www.everledger.io/industry-applications

34. Susan van den Brink et al., "Approaches to responsible sourcing in mineral supply chains," Resources, Conservation, and Recycling, June 2019. https://www.sciencedirect.com/science/article/pii/S092134491930103X

35. Jo Lang, "Three uses for blockchain in banking," IBM Blockchain Blog, Oct. 23, 2017, https://www.ibm.com/blogs/blockchain/2017/10/three-uses-for-blockchain-in-banking/

36. "J.P. Morgan Creates Digital Coin for Payments," Feb. 14, 2019, https://www.jpmorgan.com/global/news/digital-coin-payments

37. Takashi Nakamichi and Takako Taniguchi, "JPMorgan Sees Client Interest in JPM Coin for Bond Transactions," Bloomberg, June 25, 2019, https://www.bloomberg.com/news/ar ticles/2019-06-25/jpmorgan-sees-client-interest-in-jpm-coin-for-bond-transactions

38. Antony Peyton, "IBM and eight banks unleash we.trade platform for blockchain-powered commerce," bankingtech.com, Oct. 17, 2017, https://www.bankingtech.com/2017/10/ibm-and-eight-banks-unleash-we-trade-platform-for-blockchain-powered-commerce/

39. See "Could an Artificial Intelligence Be Considered a Person Under the Law?" by Roman V. Rampolskiy, blog of October 5, 2018. https://theconversation.com/could-an-artificial-intelligence-be-considered-a-person-under-the-law-102865

40. "The long arm of the list," *The Economist*, July 15, 2017, pp. 10–12.

41. Klint Finlet, "The Wired Guide to the Blockchain," *Wired*, Feb. 1, 2018, https://www.wired.com/story/guide-blockchain/

42. Tom Serres and Bettina Warburg, "Introducing Asset Chains: The Cognitive, Friction-free, and Blockchain-enabled Future of Supply Chains," foreword by Don Tapscott, Blockchain Research Institute, Nov. 28, 2017.

43. "The Blockchain In Banking Report: The future of blockchain solutions and technologies," *Business Insider*, March 20, 2017, https://www.businessinsider.com/block chain-in-banking-2017-3

44. "The Blockchain In Banking Report: The future of blockchain solutions and technologies," *Business Insider*, March 20, 2017, https://www.businessinsider.com/block chain-in-banking-2017-3

45. "What's Next In Blockchain," CB Insights, 2019, available at https://www.cbinsights.com/research/report/blockchain-trends-2019/

46. Mike Orcutt, "In 2019, blockchains will start to become boring," *MIT Technology Review*, Jan. 2, 2019, https://www.technologyreview.com/s/612687/in-2019-blockchains-will-start -to-become-boring/

47.  https://essentia.one/

48.  Loi Luu, "With Blockchain, Knowing Your Customer Is More Important Than Ever," *Forbes*, May 17, 2018, https://www.forbes.com/sites/luuloi/2018/05/17/with-blockchain-knowing-your-customer-is-more-important-than-ever/#1462011e559c

49.  "Nailing it," *The Economist*, Technology Quarterly, Sept. 1, 2018, p. 10.

50.  Ibid.
     [1] https://essentia.one/

51.  "Nailing it," *The Economist*, Technology Quarterly, Sept. 1, 2018, p. 11.

52.  Catherine Tucker and Christian Catalini, "What Blockchain Can't Do," *Harvard Business Review*, June 28, 2018, https://hbr.org/2018/06/what-blockchain-cant-do

53.  "Blockchain Startups," Crunchbase, https://www.crunchbase.com/hub/blockchain-startups#section-overview accessed Jan 9. 2019

54.  "What Employers Want from Coders," *IEEE Spectrum*, May 2019, p. 18.

55.  Matt Higginson, Marie-Claude Nadeau, and Kausik Rajgopal, "Blockchain's Occam problem," McKinsey & Company, Jan. 2019, https://www.mckinsey.com/industries/finan cial-services/our-insights/blockchains-occam-problem?

56.  "Rockefellers Go Long on Cryptocurrencies to Invest in Blockchain Startups," CCN.com, April 10, 2018 https://www.ccn.com/rockefellers-go-long-on-cryptocurrencies-to-invest-in-blockchain-startups/

57.  https://www.gartner.com/en/research/methodologies/gartner-hype-cycle

58.  "Gartner Identifies Five Emerging Technology Trends That Will Blur the Lines Between Human and Machine," Gartner, press release, Aug. 20, 2018, https://www.gartner.com/ en/newsroom/press-releases/2018-08-20-gartner-identifies-five-emerging-technology -trends-that-will-blur-the-lines-between-human-and-machine

# Chapter 8

1.  Douglas Adams, *The Ultimate Hitchhiker's Guide to the Galaxy: Five Novels in One Outrageous Volume* (p. 677). Random House Publishing Group. Kindle Edition.

2.  "Digital payment platforms primed to topple cash," U.S. Bank, news release, Aug. 16, 2017, https://www.usbank.com/newsroom/news/digital-payment-platforms-primed-to-topple-cash. html

3.  Andrew Perrin, "More Americans are making no weekly purchases with cash," Pew Research Center, Dec. 12, 2018, https://www.pewresearch.org/fact-tank/2018/12/12/ more-americans-are-making-no-weekly-purchases-with-cash/

4.  Jonathan Brugge et al., "Attacking the cost of cash," Mckinsey.com, Aug. 2018, https:// www.mckinsey.com/industries/financial-services/our-insights/attacking-the-cost-of-cash

5.  Brad Jones, "Cash Is Quickly Becoming Obsolete in China," Futurism.com, Oct. 2017, https://futurism.com/cash-is-quickly-becoming-obsolete-in-china/

6.  Clemens Jobst and Helmut Stix. "Doomed to Disappear? The Surprising Return of Cash Across Time and Across Countries." Centre for Economic Policy Research Discussion Paper No. DP12327, September 2017.

7.  "Is Cash Still King?" by Tim Sablik, Federal Reserve Bank of Richmond, February 2018. https://www.richmondfed.org/publications/research/econ_focus/2018/q2/feature2

8.  Ibid.

9.  "Is Cash Still King?" by Tim Sablik, Federal Reserve Bank of Richmond, February 2018. https://www.richmondfed.org/publications/research/econ_focus/2018/q2/feature2

10. Ruth Judson, "Crisis and Calm: Demand for U.S. Currency at Home and Abroad from the Fall of the Berlin Wall to 2011," Board of Governors of the Federal Reserve System, International Finance Discussion Papers, IFDP 1058, Nov. 2012. Available at https://www.federalreserve.gov/pubs/ifdp/2012/1058/ifdp1058.pdf

11. https://www.federalreserve.gov/faqs/currency_12771.htm

12. Jonathan Brugge et al., "Attacking the cost of cash," Mckinsey.com, Aug. 2018, https://www.mckinsey.com/industries/financial-services/our-insights/attacking-the-cost-of-cash

13. "New Research from IHL Group Shows Retailers' Cash-handling Costs Range from 4.7% to 15.3%, Depending on Retail Segment," IHL Group press release, Business Wire, Jan 30. 2018, https://www.businesswire.com/news/home/20180130005244/en/New-Research-IHL-Group-Shows-Retailers%E2%80%99-Cash-handling

14. Bhaskar Chakravorti, "The Hidden Costs of Cash," *Harvard Business Review*, June 26, 2014, https://hbr.org/2014/06/the-hidden-costs-of-cash

15. Richard J. Cebula and Edgar L. Feige, "America's unreported economy: Measuring the size, growth and determinants of income tax evasion in the U.S.," *Crime, Law and Social Change*, Aug. 2012, Vol. 57 Issue 3, pp. 265–285. doi:http://dx.doi.org/10.1007/s10611-011-9346-x

16. "India scraps 500 and 1,000 rupee bank notes overnight," BBC News, Nov. 9, 2016, https://www.bbc.com/news/business-37906742

17. "Of Indian banknotes cancelled last year, 99% are accounted for," *The Economist*, Sept. 2, 2017, https://www.economist.com/finance-and-economics/2017/09/02/of-indian-banknotes-cancelled-last-year-99-are-accounted-for

18. Jeffrey Gettleman, "Modi's Cash Crackdown Failed, Indian Bank Data Shows," The New York Times, Aug. 30, 2018, https://www.nytimes.com/2018/08/30/world/asia/modi-india-rupee-cash.html

19. "Global Cash Index," PYMNTS.com, March 2018, available at https://www.pymnts.com/cash/2018/usa-global-cash-index-digital-dollar-cardtronics/

20. http://cashlessindia.gov.in/

21. Renita d'Souza, "Two years after demonetisation: Cashless India still a distant dream," Observer Research Foundation, Nov. 23, 2018, https://www.orfonline.org/expert-speak/two-years-after-demonetisation-cashless-india-still-a-distant-dream-45682/

22. Andy Mukherjee, "India Going Cashless Could Be a Model for the World," Bloomberg Quint, June 5, 2019, https://www.bloombergquint.com/opinion/india-mobile-payments-link-facebook-to-google-to-amazon
    Copyright © BloombergQuint

23. Glenn Zorpette, "The Beginning of The End of Cash," *IEEE Spectrum*, May 2012, https://spectrum.ieee.org/at-work/innovation/the-beginning-of-the-end-of-cash

24. Dave Briggs, "Politicians target cashless businesses," CNN, Feb. 15, 2019, available at https://www.cnn.com/videos/business/2019/02/15/cashless-businesses.cnn-business

25. Scott Calvert, "Philadelphia Is First U.S. City to Ban Cashless Stores," *The Wall Street Journal*, March 7, 2019, https://www.wsj.com/articles/philadelphia-is-first-u-s-city-to-ban-cashless-stores-11551967201

26. JR Minkel, "The 2003 Northeast Blackout–Five Years Later," *The Scientific American*, Aug. 13, 2008, https://www.scientificamerican.com/article/2003-blackout-five-years-later/

27. Rev. 13:16–17, NRSV

28. Maddy Savage, "Thousands of Swedes Are Inserting Microchips Under Their Skin," NOPR, Oct. 22, 2018, https://www.npr.org/2018/10/22/658808705/thousands-of-swedes-are-inserting-microchips-under-their-skin

29. Ibid.

30. Bhakti Mirchandani, "Laughing All The Way To The Bank: Cybercriminals Targeting U.S. Financial Institutions," *Forbes*, Aug. 28, 2018, https://www.forbes.com/sites/bhakti mirchandani/2018/08/28/laughing-all-the-way-to-the-bank-cybercriminals-targeting-us-financial-institutions/#2ec7a9866e90

31. "Banks Under Attack: Tactics and Techniques Used to Target Financial Organizations," Trend Micro, Feb. 8, 2019, https://www.trendmicro.com/vinfo/us/security/news/cyber crime-and-digital-threats/banks-under-attack-tactics-and-techniques-used-to-target-financial -organizations

32. Angela Moon, "State-sponsored cyberattacks on banks on the rise: report," *Reuters*, March 22, 2019, https://www.reuters.com/article/us-cyber-banks/state-sponsored-cyberattacks-on-banks-on-the-rise-report-idUSKCN1R32NJ

33. Alan Taylor, "Photos: 15 Years Since the 2003 Northeast Blackout," *The Atlantic*, Aug. 13, 2018, https://www.theatlantic.com/photo/2018/08/photos-15-years-since-the-2003-northeast-blackout/567410/

34. Jeremy Hsu, "The Earth Was Lucky to Dodge a Massive Solar Magnetic Storm in 2012," *IEEE Spectrum*, March 19, 2014, https://spectrum.ieee.org/tech-talk/aerospace/astrophys ics/earth-dodged-solar-magnetic-storm-bullet-in-2012

35. Robert Sanders, "Fierce solar magnetic storm barely missed Earth in 2012," *Berkeley News*, March 18, 2014, https://news.berkeley.edu/2014/03/18/fierce-solar-magnetic-storm-barely-missed-earth-in-2012/

36. David E. Sanger and Nicole Perlroth, "U.S. Escalates Online Attacks on Russia's Power Grid," *New York Times*, June 15, 2019, https://www.nytimes.com/2019/06/15/us/politics/trump-cyber-russia-grid.html

37. For a detailed assessment of EMP risks, see Jena Baker McNeill and Richard Weitz, "Electromagnetic Pulse (EMP) Attack: A Preventable Homeland Security Catastrophe," The Heritage Foundation, Oct. 20, 2008, https://www.heritage.org/homeland-security/re port/electromagnetic-pulse-emp-attack-preventable-homeland-security-catastrophe

# Index

https://doi.org/10.1515/9781547401116-012